THY KINGDOM COME

BY

Ludvig Hope

TRANSLATED BY
OLAF LYSNES

Published by
AUGSBURG PUBLISHING HOUSE
MINNEAPOLIS MINNESOTA

THY KINGDOM COME

Manufactured in the United States of America

FOREWORD

AUGSBURG Publishing House is happy to offer a book of daily devotions by Ludvig Hope. Mr. Hope has a large following among the Lutherans of our country. His meditations are the fruit of many years of Bible study and Christian experience. They are Christ-centered and cross-centered, are sound and helpful. The appeal of this book will be as wide as the interests of Christian people since the author has an acquaintance, knowledge, and sympathy that are not limited to any one particular group. Readers will find brilliant thought as well as spiritual nourishment.

JANUARY 1

And he answering saith unto Him, "Lord, let it alone this year also, till I shall dig about it, and dung it: and if it bear fruit thenceforth, well; but if not, thou shalt cut it down." Luke 13:8-9

TODAY we are at the sunrise of another year. We ask ourselves, What will this year bring us? When a humble Christian looks back over years that are past he sees God's love and grace woven into his life; and from the depths of his soul comes the confession: "Lord, Thou hast done all things well!" But even as you thus give thanks you heave an anxious sigh. Through the corridors of time cold winds blow that seem to warn us of storms, punishment, and hard days. It is as though we heard the flapping of the wings of the angel with the vials of wrath that are to be poured out on us.

And yet—in the midst of all that causes us to fear difficult times, there stands a Man who until this day has always prevented the worst from happening. When the righteous hand lifted the axe for a stroke, and when the vials were to be poured out on us, then He interposed and prayed for a time of respite: "Lord, let it alone this year also. True, I have offered the same prayer before; but oh, grant this year too, Lord! Let me dig about it and dung it one year more!" In this way the Vinedresser has not only prevented the worst from happening, but He has also given years of grace in which many have been saved.

This year too He prays the same prayer for people and country, and because of this Savior-love, God will again give us a year of grace for grace. If this shall prove to be the last year here in time for some of us, then He will take such believing sinner and carry him through death into eternal day.

A few more years shall roll,
A few more seasons come,
And we shall be with those that rest,
Asleep within the tomb.
A few more suns shall set
O'er these dark hills of time,
And we shall be where suns are not,
A far serener clime.

Anniversaries and Birthdays

JANUARY 2

And when eight days were fulfilled for circumcising Him, His name was called JESUS, which was so called by the angel before He was conceived in the womb. Luke 2:21

NO one of us knows what the year we have just entered will bring us. We know only that the inheritance we received was sin and sorrow and sickness and death, and we know also that to this inheritance much cleaves that is against us. It is therefore easy to predict that this year too we will often be helpless and discouraged both in temporal and in spiritual matters.

We surely do the right thing in taking these facts into consideration. Nevertheless the greatest and best thing of all is that God considers these facts both in your case and in mine.

God has given us the right to count on something else also: We may use the name of Jesus. God has bound all His promises to this Name: there He has put our entire future filled with light and hope. In this Name there is forgiveness for all our sin, and the right to go to God boldly to get all that we need. It was this Name that Jesus left here below. He gave us the right to use this Name when we appear before God, needy and helpless, so that we may receive everything that we ask of the Father in this Name. Yea, in His Name we may go out into all the world and proclaim repentance and forgiveness of sins for all people.

Considering this, can we not look into the future with confidence and hope?

"Go!" says Jesus. "Go! Go through this year too at my expense and on my responsibility!" Go through everything that meets you! Go through life and death! Jesus will go with you.

Blessed Name of Jesus!

Jesus, only name that's given
Under all the mighty heaven,
Whereby man, to sin enslaved,
Bursts his fetters, and is saved.

Jesus, name of wondrous love,
Human name of God above:
Pleading only this we flee,
Helpless, O our God, to Thee.

Anniversaries and Birthdays

____

____

____

____

JANUARY 3

Jesus Christ is the same yesterday and today, yea and forever.
Hebrews 13:8

AS a great rock stands in the middle of a waterfall, so Jesus stands in the midst of humanity, mighty to save. As the sun rises over the earth every day, with no demand except to be permitted to give light, warmth, and life, so the grace of Jesus Christ is new upon us each day. Outside of Him everything is night and death; in Him is light and life; in Him we find the meaning and goal of life—and only in Him! No one can understand the divine miracle that we were chosen in Him before the foundation of the world. Nevertheless it is this fact that makes salvation so unshakable, and so entirely of grace.

That which was ruined by Adam is created again in Christ. He is the Spirit that gives life, the eternal life, and He gives it to all those of the race of Adam who can be gathered out and who believe on His name. Where Adam planted the seed of death, there Christ plants the seed of life; and he who with full confidence surrenders to Him shall never die.

Let everything else fail and be destroyed. This is a solid Rock to stand on, this is light in darkness, this is life in the land of death. This is the only safe point of departure for the journey to the kingdom where life never ceases and where the sun never sets. By Him the Lord makes us entirely capable of doing that which is good, and by Him the Lord accomplishes in us what is well pleasing to Him.

"Fear not; I am the first and the last, and the Living one; and I was dead, and behold, I am alive for evermore, and I have the keys of death and of Hades" (Rev. 1:17-18).

In Jesus' name
We praise our God on high,
He blesses them who spread abroad His fame,
And we do His will thereby.
E'er hath the Lord done great things by His Word,
And still doth bare His arm His wonders to perform;
Hence we should in every clime
Magnify His name sublime,
Who doth shield us from all harm.

Anniversaries and Birthdays

____

____

____

JANUARY 4

It is good for a man that he bear the yoke in his youth. Lam. 3:27

THE youth who wastes his days in idleness, without work, drudgery, and adversity, verily has little to boast of, even though he wallows in gold and pretends to be great because of what his ancestors were. To prevent wilting away in the warm winds of summer, and in order to be able to hold one's own in the severe autumn storms, it is necessary to send roots deep down while one still is in the springtime of life.

Those who were given the chance to do great things, and did them, usually grew up in straitened circumstances, or at least bore a "yoke" of one kind or another. Joseph was sold into slavery, and David began as a shepherd boy. Gideon's family was the poorest in Manasseh, and Gideon was the least in his father's house. Daniel was carried away to a strange land as a young boy. When Jesus chose men to preach the Word about Him to the nations, He did not go to the rich or to the learned, but to poor fishermen and farmers. Thus it was, thus it is now, and thus it will be to the end of time.

I want to shout to all parents: "Teach your children to work, and to be contented with only a little!" And to you young people: "Be glad to bear the yoke in your youth!" To the one who in faith and confidence struggles through hard times in his youth, God can give a victor's wreath which he is able to bear in a life of thankfulness and humility.

So, go to your work today too with joy and thankfulness.

I rest upon Thy Word;
The promise is for me;
My succor and salvation, Lord,
Shall surely come from Thee:
But let me still abide,
Nor from my hope remove,
Till Thou my patient spirit guide
Into Thy perfect love.

Anniversaries and Birthdays

JANUARY 5

Wherefore lift up the hands that hang down, and the palsied knees; and make straight paths for your feet, that that which is lame be not turned out of the way, but rather be healed.

Heb. 12:12-13

WHEN our knees are palsied we cannot walk, and when our hands hang down we are unable to work.

The great question for us Christians is the question of strength, strength to live a truly Christian life, strength to *walk*. For most of us it is not hard to *talk* like Christians: it is a more difficult art to *live* as Christians. Many strong forces both in us and around us are at work to make the Christian life loud-mouthed, vapid, and weak. But it was God's intention that we should honor His name by a truly Christian manner of life, and show an earth-bound and perverse generation that there is something more and greater to live for than this world.

But where will we get power?

Learned people say that one may get palsied knees, though one eats well, when the food does not contain all the needed nutritive ingredients. There may be a plenty of good food but if it lacks the elements that build cartilage and bone, knees will tremble.

We surely have something to learn here, if we apply this to the Christian life. If we accept only *one* side of God's Word, we will not get from the Word the strength that the Christian life needs. The person who will not accept the correction and teaching that the Word offers, will in the long run have no place for the comfort and forgiveness of grace. Let us therefore open ear and heart to the whole counsel of God unto salvation; then new strength will flow into the hands that hang down, and into the palsied knees.

Come, tenderest Friend, and best,
Our most delightful Guest,
With soothing power:
Rest, which the weary know,
Shade, 'mid the noontide glow,
Peace, when deep griefs o'erflow,
Cheer us this hour!

Anniversaries and Birthdays

JANUARY 6

God, having of old time spoken unto the fathers in the prophets by divers portions and in divers manners, hath at the end of these days spoken unto us in His Son. Heb. 1:1-2

GOD has spoken to us. It is great to think of this and comforting to know it. But it is greatest of all that He has spoken to us by His own *Son.* His speech is not piecemeal, in the only way that He can speak through us men. Looking out over the expanse of time, the Son does not see only a mountain top here and there. He sees everything and knows everything just as certainly as God Himself does. He sees every valley, and everything even to the very least that was and is and shall be. "No one knoweth the Son, save the Father; neither doth any know the Father, save the Son, and he to whomsoever the Son willeth to reveal Him" (Matt. 11:27). "The only begotten Son, who is in the bosom of the Father, He hath declared Him" (John 1:18).

A man of God once said: "The Son is not only a messenger from God; He is Himself the message. He is everything that God has to say to us: all of God's thoughts, all of God's wisdom, all of God's will, all of God's power. Christ is the Word in the written word."

"Who is the image of the invisible God, the firstborn of all creation; for in Him were all things created, in the heavens and upon the earth, things visible and things invisible, whether thrones or dominions or principalities or powers; all things have been created through Him, and unto Him" (Col. 1:15-16).

Oh, what blessing to be near Thee,
And to hearken to Thy voice;
May I ever love and fear Thee,
That Thy Word may be my choice.
Oft were hardened sinners, Lord,
Struck with terror by Thy Word;
But to him for sin who grieveth
Comfort sweet and hope it giveth.

Anniversaries and Birthdays

JANUARY 7

Jehovah is my light and my salvation;
Whom shall I fear?
Jehovah is the strength of my life;
Of whom shall I be afraid? Psalm 27:1

THE world leaves us in darkness where we long most earnestly for light. We ask, yea, we shout from the depth of our souls: Where did we come from? Whither are we going?—and we get no answer.

Then we realize how unspeakably wonderful it is that a light has been given us by which we can see beyond the confines of this life. The Lord is our light *in God's Word*. There we see both the origin of life and the goal of life. There we also see our sin and feebleness, and there we see our salvation.

We see all this and much more in the Lord through His Word. How easily we forget the treasure that we have in God's Word! Think of all those who must live and die without this light! Of what lies beyond the grave they see nothing except their own speculations and dreams. They see no Savior and no heaven: they must live and die in darkness.

A word to all of you who are so inclined to look only within your own selves, and out into the dark night of death: Come and look into God's book! There you will see again the Possessor of the light of life who wants to be our salvation. He will give light unto our feet, so that we find the way home to Him. It is the *Lord* we are to see; He is our light, not we ourselves. He has taken our right hand, He will lead us through the darkness, yea, also through death.

When all my mind is darkened o'er,
And human help can do no more;
Then come, Lord Jesus! come with speed,
And help me in my hour of need;
Lead me from this dark vale beneath,
And shorten then the pangs of death.

Anniversaries and Birthdays

____

____

____

JANUARY 8

Whom have I in heaven but Thee?
And there is none upon earth that I desire besides Thee.

Psalm 73:25

WHEN Asaph gazed upon the earth and looked down instead of up, he got into so great a danger that he was at the point of falling away from God. If he had not torn himself loose from that vision, that fine man of God would have been earthbound. But fortunately he again looked toward the sanctuary. Then he asked no more about what he had on earth, but about heaven, and thus he was saved.

Does not the same danger threaten us Christians today? We begin to inquire about what we have on earth, and then our life with God is endangered without our seeing it. If we discover that others are better off than we are, then jealousy, love of the world, and unbelief take our heart captive. We demand exemption from adversity, shame, and sorrow; and if we do not get what we want, and if we do not get off easily when we desire to be exempt, well, then God is not good to us, and there we are in the midst of danger.

But this is not what we were called to! We were bought from the earth to God! Look up, citizen of heaven, and inquire about the things that await you in your true fatherland. Let thought and heart enter the land where Jesus is your Savior, God your Father, and the angels your servants, and where the inheritance awaits you.

See and believe, and you are saved.

"If then ye were raised together with Christ, seek the things that are above, where Christ is, seated on the right hand of God" (Col. 3:1).

There, at my Savior's side,
Heaven is my home;
May I be glorified,
Heaven is my home;
There are the good and blest,
Those I love most and best,
Grant me with them to rest;
Heaven is my home.

Anniversaries and Birthdays

JANUARY 9

Have this mind in you, which was also in Christ Jesus. Phil. 2:5

WHAT counts for most in our Christian conduct is not what we do, but what we are. Many big words may fall to earth powerless, while the simplest everyday expressions may give us grace and strength.

What does the child care for mother's godly talk or father's preaching, if they have not the mind of Christ in daily life? Christianity is not talk, and not chapel and church and well dressed people who indulge in much pious talk. Oh, that we once and for all could understand that! No, Christianity is the inner harmony of life, life from God, and in God. Christianity is righteousness, peace, and joy in the Holy Spirit. Christianity is spirit and life.

Though it is quite impossible to see and measure this holy power, nevertheless we are sure to meet it in holy people. It is this power and this mind that the Word asks us to have, and it is this mind that God can use to influence other people. Without this mind our Christianity is sounding brass or clanging cymbal. All Christians desire to possess this power, but many of them have little of it: the reason is that they are unwilling to take up the cross that lies at the entrance to the sanctuary. We think it is too heavy. Still, let us submit, and look to Him who humbled Himself even unto death. There is the strength we need to walk in His footsteps.

Where the mind of Christ has full sway, the fruit is ripened that God can use for seed in the souls of men. The good seed is not only the Word of God, but also the children in His kingdom.

Oh, where are the reapers that garner in
The sheaves of the good from the fields of sin?
With sickles of truth must the work be done,
And no one may rest till the "harvest-home."

Anniversaries and Birthdays

JANUARY 10

Him that cometh to me I will in no wise cast out. John 6:37

THE door leading into the kingdom of God is here thrown so wide open for us that it is impossible for anyone to say that he cannot enter. The only requirement is to come. Not a word is said about how one is to come, or how one is to be when he comes. He assures us that we shall not be turned away when we do come.

It is positively thrilling to see how simple a matter it is to be saved. When one has found the way, and knows how simple it is, he marvels that others do not see it too.

It was a Sunday when there was preaching in the church. The church door stood open, and by chance a bird flew in. When the bird in terror flew from window to window and perched on chandelier and posts, people said to each other, "How strange that it does not see the door!" At last the bird fell to the floor, tired and weary of wing. Then it saw the open door and flew out.

Among us humans there are many such "birds" who race from pillar to post to find liberty and salvation, and find nothing. You tired bird! The door is wide open. Listen! "Him that cometh to me I will in no wise cast out." That is the open door.

Just come to Him, and you are saved and free! "I will give unto him that is athirst of the fountain of the water of life freely" (Rev. 21:6).

Do you not feel, dear brother,
His Spirit now striving within?
Oh, why not accept His salvation,
And throw off your burden of sin?

Why do you wait, dear brother?
The harvest is passing away;
Your Savior is longing to bless you,
There's danger and death in delay.

Anniversaries and Birthdays

____

____

____

____

JANUARY 11

When thou passest through the waters, I will be with thee; and through the rivers, they shall not overflow thee: when thou walkest through the fire, thou shalt not be burned, neither shall the flame kindle upon thee. Isaiah 43:2

TO pass through this world is not at all so simple a matter as we often thought in younger years—least of all for a Christian. The longer we live, the more fully we are woven into life's texture, and with that also into life's struggle.

We used to think that when we had only got past *that* difficulty and *that* time, we should see brighter times and be better off. But for many there were more deep rivers to cross, and a new fire to temper the steel. We are slow at learning that the way is narrow to the very end.

But then there is something else that is true, too, namely, that God has promised to be with us and to carry us through both the fire and the water. The reason that we experience the fellowship of God most vitally when things look most hopeless, is that He is with us where we cannot possibly help ourselves.

In the den of lions Daniel got the assurance that God was with him, and in the fiery furnace one like a son of the gods walked with his three friends. When we behold God's face and get His help in that way, life's heaviest burden is transformed into its greatest joy. When we went through fire and water, and God was with us, we learned one of the most beautiful melodies to be found in a Christian heart, one that will be heard through all eternity in the song about the Lamb.

I was lost, but Jesus found me,
Found the sheep that went astray,
Threw His loving arms around me,
Drew me back into His way.

Yes, I'll sing the wondrous story
Of the Christ who died for me,
Sing it with the saints in glory,
Gathered by the crystal sea.

Anniversaries and Birthdays

JANUARY 12

Blessed are the merciful: for they shall obtain mercy. Matt. 5:7

IT is great riches to have a sympathetic disposition that suffers with those that are in trouble, and rejoices to wipe away a tear and bring a smile to faces long sad. Above all is it good fortune for the person himself, but also for others. He who has endured cold treatment and hard judgments blesses the day that he met a merciful person. Jesus will be blessed in all eternity because He was rich in mercy.

There was never another like Jesus on earth,
So compassionate, loving, and mild.

Then when we learn of Him to go through life with kindness, we get the grace to be a little like Him who wept because of our distress, and was merciful unto death.

How poor and unhappy those people are who have trained themselves to be hard and dry and cold in the presence of distress and tears. When love of the world takes possession of the heart, it dries up and becomes a money bag. And if you think that it is only among worldly people that we find such persons, then you must think again. Christians too can be seized by this spirit of coldness, and if it once gets a hold it is difficult to dislodge.

He who was moved with compassion for the people, is eager to give the same mind to all those who are His own. The world longs for people who have a heart and some sympathy. Let us be numbered among those who satisfy this longing with a helping hand. Then God will be merciful to us too.

In sickness, sorrow, want, or care,
What'er it be, 'tis ours to share;
May we, where help is needed, there
Give help as unto Thee.

Anniversaries and Birthdays

JANUARY 13

Ask, and it shall be given you; seek, and ye shall find; knock, and it shall be opened unto you. Matthew 7:7

WHEN we go to God to ask for something, we do not knock at a closed door that no one opens, nor do we go to a narrow-hearted Dives who would rather have us stay away. No! We go to Him who has sent for us, and has taught us to pray, and has promised that we shall receive.

Many consider prayer a commandment and a dreary duty that God has laid on us, a burden that is to show us our impotence and His omnipotence. That is not true. Prayer is a door that opens to the throne of grace where we may receive mercy, and may find grace to help us in time of need. Prayer is not a yoke but wings, not duty but a right. Prayer is the right of the helpless one.

When all doors are closed against us in this world, when all earthly power is impotence, then we can fold our hands, appear before God, and ask Him for what we need. We may speak to God about everything that happens to us in this life from praying for salvation and the forgiveness of sins, down to the smallest trifles in the daily grind. None of all the things that His children struggle and work with in this world is too insignificant for Him to hear about. Today too we can bring life and work, health and sickness to Him in prayer.

"And ye shall call upon Me, and ye shall go and pray unto Me, and I will hearken unto you. And ye shall seek Me, and find Me, when ye shall search for Me with all your heart" (Jer. 29:12-13).

While I am a pilgrim here,
Let Thy love my spirit cheer;
Be my guide, my guard, my friend;
Lead me to my journey's end.

Anniversaries and Birthdays

JANUARY 14

Follow after peace with all men, and the sanctification without which no man shall see the Lord. Heb. 12:14

THE Christian, who is not dissatisfied with himself and who does not feel the need of more of the mind of Christ, is in great danger. To be blessed is to hunger and thirst after righteousness and to be poor in spirit. To be poor in spirit is not the same as poverty of spirit. To long as new-born babes for the spiritual milk which is without guile, and to press on toward the goal that we may lay hold on Him who has laid hold on us,—that is Christian life making growth. The spirit that hungers and thirsts has sound Christian life; but where no hunger and thirst are found, sickness and death are at the controls. He who tries to be at peace with God and men, and follows after holiness, will see Him who said: "Blessed are the eyes which see the things that you see."

"He hath put down princes from their thrones,
And hath exalted them of low degree.
The hungry He hath filled with good things;
And the rich He hath sent empty away"
(Luke 1:52-53).

One has correct, Christian eyesight when he sees that he is impotent and helpless.

You who weep over yourself and see that you need grace, you must rejoice and thank God. Praise Him who has kept alive in your heart the craving for more of the power of Jesus Christ.

Go to Him who gives to all liberally without upbraiding, and ask Him for grace and power to meet the demands that you put on yourself.

O that I only might learn consecration,
Make full surrender of heart day by day!
O that my Jesus might be my sole portion,
I am, alas! all too far, far away.
Jesus, whose voice full of love's gentle warning,
Gladly I follow, O give me Thy hand,
That in pure holiness, faith's bright adorning,
Like a true Christian I walk to the end.

Anniversaries and Birthdays

____

____

____

JANUARY 15

Because thou hast done this thing, and hast not withheld thy son, thine only son, in blessing I will bless thee. Gen. 22:16-17

WHEN one of God's elect faithfully walks the road that God has staked out for him, no matter how narrow it is, God meets him there with His power and blessing. And the more burdensome walking becomes, the more grace and help God gives.

When life seems to be arranged according to our will, we must often walk without seeing the Lord; but He is our strength where the hill is steep and the burden too heavy. Many a time we have thoughtlessly prayed that we might be spared from sacrifice and adversity; but that prayer was usually unwise. If God had heard that prayer, we should have been in danger of losing the grace of God. By comparison it is much more blessed to go the way where God leads us into suffering and sacrificing. That is where we learn to say with Paul, "We glory in our tribulations."

God's best people were not brought up in hothouses. The way of the Christian leads to the place of sacrifice that he may give back to God what He gave us first. There God reveals Himself to His own and gives them life's greatest happiness. He who accompanies Abraham to the sacrificial altar is permitted also to enter with him to God's blessings. The greater the sacrifice, the greater the blessing. When Abraham gave Isaac, God's promise to him was not only of a blessing, but of a great blessing. He who surrenders most fully to the will of God, receives most from His power.

Lord Jesus! bounteous giver
Of light and life divine,
Thou didst my soul deliver,
To Thee I all resign:
Thou hast in mercy bought me
With blood and bitter pain;
Let me, since Thou hast sought me,
Eternal life obtain.

Anniversaries and Birthdays

JANUARY 16

But seek ye first His kingdom, and His righteousness; and all these things shall be added unto you. Matthew 6:33

NOT many people are flippant enough to reject the kingdom of God in a shameless manner, determined never to have anything to do with it. Seldom does the deceiving guile of Satan plan to get people to say that they for all time give up all right to everything that belongs to the kingdom of God. Satan's usual tactics are to get us to postpone seeking God "till some other time." First one must use the years of youth for play, joy, and fun. Then one must build his own home and his future, and after that perhaps one might see whether it was the right time to seek God, and plan for eternal welfare. And if even then there is not time to seek the kingdom of God, I think God will accept me nevertheless—after death. God is gracious and loving and cannot endure to see anyone go to perdition.

That is the way most people think and live, and so far as eye can see, many pass quietly into eternal death on the strength of this deceit of Satan.

Reader, listener, are you being allured by this falsehood? If you are, I beseech you to wake up! Repent! Seek the kingdom of God today! That is your salvation. Make haste and save yourself!

You who are a Christian must remember that your life, your day, your work, everything that you have are to be entered in the kingdom of God first. Then you have for always the great promise that all other things shall be added unto you.

What more do you need for a happy life and a blessed death?

> I, the Lord, am with thee, be not thou afraid;
> I will help and strengthen, be thou not dismayed;
> Yea, I will uphold thee with mine own right hand;
> Thou art called and chosen in my sight to stand.

Anniversaries and Birthdays

____

____

____

JANUARY 17

**"... in holy array
Out of the womb of the morning
Thou hast the dew of Thy youth." Psalm 110:3**

A YOUNG man won for God is not only a soul won for heaven: it is also a life won that can win others for God.

Christian young people can best lead other young people to Christ. It is those who are young today who will build the new homes of our people, and who will fashion the coming generation. We look to them to fill our missionary training schools and to go out with the Word of peace to the ends of the earth. If they do not go, no one can go. The young people take possession of our school houses, kitchens, and nurseries, and it is they who must care for the sick and the dying in home and hospital, in town and country.

In grievous times when everything seemed headed for destruction, it was among the young men that God found those He could use as life-savers. He found Joseph, Samuel, Daniel, and many other young men. In Norway He found a young man in the southern part of the country. He came indeed as dew out of the womb of the morning and gave us a new day from God with springtime and awakening life.

If the young people of our day who have Christian knowledge would turn and accept Christ, the earth would yet once again have a springtime of life.

Young friend, come, and give Christ your one precious life! He will clothe you in holy array and make of you a drop of dew through which the sun of grace will shine to bring joy and happiness to you and many others.

*"For Thou art my hope, O Lord Jehovah:
Thou art my trust from my youth"*
(Psalm 71:5).

Thine for ever! Lord of life,
Shield us through our earthly strife;
Thou the life, the truth, the way,
Guide us to the realms of day.

Anniversaries and Birthdays

____

____

____

JANUARY 18

But grow in the grace and knowledge of our Lord and Savior Jesus Christ. II Peter 3:18

IF we have found Christ and are born of God, we are expected to grow. As the life with God is spiritual, the growth must also be spiritual. It is this growth that must appear in our daily life. We must grow not only in godliness but also in good works. If there is poverty of good works, there is also poverty of godliness.

We must especially be on our guard lest we get into a way of living that will stop the growth of the Christian life. For then there is real danger, and this is a danger that we can get ourselves into. That is the reason the Word puts the responsibility on us: *We* must grow.

But then comes the question, What is it to grow? The Word we are considering says that we are to grow in the grace and knowledge of Christ. We must not grow so that in our own eyes we appear to be greater and better Christians; but we must grow in grace.

How do we grow when we grow in grace? Then we grow downward in our own eyes, first and last. Then we see more of our own folly, our perverted nature, and the deep depravity of our hearts. We see ourselves as greater sinners. We cannot grow in grace and in knowledge of Christ, if we do not see that we need grace. It is where sin abounds that grace abounds more exceedingly. Thus do we grow in the grace and knowledge of Christ.

God grant that we all may grow thus!

I bring my guilt to Jesus,
To wash my crimson stains
White in His blood most precious,
Till not a spot remains.

Anniversaries and Birthdays

JANUARY 19

But to him that worketh not, but believeth on Him that justifieth the ungodly, his faith is reckoned for righteousness. Rom. 4:5

THERE come times for even the best Christian when everything seems to fail him. All that he sees in his heart and in his works accuses and condemns him. Everything looks like sores and sin and hypocrisy. "I was not what I pretended to be," his heart moans. His inner man looks like an ocean full of wreckage and nastiness. "I used to go to God as a child to his father. Now I dare not believe that I am saved, and cannot call God Father. I have lost the spirit of adoption, and the Spirit of God does not bear witness with my spirit that I am a child of God."

Faith will fail, and hope will waver;
The sun is gone, there is night in the soul.

Many who used to live a Christian life in confidence and liberty, lament in this way.

A word to you who have gotten into this night! I want to remind you that if you really have lost the rights of a child, you still have one right left: the right of the ungodly. And you cannot be anything worse than an ungodly person. So when everything fails you, you still have this left: you can believe on Him who justifies the ungodly. Lay hold on that right! When all that is your own is crushed and ruined, you are saved by that right.

All that I was, my sin, my guilt,
My death, was all my own;
All that I am, I owe to Thee,
My gracious God, alone.

Anniversaries and Birthdays

JANUARY 20

Be ye free from the love of money; content with such things as ye have: for Himself hath said, I will in no wise fail thee, neither will I in any wise forsake thee. Heb. 13:5

GOLD has a wonderful drawing power. As serpent eyes draw the flying bird to serpent mouth when once they have caught the eyes of the bird, so money draws the human heart to itself when it has caught our eye. Of all the sins that can get power over us, the love of money is one of the worst, and it is the hardest to overcome. More than all other sins it blinds our spiritual vision, and destroys whatever of true Christianity and true humanity there is in us.

Where the love of money comes in, sympathy for fellow men must go out. Love for gold makes of man a machine and a money bag. As a rule there is more heart in the worst harlot and the greatest criminal than there is in the stingy person. We are surprised when we read of Israel dancing around the golden calf at the foot of the mountain of God. Oh, that we may see how easy it is to do the same thing very near to Calvary! Gold is our time's most beautiful god.

In order to manage to get by this idol without kneeling and dancing, the Christian must see the danger and pray to God for help. *But the greatest danger is, I suppose, that we do not see the danger.* Where is the Christian who fears that he is covetous? It is sad to see Christian people lose in life's race under the weight of gold.

Christian! Let your manner of life be free from the love of money! Be content with what you have, and the Lord will never forsake you.

Go, then, earthly fame and treasure!
Come, disaster, scorn, and pain!
In Thy service pain is pleasure;
With Thy favor, loss is gain.
I have called Thee Abba, Father;
I have stayed my heart on Thee;
Storms may howl, and clouds may gather,
All must work for good to me.

Anniversaries and Birthdays

JANUARY 21

Come unto Me, all ye that labor and are heavy laden, and I will give you rest. Matt. 11:28

TOIL and heavy burdens are our lot in this life. Most people must work with all their might from morning till evening just to make a living. Poets and popular orators can indeed make many pretty words and phrases about the blessing there is in work, and in a way they have a right to do that: under present conditions work is a blessing. Nevertheless, work bears the mark of the judgment: "in the sweat of thy face shalt thou eat bread."

But is that the kind of tired people that Jesus invites to His rest?

I dare not say that; I know only that also he who is physically tired can find rest with Him.

Still the truth is that our heaviest burden will be the struggle with ourselves. We can lay down a spade and a sledge, but bad thoughts, a sore conscience, and memories of injustice one has been guilty of,—these are not so easily tossed aside. When, tired of all these, we find our way to Christ and see our full salvation in Him, then we find rest for our souls. Then every promise becomes a resting place, a shelter where we can find refuge in the evil day.

In faith there is rest in the midst of strife. But because it is not the perfect rest, we sigh and look forward to the sabbath rest with God. For the majority of us, perhaps for all of us the way to that rest passes through death. But over the grave Jesus wrote this: "Blessed are the dead who die in the Lord from henceforth: yea, saith the Spirit, that they may rest from their labors; for their works follow with them."

"Come unto Me, ye weary,
And I will give you rest."
O blessed voice of Jesus,
Which comes to hearts oppressed;
It tells of benediction,
Of pardon, grace, and peace,
Of joy that hath no ending,
Of love which cannot cease.

Anniversaries and Birthdays

JANUARY 22

The opening of Thy words giveth light;
It giveth understanding unto the simple.
Psalm 119:130

THERE is a way that leads back of the letter and into the divine content of the Bible. He who does not find that way will never find the salvation that God has given us in Christ, and he will never possess the strength he needs to live a truly Christian life. God Himself must open for us the door that leads to the vital power that is in the Word. If He is not permitted to do that, the door will always remain closed.

Not until our eyes are anointed by Him who gave sight to the blind do we behold wondrous things out of God's law. Then the Lord giveth understanding unto the simple. Then even the unlearned finds God's wisdom, God's light and grace, and *can see* where all the wise men of the world grope in darkness.

But this door will not open if we just sit around and wait for God's light. We must use the Word if we want God's help to find the heavenly treasure back of the letter. We must use the Word prayerfully and with a heart willing to be guided by what the Word says. He who lays his Bible away and believes that he is wiser than the Word, will always be found groping in darkness. But he who reads, and permits the Word to give him light and to judge the thoughts and intents of the heart, to him light shall be given and he shall find the way to his Savior. Strength will also be given him to fight the good fight, and to win.

"I have more understanding than all my teachers:
For Thy testimonies are my meditation" (Psalm 119:99).

Father of mercies, in Thy Word
What endless glory shines!
For ever be Thy name adored
For these celestial lines.

Here may the blind and hungry come,
And light and food receive;
Here shall the lowliest guest have room,
And taste and see and live.

Anniversaries and Birthdays

____

____

____

JANUARY 23

But as many as received Him, to them gave He the right to become children of God, even to them that believe on His name. John 1:12

IT is an honor to be a child of good parents who belong to the nobility; but to be God's child is life's highest nobility and honor. In this life we can never fully understand the happiness and the future that we own as the children of God. Occasionally we have an inkling of something unspeakably great when we think of our sonship with God. When our soul grasps this thought with confidence, earth pales away as a withering leaf, and an inexpressible joy carries us in the spirit up toward our true fatherland. "Behold what manner of love the Father hath bestowed upon us, that we should be called children of God; and such we are." But then we are also "heirs of God, and joint-heirs with Christ." More than any earthly father He bears all His own in His Father care; and He watches over us more than any mother over her weak and sick child.

It is right that we see our folly and sin, but it is also right to lift our eyes to Golgotha and to look into heaven, where our Brother and Father are, and where the inheritance awaits us. Child of God, do not forget your high estate and your bright future! The goal of our faith will strengthen us in the strife.

May you, who have no part in all this because you rejected Christ, soon see that that is your eternal misfortune, and the greatest sin you ever committed. Perhaps then you will make haste to receive Him who casts no one out.

Weary of earth and laden with my sin,
I look to heaven and long to enter in,
But there no evil thing may find a home;
And yet I hear a voice that bids me, "Come!"

Anniversaries and Birthdays

JANUARY 24

God is Spirit: and they that worship Him must worship in spirit and truth. John 4:24

TO worship God is not the same as to pray. Worship is the highest form of thanksgiving, admiration, and trust. It is humbly to lift one's spirit up to God. It is to let the inner man kneel and acknowledge that God is God, almighty, eternal, and gracious, and that we are helpless creatures who have no one else to depend on but Him. This veneration of God, this longing to honor and thank Him cause the soul to yearn deeply for the refuge of His divine power and grace, and they create in us a holy desire to do His will.

To worship is not to beg for food or health or other earthly things. It is to feel that you are very, very small, and that God is unspeakably great and good. The wings of the spirit then grow larger and stronger, so that we more easily get away from ourselves and move up to God, away from distrust and impotence. Then we forget life's little sorrows, and we bless and praise Him who does all things well. Worship lifts us a step nearer God and ennobles our spirit, so that we become holier men. When once we enter heaven and stand in God's presence, then we will join in worship with angels, and with people from all races and countries.

May we learn more of the blessed art of worship while we are still on the way home.

"Such doth the Father seek to be His worshippers."

Holy, holy, holy, merciful and mighty!
All Thy works shall praise Thy name, in earth and sky and sea;
Holy, holy, holy, merciful and mighty!
God in three persons, blessed Trinity!

Anniversaries and Birthdays

JANUARY 25

Jesus saith unto him, "I am the way, and the truth, and the life: no one cometh unto the Father, but by Me." John 14:6

THOMAS does not know the way. Everything gets tangled and obscure for him. He does not know whither Jesus is going, and he does not know where he himself is going.

Thomas is not the only one whose thoughts have gotten twisted. Many a time both you and I ask: Am I on the way to heaven? Will I be among the saved if I die now? What if I am only deceiving myself! How happy I would be if I were entirely certain that I am on the way! And while we are asking, we in the manner of genuine "reason" and unbelief, go to our own heart for the answer. We permit ourselves to be led into this dark, primeval forest, even though we know that that is wrong.

But Jesus gives us the answer, the light, and the ransom. He says that He is everything for us. This means not only that He has *given* us the truth and the life, and built a new way for us, but also that He Himself first and foremost *is* all this for us. So if we have received Him and are with Him, then we are in the truth and life, then we are on the way. He who is with Jesus is on the way because Jesus Himself is the way. As the automobile, the elevated, and the train carry us toward our destination when we have entered the car, so Jesus takes us to heaven when we are in Him. The way is alive. The way itself travels, because Jesus is the way.

"Commit thy way unto Jehovah;
Trust also in Him, and He will bring it to pass"
(Psalm 37:5).

Thou art the Way, the Truth, the Life:
Grant us that Way to know,
That Truth to keep, that Life to win,
Whose joys eternal flow.

Anniversaries and Birthdays

JANUARY 26

One soweth, and another reapeth. I sent you to reap that whereon ye have not labored: others have labored, and ye are entered into their labor. John 4:37-38

THERE were Christians who lived and worked before us; God takes into consideration what they did, too. If their work had not been done, we would not be gathering fruit.

Granted that sometimes the work of our ancestors was primitive and unimpressive—nevertheless mother often took us in her lap and folded our child hands in prayer. She told us about God, about Jesus, about the angels and heaven, and about evil that lurks around us. We had our seat in school, too, with Bible history, catechism, and hymn book; and we sat in church and chapel and heard the Word of God. Then was good seed sowed in our heart, too.

It is a privilege to have a part in times of great spiritual awakenings, and to help people to find peace with God. But we must never forget those who worked before us. *God* does not forget them. The work of every prayerful and believing laborer in the kingdom of God will bear fruit. Even though we do not see it now, the fruit will appear in due time. We will believe what God has said, and then we will be made strong to hold out.

"In due season we shall reap, if we faint not."

Jesus, Master! at Thy Word
I will work whate'er betide me,
And I know Thou wilt, O Lord,
By Thy Word and Spirit guide me;
At Thy Word my faith shall see
All things work for good to me.

Anniversaries and Birthdays

JANUARY 27

For whosoever would save his life shall lose it: and whosoever shall lose his life for my sake shall find it. Matt. 16:25

THE life that Jesus says we must lose, if we are to save our lives, is everything in us which is contrary to the personality and will of God.

It was this sin-life and death-life that conquered our first parents when Satan overpowered them. We inherited that life, and it has created an abyss of sin in us. Evil forces have captured spirit, soul, and body. We are governed by hatred for God and by love for evil. About this life of ours God's Word says:

"They have all turned aside, they are together become unprofitable;
There is none that doeth good, no, not so much as one."

This is the life we must lose, if the life that God gave us is to be saved. If our human life is not ransomed and set free from the life of sin, we are lost.

But how shall we lose our life so that we save it?

Jesus says we must deny ourselves, take up the cross, and follow Him. We must give ourselves to Christ. As He gave Himself wholly for us, so we are to give ourselves wholly to Him. By the life we then get from Him, the sin which is in us will be delivered up to death. The man of sin will then be crucified with Christ.

At the cross of Jesus we get power to die with Him, so that we can live in all eternity. The road away from sin and into life passes through death.

"For Thy sake we are killed all the day long;
We were accounted as sheep for the slaughter.
Nay, in all these things we are more than conquerors through Him that loved us" (Rom. 8:36-37).

Love of God, so pure and changeless;
Blood of God, so rich and free;
Grace of God, so strong, and boundless,
Magnify it all in me—
Even me.

Anniversaries and Birthdays

____

____

____

JANUARY 28

And Jesus answering said, "Were not the ten cleansed? but where are the nine?" Luke 17:17

THE man who believes and gives thanks is a happy person. Gratitude drives despondency and bad humor away and makes other people happy. Those who are always complaining and always demanding something are a burden both to themselves and to others. They banish the last bit of joy.

If we look at life honestly we will find that God has given us grace for grace, and has dealt with us more lovingly and faithfully than a mother. Still there are many Christians who see only the blackness of darkness. Instead of being thankful for great benefits, we complain again. Christians, wake up, reflect, and be renewed in the spirit of your mind!

The effect is dreary and depressing when Christians grow more impatient, dissatisfied, and full of complaints as the years pass; but it is a great joy to meet people who, while approaching life's sunset, have a smiling face and a soul full of thanksgiving. They grow and retain their freshness until the late autumn of life, and they are blessed by both God and man in time and eternity.

"Giving thanks always for all things in the name of our Lord Jesus Christ to God, even the Father." "Thanks be to God for His unspeakable gift."

"It is a good thing to give thanks unto Jehovah,
And to sing praises unto Thy name, O Most High;
To show forth Thy lovingkindness in the morning,
And Thy faithfulness every night.
For Thou, Jehovah, hast made me glad through Thy work:
I will triumph in the works of Thy hands"
(Psalm 92:1, 2, 4).

For the joy Thy birth doth give me,
For Thy holy, precious Word;
For Thy baptism which doth save me,
For Thy gracious festal board;
For Thy death, the bitter scorn,
For Thy resurrection morn,
Lord, I thank Thee and extol Thee,
And in heaven I shall behold Thee.

Anniversaries and Birthdays

______

______

______

JANUARY 29

For the Word of God is living, and active, and sharper than any two-edged sword, and piercing even to the dividing of soul and spirit, of both joints and marrow, and quick to discern the thoughts and intents of the heart. Heb. 4:12

THE Word of God is living because God is in the Word. And God's Word reveals what would otherwise be hidden, because God has spoken this Word.

It is by the Word of God that we attain to eternal life, and by it light is cast on the future. Without this Word everything would lie in darkness. It is only the Word of God that throws light beyond the grave and that tells us what secrets eternity has in its bosom. The most learned men can dig for a distance into the earth, and they can look far out into the universe, but not one of them knows how the numberless planets and groups of stars were created. But the Word of God tells us about the origin of everything, and the purpose of everything. It reveals to us a world outside the one we see, and gives us a sure promise of a life after that which we now know.

When this Word finds lodgement in the heart, it crushes the stony soul-resistance, and takes root downward where there never was life before. It can bring the proudest man to his knees. It can open a way to the deepest sources of life, to thought, will, and on into the most secret wishes and longings. It gives light, cleaves, severs, and separates. But it creates new life, too; it raises up the worst criminal, it makes good and peaceful people out of murderers, transforms liars and hypocrites into truthful and honest people, and makes a paradise out of the worst home.

God's Word is our great heritage,
And shall be ours for ever;
To spread its light from age to age
Shall be our chief endeavor;
Through life it guides our way,
In death it is our stay;
Lord, grant while worlds endure,
We keep its teachings pure,
Throughout all generations.

Anniversaries and Birthdays

____

____

____

JANUARY 30

The Lord is at hand. **Philippians 4:5**

WE are all inclined to think of God as being far away. We like to harbor the thought that God is up in heaven, and we down here on earth very far from God. Thus unbelief makes a great vacuum between God and us.

In this space Satan takes his place and tries to entice us to sin. And here he has a free hand. When unbelief has moved God far away from us, we are like lambs among wolves. That is the reason Satan does all he can to get us to believe that the Lord is far away. For then we are easily ensnared.

But when we have the inner certainty that God is where we are, then we become strong in the Lord, and we walk carefully. To know that the Lord is near gives wonderful power to overcome temptation. How blest to begin the day's struggles in the firm faith that God is near us! What strength, what defense, what hope there is in this! Was it not when you believed that you were near the Lord that you were lifted away from evil, and up to God?

But the Word, "The Lord is at hand," also tells us that our time is short. Before the day is over He may come for us. He may come through death or judgment at any time.

"O Jehovah, Thou hast searched me, and known me.
Thou knowest my downsitting and mine uprising;
Thou understandest my thought afar off.
Thou searchest out my path and my lying down,
And art acquainted with all my ways.
For there is not a word in my tongue,
But, lo, O Jehovah, Thou knowest it altogether"
(Psalm 139:1-4).

Praise the Lord, for He is glorious;
Never shall His promise fail;
God hath made His saints victorious;
Sin and death shall not prevail.
Praise the God of our salvation;
Hosts on high, His power proclaim;
Heaven and earth, and all creation,
Laud and magnify His name.

Anniversaries and Birthdays

JANUARY 31

My little children, these things write I unto you that ye may not sin. And if any man sin, we have an Advocate with the Father, Jesus Christ the righteous: and He is the propitiation for our sins; and not for ours only, but also for the whole world.

I John 2:1-2

"IF we say we have no sin, we deceive ourselves, and the truth is not in us." Everyone that commits sin is of the devil. "If any man sin, we have an Advovcate with the Father."

In these Bible passages we see three degrees of sin: to have sin, to sin, and to commit sin. A Christian has sin so long as he is here in the time of grace; and he may happen to sin, if he forgets to keep watch at his post. But if this should happen, he must not despair, because Christ is the propitiation for our sins, and His blood cleanses from all sin, if we only confess our sins to Him. But he, who in unbelief turns away from Christ, he commits sin and is of the devil, no matter how he lives otherwise.

In the soul of a Christian the voice that shouts warnings against sin must never die. He who is not afraid of sin but caresses it, is dangerously near to a fall. So many ask, May I not do that if I am a Christian? Is that sin, too? There is little Christianity in those questions. The Word knows only one reason that gives a Christian the right to risk his life at the edge of an abyss, and that is to try to help others out of sin. Then one can be certain that God goes with him.

Lord Jesus, King of Paradise,
O keep me in Thy love,
And guide me to that happy land
Of perfect rest above;
Where loyal hearts and true
Stand ever in the light,
All rapture through and through,
In God's most holy sight.

Anniversaries and Birthdays

FEBRUARY 1

It is the spirit that giveth life; the flesh profiteth nothing: the words that I have spoken unto you are spirit and are life.

John 6:63

IT is well to have knowledge of God. All that we know of the things that pertain to the kingdom of God make up a rich treasure to take with us out into life. He who despises this heritage sins against Him who gave us the light.

But this knowledge is not enough. Though we know ever so much about God, we may yet be eternally lost. The best and most complete electric installation is worthless if there is no current. So the knowledge of God is unprofitable if the Spirit of God does not make it living in the heart. "For the letter killeth, but the spirit giveth life." There are many who know just about everything about God, who yet do not know Him because they close their hearts against the Spirit of God.

The great multitude is satisfied with knowledge alone, and think that they will be saved some time by what they know about God, without being converted and pondering the Word in their hearts. This danger is so great that it threatens also them to whom the life with God has once been given. To trust in what you have once experienced in God's fellowship is living on power that has been used up. In that way many Christians have lost the life with God.

All those who would cherish the hope of being permitted to "enter in by the gates into the city" must have the Spirit of God. It is the Spirit who transmits eternal life from Christ to the person who has knowledge of Him. Let us pray, saying, "God, cast us not away from Thy presence, and take not Thy Holy Spirit from us."

Come, holy Comforter,
Thy sacred witness bear
In this glad hour;
Thou who almighty art,
Now rule in every heart,
And ne'er from us depart,
Spirit of power!

Anniversaries and Birthdays

____

____

____

FEBRUARY 2

Fear not, for I have redeemed thee; I have called thee by thy name, thou art Mine. Isaiah 43:1

MANY think it would be easier to find comfort and assurance of salvation if God stood by our side, so we both saw and heard Him, and He said these words: "I have redeemed thee, I have called thee by thy name, thou art mine." Just think if God Himself spoke these glorious words to me!

But if we think it over we will doubtless find that the way it is, is the best way: the Word of the Bible is God's Word. There the Lord speaks to us. There we hear His voice. That we could much more easily be assured of salvation and find comfort in God's Word if we saw Him and heard Him speak, is an entirely false supposition. There was a time when God was on earth so that people saw Him and heard words from His own mouth, but were there many who accepted and believed His words? Why then did Jesus sit on the foal of an ass and weep because the people would not accept salvation? No! If the heavens were opened above us, if the air were filled with angels, and if God Himself from the midst of the heavenly host shouted down to us, "I have redeemed thee; I have called thee by name; thou art mine!" we would have the same uncertainty and doubt, if we did not believe what He said.

Therefore let us take the Word in the Bible as God's Word to us—the Word for today, too—and then we shall get what the Word promises.

O may these heavenly pages be
My ever dear delight;
And still new beauties may I see
And still increasing light.

Divine Instructor, gracious Lord!
Be Thou for ever near;
Teach me to love Thy sacred Word,
And view my Savior there!

Anniversaries and Birthdays

FEBRUARY 3

If therefore the Son shall make you free, ye shall be free indeed.
John 8:36

A CHRISTIAN is not free in the sense that he can go through life without meeting adversity. Sickness, suffering, sorrow, and death come to us all. The struggle for existence is just as intense for a Christian as for an unbeliever. Nor is the Christian without temptation and sin. "If we say that we have no sin, we deceive ourselves, and the truth is not in us."

It is in Christ that we have our charter of liberty. In Him we have forgiveness of sins and fellowship with God. One of the greatest experiences that a Christian can have in this world is that his happiness grows greater as he approaches nearer to God. When through the Word of God and prayer, and through fellowship with the people of God we know the fragrance of the sanctuary, then we say with the poet: "These are the most delightful hours that we can attain to here on earth." The Christian is freed from the condemnation that the feeling of guilt lays over us. Conscience, which was as terrified as an animal wounded by the hunter, has found peace. The soul that trembled in expectation of punishment, looks up to God as a child to father and mother; and the spirit that was imprisoned is free and happy.

A Christian is free indeed because the inner man is free. Exactly the opposite is true of the person who is not a Christian. If he thinks that God is approaching he becomes unhappy and frightened.

The Christian is free because he is saved through Jesus Christ, and God is his Father.

Jesus, Jesus, only Jesus,
Can my heartfelt longing still;
See, I pledge myself to Jesus,
What He wills, alone to will.
For my heart, which He hath filled,
Ever cries: Lord, as Thou wilt!

Anniversaries and Birthdays

____

____

____

FEBRUARY 4

Have mercy upon me, O Jehovah; for I am withered away:
O Jehovah, heal me; for my bones are troubled.
My soul also is sore troubled:
And Thou, O Jehovah, how long? **Psalm 6:2-3**

IN olden days the people of God often spoke of "an attacked faith." What is "an attacked faith"? It is spiritual darkness, a hard soul-struggle, and doubt. Sharp arrows stick fast in the soul, and seem to say: "I am no longer right with God. I have lost the joy in God, peace, and my sonship. Sin and Satan now rule over me, and the Spirit of God is gone. I no longer find any comfort in God's Word. Everything that I read condemns me, and if I pray I get no answer."

"He hath walled me about, that I cannot go forth; He hath made my chain heavy.
Yea, when I cry, and call for help, He shutteth out my prayer."

What then is the reason that Christians have such experiences?

The reason may be found in a slovenly Christian life, in frayed nerves, in Satan's temptations, or in God's gracious plan for our lives. An old Christian once said: "God makes a lost sinner of the person that He wants to make God-fearing; the man that He desires to make alive He puts in the jaws of death; and the one that He wishes to get to heaven, He sends to hell."

So when God leads us out of "the night of an attacked faith," He gives comfort not only for our sake, but also that we may be able to comfort others with the same comfort wherewith we were comforted of God. This is the most advanced education that God gives His children in this world. Blessed is the man that passess the examination.

Thou, our Savior, from the throne
Listenest to Thy people's moan;
Thou, the living Head, dost share
Every pang Thy members bear;
Full of tenderness Thou art,
Thou wilt heal the broken heart;
Full of power, Thine arm shall quell
All the rage and might of hell.

Anniversaries and Birthdays

____

____

____

FEBRUARY 5

Come; for all things are now ready. **Luke 14:17**

JESUS has put these words in the mouth of His witnesses. He has commanded them to go into all the world and say to all men that they may come to God, because all things are now ready. Whosoever will may now come, the bad and the good, without money and without price. Sin is atoned, the debt is paid, death is conquered, and we have received of Jehovah's hand double for all our sins. Where sin abounded, grace abounded more exceedingly, "for of His fulness we all received, and grace for grace."

The question no longer is whether we can get help, but it is whether or not we will come. There is the rub: People will not come! It is more fun to enjoy the pleasures of sin on the edge of the eternal abyss, than to grasp the saving hand. And so people are lost in spite of the fact that all things are ready. It will surely be hard to "be cast forth into the outer darkness," where no one any more cries, "Come!"—and to know that this happens because one disdained the Savior-hand while yet there was time. That must be hell.

If you are one of those who have not yet come, then I beg of you: Come now, come to Him who has made all things ready!

And you who are digging in your own heart, and find only poverty: Lift your eyes to Him who has everything that you need! He is rich enough for everybody, also for you.

O come, if sinner be thy name,
And sin's sore burden thou art feeling,
To Him who never put to shame
The suppliant at His foot-stool kneeling.
Why wilt thou gloom for glory choose,
And His free gift of life refuse?
Wilt thou vile bondage love for ever,
When He proclaims the word, Deliver?
Ah! cease thy dearest Friend to grieve,
My Savior sinners doth receive.

Anniversaries and Birthdays

____

____

____

____

FEBRUARY 6

If any man willeth to do His will, he shall know of the teaching, whether it is of God, or whether I speak from Myself. John 7:17

HERE Jesus indicates the course of action that must be followed by everyone who wants to experience the truth of what He has said.

And the demand that is put into this law is just. When a man has promised to give us something, provided we will come and get it where it is, we cannot say that that man is unreliable if we get nothing, when we do not do what he said we should do, if we wanted the things promised.

But just that is what most people do when asked to believe in Jesus. If they are to believe in Him, they demand that He give them everything He has promised, without their doing what He says they must do. Then when they do not receive, they will not believe. Many, who in other matters are wise, are just that perverted and unreasonable in this question of faith.

It is God's will that we repent, confess our sins, and give Him our life. It is God's will that we believe that we are saved because of what God has done for us in Christ, and trust in Him alone. On condition that we do this, God has promised to make us happy, to give us peace, to cleanse our conscience, to transform us into new beings, and to let His Spirit bear witness with our spirit that we are children of God.

A question to all you who desire to think your way into the fellowship of God: Do you not know that this is impossible? Come to God as a child to its mother, and act according to His Word: then you will get what He has promised.

The way is open for all of us today. Come, and let us walk in that way!

Thy Word, a wondrous guiding star,
On pilgrim hearts doth rise,
Leads those to God who dwell afar,
And makes the simple wise.
Let not its light e'er sink in night;
In every spirit shine,
That none may miss heaven's final bliss,
Led by Thy light divine.

Anniversaries and Birthdays

FEBRUARY 7

Pray without ceasing. **I Thessalonians 5:17**

TO pray without ceasing seems not only to be difficult, but for many quite impossible. And if we believe that words must always be used, it is impossible to pray without ceasing. But God has not arranged it that way for us. We can pray without words. And then we can pray wherever we wish and whenever we wish.

So we must inclose this Word about praying without ceasing in the Word about praying in the spirit. For every person who knows his own helplessness, it should be a great comfort to know that God hears our prayers even if we do not use words. Our spirit and God's Spirit can bring a prayer to God more swiftly than the telegraph carries a report around the earth. He who Himself is Spirit hears the praying spirit. The Father seeks those who worship in spirit and truth.

I know very well that this comfort for the people of God can be used as false comfort by those who never will and never can open their mouths to pray. But the Word about praying in the spirit is the truth for all that. A Christian always considers it a great privilege to be permitted to open his mouth in prayer to God. But when the mouth is unable to be interpreter for the heart, it is well to know that,

Then He puts His ear up close to my faint heart:
I note that He can hear though not a word be said.

So no matter where you are, in the quiet valley, on the wild ocean, or in the midst of a crowd of raw and godless people: the prayer that lives in your heart reaches God.

I praise Thee, O my God and Father,
For all I am and all I have,
The blessings that we daily gather,
E'en from our cradle to our grave;
For Thy rich grace hath scattered here
Whate'er we need to help and cheer.

Anniversaries and Birthdays

FEBRUARY 8

I do not make void the grace of God: for if righteousness is through the law, then Christ died for naught. Gal. 2:21

THE road from Golgotha to Sinai is not always long, and many Christians have walked it and thought that they did right. It appears so right and wise to do that, because our nature so much prefers to help itself rather than to live on grace. In all times it has become evident that the great danger that threatens the people of God is this: to glide away from grace and into the works of the law. To carry an empty container and just have something given to you from day to day, from year to year, from generation to generation—that might easily be mistaken for sinning on grace. In such times there is among Christians fertile soil for bondage under the law, and for the teaching of sinlessness.

Neither has Satan any objection to telling us how a Christian should live and what he should be, if thereby he can separate us from grace. For there is no way that more certainly leads to eternal death than the Pharisaic way of works. Wherefore Jesus also has said that we must above all things beware of the leaven of the Pharisees.

To be saved by grace alone, and then in addition to that to be permitted to live and die, saved by grace alone: that is the road leading home to heaven again that God has built for sinners. On that road we can be completely saved in sorrow and in joy, in light and in darkness, when our soul feels lifted toward God, and when our heart condemns us.

"And he hath said unto me, My grace is sufficient for thee: for My power is made perfect in weakness. Most gladly therefore will I rather glory in my weaknesses, that the power of Christ may rest upon me" (II Cor. 12:9).

Lord, my sins they are many,
  Like the sands of the sea,
But Thy blood, O my Savior,
  Is sufficient for me;
For Thy promise is written
  In bright letters that glow,
"Though your sins be as scarlet,
  I will make them like snow."

Anniversaries and Birthdays

FEBRUARY 9

Blessed are the meek: for they shall inherit the earth. Matt. 5:5

NO doubt we think when we fly into a rage, that we shall now conquer both people and country; but soon we ourselves are beaten. He that ruleth his spirit is better than he that taketh a city, and that person is a winner who can be silent when others scold.

Not all people are by nature hot-tempered. Some are born with so patient a spirit that hardly anything can destroy their poise. There is little reason to thank such people for not being over-zealous. But the one who is victorious over self is he who by nature is hasty and ungovernable, and yet in spite of that can take a blow calmly. There will be no sanctification and growth in grace in those who are unacquainted with the war against evil. But where the enemy storms ahead with a force that we cannot resist, and then the power of God finds a place in us, so that we win—that is sanctification, that is growth in grace, that is the power of God made perfect in the helpless one.

When the ungovernable nature is held in check, when the quick-tempered man controls his anger, when the loose tongue is silent and neither wounds nor gossips, and when the hard-hearted person becomes mild and tender—that is victory. That is the meek person who is blessed. Over his life God has written this: He shall inherit the earth. What this promise means, I cannot say, but we can be sure that it is something great and good.

God grant that we be found among the meek.

> Nearer is my soul's salvation,
> Spent the night, the day at hand;
> Keep me, in my lowly station,
> Watching for Thee, till I stand,
> O my Savior,
> In Thy bright, Thy promised land.

Anniversaries and Birthdays

____

____

____

____

FEBRUARY 10

For of His fulness we all received, and grace for grace. John 1:16

GRACE does not take virtue and good deeds into consideration. It asks only whether we are human beings, and then we can be anything at all: Kaiser or beggar, in the eyes of men unblemished, or dirty with sin and shame. Grace does not distinguish between virtue and vice: if it did, it would no longer be grace. We are saved by grace and may live on grace all our lives. As the air surrounds us wherever we go, so grace surrounds all those who enter the kingdom of God. There is grace to walk into the presence of God as His child, grace for the fight and the victory, grace to get our wounds cleansed and healed, grace to keep us from growing weary and losing courage.

The Christian who desires to be genuine and whole in his Christianity, easily gets discouraged. When he looks at himself, what he is and what he ought to be, then from the depths of his heart this sigh often becomes vocal: "I am not making the grade, my Christian life is not up to the standard, I guess I am losing out." Surely if we are going to look at ourselves and our Christianity, we must give up: but God has not spoken thus. He has given us grace for grace, yea, grace overflowing so that where sin abounds grace abounds more exceedingly. Discouraged Christian, behold that way, and then you are saved.

Then our text says that of His fulness we all received. Have we all received? Yes, so God loved the world. All have received, but not all have accepted what was given them, and the result has been disastrous. Sinner, accept what is given you, and then you too are saved.

Praise, my soul, the God that sought thee,
Wretched wanderer, far astray;
Found thee lost, and kindly brought thee
From the paths of death away:
Praise, with love's devoutest feeling,
Him who saw thy guilt-born fear,
And, the light of hope revealing,
Bade the blood-stained cross appear.

Anniversaries and Birthdays

FEBRUARY 11

The kingdom of heaven is like unto a treasure hidden in the field; which a man found, and hid; and in his joy he goeth and selleth all that he hath, and buyeth that field. Matt. 13:44

WHEN we find Christ we get the purest joy and greatest riches that we can obtain in this world. But what is hard and offends many is that we must give up everything for that One. Why may we not be Christians, and then own and love whatever we wish? Most people think this must be right, and so they go away in anger, and say that Christianity is unreasonably strict in its demands.

If that is your opinion, let us ask you what you would say about the wife or husband who wanted to share love and life with many men and women? Do you think that would work? You know that that is impossible, and yet you demand this impossibility when you wish to become a Christian.

We can never own Christ, life's most precious treasure, if we desire to love something else just as much as Him. "He that loveth father or mother more than Me is not worthy of Me." . . . "Son, daughter, give me thy heart."

If you desire to be rich and to have life's greatest success, and if you wish to wear the pearl that will adorn you in life, in death, and in all eternity, then give yourself wholly to Christ. And you who were wise enough to choose Him to be the only One to own you entirely, praise Him who accepted you, and who loves you as His bride.

Jesus, priceless treasure,
Source of purest pleasure,
Truest friend to me:
Ah, how long I've panted
And my heart hath fainted,
Thirsting, Lord, for Thee.
Thine I am, O spotless Lamb!
I will suffer naught to hide Thee,
Naught I ask beside Thee.

Anniversaries and Birthdays

FEBRUARY 12

Whom He appointed heir of all things, through whom also He made the worlds. Heb. 1:2

NO one can show us the eternal riches of God. The shadow of the earth and of sin obscures our sight. But we believe that God is rich, as rich as He is eternal: the inheritance that the Son has received must then be unspeakably great.

"Father, Thou gavest Him authority over all flesh." He has created everything, He has bought everything, and He has inherited everything. And He who is not ashamed to be called our brother, He has also promised to share the inheritance with us. "If children, then heirs; heirs of God, and joint-heirs with Christ." An inheritance incorruptible, and undefiled, and that fadeth not away is reserved for us in heaven.

But it may be that there is one part of the inheritance that the Son especially considers His inheritance. That is all those who are saved. A heaven full of saved sinners! A multitude that no man can number, "out of every nation and of all tribes and peoples and tongues": that must be Jesus' greatest and dearest inheritance. The saved are His crown of glory, the full-blown flower that never withers, and pearls in the Savior-crown of Jesus Christ. They take heaven's highest notes, and sing heaven's most beautiful song. A heaven full of saved sinners—that is proof that the miracle of God's love is completed.

How wonderful it will be when by grace I too shall be permitted to be there.

Jesus, name of priceless worth
To the fallen sons of earth,
For the promise that it gave,
"Jesus shall His people save."

Anniversaries and Birthdays

FEBRUARY 13

For we are become partakers of Christ, if we hold fast the beginning of our confidence firm unto the end. Heb. 3:14

EVERY Christian knows of a time when life lay before him sinful and defiled. We could undo nothing. What had been done, had been done, and we could do nothing about it. But just as all our own resources were used up, when the last hope had died, an invisible hand came and turned our eyes away from ourselves, and to Him who saves sinners. As a bird sings on a fair spring morning, so we sang then about salvation full and free. Then was given us the beginning of our confidence, that which our text exhorts us to hold fast firm unto the end.

But life has taught us that this is more easily said than done. To keep ourselves quite independent of ourselves both in what we are and in what we are not, and to have everything in Jesus alone, that is the high art of Christianity, an art that no one learns except by the grace of God. Our evil nature and our human understanding continually draw us back to ourselves, and before we know it we are expecting more from our own Christianity than from Christ. Then we look at ourselves when we should be looking at Him, with resulting doubt, anxiety, and lost peace. When we feel glad, good, and spiritual we think that all is well; but when our heart feels cold and evil, we doubt.

But this is not being firm in the beginning of our confidence. This is believing in yourself instead of in Christ. He alone is entirely sufficient for our salvation—always.

Not the labors of my hands
Can fulfill Thy law's demands;
Could my zeal no respite know,
Could my tears forever flow,
All for sin would not atone;
Thou must save, and Thou alone.

Anniversaries and Birthdays

___

___

___

___

FEBRUARY 14

And He answereth them and saith, "O faithless generation, how long shall I be with you? how long shall I bear with you? bring him unto Me!" Mark 9:19

WE feel that it is a shame and a disgrace that Jesus so often must complain about our unbelief. If we had had more confidence in Him, then He could have helped many unhappy people through us. But because of our unbelief many of those that God wanted us to help must go unhelped. And yet, in the midst of all that settles down on us to our shame and chastening, we have one great comfort: what we cannot do, He can. And He invites us to bring everything to Him.

Mother and father and whoever you are, toiling at many tasks, with disobedient and godless children too, you who think, are anxious, weep, and pray, and you who accuse yourself because things are as they are: Come, and give ear to these words of Jesus: "Bring him unto Me!" When the Savior asks us to bring to Him the problems we cannot master, should we not do so? Go! and lay down before Him everything that is too hard for you.

But remember, not to take back with you the burden that you brought to Him. Many do that. But you must not do that. The burden is to be left with Him. God desires not only that we pray: He also wants us to remember what He has promised, and to rely on what He has said. Then we get rid of our burden, and we show Him the confidence of which He is worthy. Then we give our Savior the opportunity to be for us what He would like to be.

They that trust in Him shall never be put to shame.

O Word of God incarnate,
O Wisdom from on high,
O Truth unchanged, unchanging,
O Light of our dark sky;
We praise Thee for the radiance
That from the hallowed page,
A lamp unto our footsteps,
Shines on from age to age.

Anniversaries and Birthdays

FEBRUARY 15

For God is not unrighteous to forget your work and the love which ye showed toward His name, in that ye ministered unto the saints, and still do minister. Heb. 6:10

THIS is really a wonderful word. Just before this, the author writes about blaspheming the Holy Spirit; and we get the impression that the Jewish Christians had been in great danger of committing this sin, because they were tempted to leave Christ. But one of the things that kept them from falling into the eternal abyss, was the love they had showed toward the name of Jesus by serving the people of God. The author of the letter to the Hebrews is certain that this awful sin will not get dominion over them, because they have served the saints, and still do serve.

I suppose it is not often that the thought gets a foothold with us Christians, that our love for the name of Jesus finds its best expression in serving the people of God, and that in this service there is power which defends against sin, and helps to hold fast to Christ. So often we are busy pondering and digging in our hearts to find out whether we love our Savior—and get no answer. But in God's Word we learn it in a quite different manner. The Word of God says that if we serve the people of God we love Jesus. There is the answer. When Peter testified to Jesus that he loved Him, he was told to serve the saints. Here he would have an opportunity to show by works that his testimony was true.

He who serves the saints loves Jesus.

Let us ask ourselves if it is in this way that we love our Savior.

> Still the weary, sick, and dying
> Need a brother's, sister's care,
> On Thy higher help relying,
> May we now their burden share,
> Bringing all our offerings meet,
> Suppliant to Thy mercy-seat.

Anniversaries and Birthdays

FEBRUARY 16

Blessed are the poor in spirit: for theirs is the kingdom of heaven.
Matt. 5:3

TO be poor in spirit is not the same as to be lacking in spirit. That misunderstanding has damaged the Christian life of many. To be lacking in spirit is to have a weak and sick life with God, a life that does not know its own poverty, and that does not hunger and thirst. To be poor in spirit is a sure sign of a life in God that is true and healthful.

The Word of God is full of comfort for all who think humbly of themselves, and who hunger and thirst after God. The self-sufficient and the sated, God has sent empty away, but the poor He has filled with good things.

Of the seven Christian churches that Jesus sent messages to by John (Rev. I, II, III), there are only two that do not get a warning and a reproof. We will find something to prove and try us if we discover what is said about these two, and not about the others. Of one we read: "I know thy tribulation, and thy poverty"; and of the other: "Thou hast a little power." This is not said of the others. On the contrary they are rebuked for not knowing their wretchedness. "Thou knowest not," we read, "that thou art the wretched one and miserable and poor and blind and naked." That is the calamity.

A true Christian never finds riches and satisfaction in himself, but he always stretches out two empty hands to Him who has promised to give to the poor.

Naught I ask for, naught I strive for,
But Thy grace so rich and free;
That Thou givest whom Thou lovest,
And who truly cleave to Thee.
||: Let me find Thee! :||
He hath all things who hath Thee.

Anniversaries and Birthdays

FEBRUARY 17

For in the day of trouble He will keep me secretly in His pavilion:
In the covert of His tabernacle will He hide me;
He will lift me up upon a rock. Psalm 27:5

NO one will ever in this world succeed in finding a solution for all the riddles of life. It will needs be sufficient for us to believe that the Lord does all things well. But for many people, that which more than anything else throws shadows across life's way, is all the opposition and the evil days. It looks almost as though some people existed just to be knocked about from pillar to post, with treatment growing steadily worse. Then the question arises: Why must I endure all this? Why must all my life be entwined with adversity? Many of us are acquainted with such questions.

But you who "know the fear of the Lord," have you not gradually, as the years have passed, gotten answers to many of your "Why's"? When all is said, were not many of the evil days the best? Was it not then that you found the most blessed peace and the supremest joy in God? Was it not especially on evil days that you found the way to the farthest recesses of the prayer rooms of God's house? And was it not so good for you to be there that in deepest earnestness and with clear conviction you could thank God for the evil days?

"Whom the Lord loveth He chasteneth." And he who humbly accepts His chastisement is drawn close in to the heart of God.

Perfect truth will love to follow
Watchfully our Master's ways;
Seeks not comfort poor and hollow,
Looks not for reward or praise.

Perfect truth from worldly pleasure,
Worldly turmoil, stands apart;
For in heaven is hid our treasure,
There must also be the heart.

Anniversaries and Birthdays

FEBRUARY 18

Suffer hardship with me, as a good soldier of Christ Jesus.
II Tim. 2:3

TO suffer because one does evil, that is the wage that sin pays, and it is always bitter to accept that wage. But to suffer for Jesus' sake, that is the Christian's honor, and that is a good wage to receive.

Timothy was that kind of soldier. When Paul called on Timothy to suffer hardship with him, the reason probably was that Timothy was losing courage. There are many who have gone under in despondency.

If we only remember that all over the world, from palace to hut, there are thousands of Christians who are struggling together with us, this will help to give the most thoroughly discouraged person joy and strength in the midst of strife. The idea that I am worse off than others, that I am the forgotten man, that idea finds a way into the heart with wonderful ease. But the truth is that at all times there is a great multitude who share the same strife, sufferings, and longings as we.

Let us also remember that the heavens rejoice at every victory we win, and all who can, thank God for us. The hymns of praise will resound mightily through the city of God, when the victory is completely won, and the people of God have come home to stay. A moment in this jubilee choir will outweigh ever so many years in the strife here.

For thee, O dear, dear country,
Mine eyes their vigils keep;
For very love, beholding
Thy happy name, they weep:
The mention of thy glory
Is unction to the breast,
And medicine in sickness,
And love, and life, and rest.

Anniversaries and Birthdays

____

____

____

____

FEBRUARY 19

I stand continually upon the watch-tower in the day-time, and am set in my ward whole nights. Isaiah 21:8

TO be on guard duty the livelong day, and night after night, that is the Christian's task so long as he is here on earth. He is assigned to this post to watch Time's clock, and to listen and learn what hour is being struck. He is also to keep an eye on the spiritual hosts of wickedness that are making war against the kingdom of God and the Christian church, so he can cry out to his brothers to make ready for battle. But especially is he to be on his guard against those enemies that would destroy him personally.

It is a difficult and wearisome position, and the person who is to fill it must tear himself loose from this world, and get his eye on his true fatherland. Many have gotten tired and have gone to sleep, because they looked toward the earth. In our best moments we too can see how easily we may forget that we should be a people doing guard duty. The danger of failing God and going to sleep was never greater than now. But do we take this into consideration? It is surely time to call to each other that we must wake up and again take our posts as sentries day and night. What of him who hears the cry and stands at his post? God Himself shall put on him the breastplate of righteousness, and make him strong to use both shield and sword in victorious conflict.

I walk with Jesus all the way,
His guidance never fails me,
Within His wounds I find a stay,
When Satan's power assails me;
And by His footsteps led,
My path I safely tread,
In spite of ills that threaten may,
I walk with Jesus all the way.

Anniversaries and Birthdays

FEBRUARY 20

And both the Pharisees and the scribes murmured, saying, This man receiveth sinners, and eateth with them. Luke 15:2

STRANGELY enough, one of the accusations that the enemies of Jesus brought against Him, was entirely true. He received sinners and ate with them. It was impossible for the Pharisees to be reconciled to this. They were fully convinced that when the Best Person of all good people came, He would join their company. But, No! Quite the contrary! He preferred the company of those of whom the Pharisees had the poorest opinion. The result was that those who considered themselves the best people bcame the worst antagonists of Jesus—and finally slew Him.

It may well be that Jesus might have lived, and said and done anything He wished, if He only had turned His back on publicans and sinners. But He could not do that without breaking faith with Himself: instead He gave His life as the Friend of sinners. It is more impossible for Jesus to turn away from a sinner that He can save, than it would be for a mother to let go her hold on her child while carrying it across an abyss.

It is great good fortune for a person to be a real sinner in his own eyes. If we are not sinners, what need have we of a Savior? He who does not see his sin and helplessness has no use for a Savior. If the result of a Christian's development is that he sees less and less of his sin, he becomes a Pharisee. But a great sinner needs a great Savior.

To me the preaching of the cross
Is wisdom everlasting;
Thy death alone redeems my loss;
On Thee my burden casting,
I, in Thy name,
A refuge claim
From sin and death and from all shame—
Blest be Thy name, O Jesus!

Anniversaries and Birthdays

FEBRUARY 21

And he said, Lord, I believe. And he worshipped Him. John 9:38

IN this world a Christian must walk by faith. Also after we have met Christ as our Savior, we must be believers. Building on what we have experienced as Christians, instead of believing, is a plan that will carry us away from Christ. "Whom not having seen ye love; on whom, though now ye see Him not, yet believing," says Peter. Even Paul, who had been in heaven and heard unspeakable words, must afterwards be a believing man. At the edge of the grave he rejoices because he has not lost his faith.

But Christian faith is not like a man who seeks without finding. He who goes ahead trusting in God's Word is not only a believer, but he also lives to see what God has promised. Christ not only tells us what we are to believe and be, but He also gives us that.

What Thou so wearily hast plowed,
Is an eternal crop for me.

So let us with the man born blind fall on our knees before Christ, and more than ever before believe His plain Word. He who has helped us so many, many times—occasionally when we least expected it—He is worthy of our confidence today too. Perhaps a difficult task awaits you just now. Remember then that he who puts his trust in the Lord will never be put to shame.

O for a faith that will not shrink,
Though pressed by many a foe,
That will not tremble on the brink
Of any earthly woe.

Anniversaries and Birthdays

FEBRUARY 22

Having therefore, brethren, boldness to enter into the holy place by the blood of Jesus, by the way which He dedicated for us, a new and living way, through the veil, that is to say, His flesh; and having a great priest over the house of God. Heb. 10:19-21

YOU and I may come into the holy place, to the living God in whose presence not even the heavens are clean. Jesus has opened the way, and by the blood of Jesus the right to walk that way has been given to us all; yea, Jesus is Himself the new and living way. If we are in Him, He brings us into the holy place, where for His sake we dare to call God Father. In ourselves we are condemned to be shut out from God forever, but in Jesus we have received the right to be the children of God.

We can draw nigh the throne
And say, Our Father,
Thy child Thou now must help!
O God, what prospects
Of bliss beyond compare!

Yes, it is lovely, and too high for thought. But God has given us this by Jesus Christ. If we fully understood this, we would shout forth His praise and honor, thank Him, and worship Him day and night.

So let us use this glorious right and go into the holy place. Our heavenly Father looks forward with joy to meeting us there. We can tell Him about everything we need, about our burdens and about everything that hurts us. He will gladly help His children today. He will help you.

Ye fearful saints, fresh courage take:
The clouds ye so much dread
Are big with mercy, and shall break
In blessings on your head.

Anniversaries and Birthdays

____

____

____

____

____

FEBRUARY 23

Looking unto Jesus the author and perfecter of our faith, who for the joy that was set before Him endured the cross, despising shame, and hath sat down at the right hand of the throne of God.

Heb. 12:2

OUR text says that Jesus received strength in His struggle and got help to endure the cross with patience, from the joy that was set before Him. As He looked to the goal and acquired power by this vision, so we must look at Him and win power for victory.

Gradually, as a Christian gets acquainted with himself, he sees more and more clearly that the true and only source of all vital power for the Christian is found in beholding Christ. If our vision of Him is not renewed, our Christian life will harden into dead forms, and we will land in bondage, using empty Christian talk. Even the use of the Word and of prayer becomes wearisome work that gives no vital power, if we do not get to see Christ through the Word and prayer. In Him "are all the treasures of wisdom and knowledge hidden." He is the fountain of life, food and drink for the soul.

So surely as we want to be saved and hold fast to the Lord, He who has promised to make us victorious, will help us to this. But then we must also expect Him to use His chastising rod. That seems to be one of the most successful methods that He has, to give us a renewed vision of Jesus.

Behold the Lamb of God!
O Thou for sinners slain,
Let it not be in vain
That Thou hast died:
Thee for my Savior let me take,
My only refuge let me make
Thy pierced side.

Anniversaries and Birthdays

FEBRUARY 24

But I am in a strait betwixt the two, having the desire to depart and be with Christ; for it is very far better. Phil. 1:23

ONE would think that a man entirely loosed from everything in this world is poorly equipped to do anything on earth. It may seem reasonable to think that people whose interests are outside of this life will fold their hands and spend their time looking toward heaven.

But the remarkable thing is that practical life shows us the exact opposite of this. He who is most strongly bound to heaven has also the greatest desire to get others with him to the same destination. Where love for the world has been drowned in the living hope, the heart is filled with a longing to help others into the fellowship of God. The desire to depart and to be with Christ draws heaven down over your home and work-a-day life and gives power to serve and to give light for others in good and in evil days. He who has Christ as his life and heaven as his home, has in Him a double pull: he wants to go home to God, and he is eager to get others with him. These are the two wishes that puzzled Paul and made him happy.

As the rays of the sun draw water into the air, and then send it down again to bless the earth, so Jesus draws His people upward. And as we gradually are loosed from everything here below, we little by little become a greater blessing on earth. For a Christian, happiness surely does not consist in being earth-bound, but in feeling freed from everything here, and in having a desire to be with God.

> There is a land of pure delight,
> Where saints immortal reign:
> Infinite day excludes the night,
> And pleasures banish pain.

Anniversaries and Birthdays

____

____

____

____

____

FEBRUARY 25

No man hath seen God at any time; the only begotten Son, who is in the bosom of the Father, He hath declared Him. John 1:18

GOD is invisible to us. He dwells in light unapproachable. But His only begotten Son who was in the bosom of the Father, and who played in His presence before the foundation of the world, He has made the Father known. He who sees Jesus, hears His Word, and follows Him from the cradle to the grave, and from the grave to the Ascension, he sees God.

There are especially two views of God that are untrue and deceiving. The one is that God is hard and cold, and delights in striking and punishing us, while Jesus is the mild Savior who always defends the sinner so that a just God shall not reach him with His righteous hand. The other view is that God is a loving Father who receives sinners without any atonement for sin by Jesus.

Both of these views give us a false picture of God. The Son is just as holy and righteous as the Father, and the Father is just as mild as the Son. We see God when Jesus accepts sinners and helps them in all kinds of need; and we see God when Jesus takes the cup of suffering and tastes of death for every man. He who desires to find a way to the father-heart of God outside the Christ who died for us and atoned for our sins, he dulls the sharp point of God's righteousness, removes the effulgence of His glory, and dishonors Him who was in Christ reconciling the world to Himself. It was God who so loved the world that He gave us Jesus as our Savior. In Christ, God is our Savior, and in Him God is our Father. No one cometh unto the Father but by the Son. He who gave us Jesus, freely gave us all things with Him.

Come, my soul thy suit prepare,
Jesus loves to answer prayer;
He Himself has bid thee pray,
Therefore will not say thee nay.

God, my Lord, my king, Thou art,
Take possession of my heart.
There Thy blood-bought right maintain,
And without a rival reign.

Anniversaries and Birthdays

____

____

____

FEBRUARY 26

Finally, be strong in the Lord, and in the strength of His might.
Eph. 6:10

WE must be strong if we are to conquer the evil forces within us and outside us. If we are not strong we must either suffer defeat, or we must get someone who is stronger than the enemy to fight for us. This Word says, "Be strong in the Lord." I think we must notice that it says "strong *in* the Lord," not *by* Him in us; but *in* Him.

It is in this "in the Lord" that the secret is hid: this that God Himself is our strength.

In one way it is easy to understand that if we only have the power of God in us, we can surely be strong. But that is certainly not the way it is meant here. Here the figure is of a little weak child resting in the arms of a strong father. The strength is not transferred to the child. What saves the child is the strength in father himself.

Jehoshaphat went out against the enemy, not to do his own fighting but to see that which had been promised him: that the Lord would fight for him. Daniel sat in the den of lions, surely as weak as anyone. But the Lord was his strength, and no lion could touch him.

To seek our strength in the Lord by trusting in that power of God that is conducted into us, is not the same as being strong in the Lord. But to be strong in the Lord means to be without power, and then in confidence to look up to God who Himself will fight for us; and that is truly the deepest mystery in our victory.

"In quietness and in confidence shall be your strength" (Isaiah 30:15).

> Why art thou cast down, my soul?
> O what mean thy sighs and sadness?
> Trust in Him who makes thee whole,
> And thy griefs can turn to gladness,—
> Often in the darkest hour
> He reveals His love and power.

Anniversaries and Birthdays

FEBRUARY 27

Surely there is not a righteous man upon earth, that doeth good, and sinneth not. **Eccl. 7:20**

MANY of those who honestly seek God dare not believe that they are saved; because in their own opinion they are too great sinners. Others expect to reach heaven with God's help when they live the best way they know; and a large multitude think they can take care of everything alone.

On a very great and solemn occasion in Norway's parliament a man stood forth and spoke about thus: "If it is not true that Christ is God, if He is not an atonement for our sins, if He did not rise from His grave, then the Christian faith no longer has any foundation, and then we no longer have the answer to life's profoundest question, the question about our salvation."

A man outside the parliament answered with these words from Luke X: "Thou shalt love the Lord thy God with all thy heart, and with all thy soul, and with all thy strength, and with all thy mind; and thy neighbor as thyself." . . . And then the same man added, on his own account: "This is the answer to the question of the anxious member of parliament."

This man seemed in sober earnest to believe that he could take care of everything alone! Sensible people can have such petty thoughts about God, and such great ones about themselves. Miserable self-deception! It is sad to think of all the people who are so thoughtless and blind about life's greatest question.

"Professing themselves to be wise, they became fools." Your life and your works are too poor a key to unlock the gate of heaven. He who does not turn and come to Christ, will be left standing outside. God's Word says that.

Come in poverty and meanness,
Come defiled, without, within;
From infection and uncleanness,
From the leprosy of sin,
Wash your robes and make them white;
Ye shall walk with God in light.

Anniversaries and Birthdays

______

______

______

FEBRUARY 28

Jesus also was bidden, and His disciples, to the marriage. John 2:2

IT was into the first home on earth that Satan forced his way and devastated human life. It was in a home too that Jesus did the beginning of His signs on earth, and manifested His glory. Where sin and Satan first had been admitted, there the Savior of the world first revealed His power.

God had ordained it that way.

The home is the place where true Christian life and all sound folk-customs can best be developed. When homes are destroyed, morals degenerate, and folk-joy and community life fare ill. Therefore Jesus accepted the invitation to the marriage. He desired to bless the home. Thereby He revealed not only His divine glory but also His true human nature. It is not only homes where sinners are begging for grace, and where Death is knocking at the door, that the Son of man enters. If permitted He also visits young people who are glad of life and who are building their homes and earthly future. There He makes wine of water, which means that He makes joy out of sorrow, and permeates the struggle for existence and the work-day with His glory. Satan poured sin, sorrow, and death into a cup till it was filled; but Jesus takes it and fills it with life, joy, and peace. He will do this most especially as we in our homes meet the problems of life in the height and depth of their demands. To invite Jesus to the marriage feast and to give Him a place in your home as Savior and King, that is building your house on a rock. Then there will be help in need, light in darkness, and hope in death.

Come Thou who spreadest joy and gladness,
Forever bide with me and mine,
And bring to those who sit in sadness
And gloom of death Thy light divine:
A voice comes from my soul within;
Thou blessed of the Lord, come in!

Anniversaries and Birthdays

____

____

____

____

MARCH 1

He had to pass through Samaria. John 4:4

WHY must Jesus pass through Samaria? Because there He would have the opportunity of saving a sinful woman, and of speaking the Word of life to people that were eager to be saved.

In Jesus there is a force that compels Him to go where He can save a sinner. He sent an angel to Cornelius while he longed and prayed, so that Peter might bring him the Word of life. The Spirit told Philip to go near and join himself to the chariot in which the treasurer of Ethiopia sat, wistfully reading. He sought you and me too and helped us. When no one understood us, when we sat lonely and hidden away like Nathanael, then He came to many of us. He did not condemn us, but drew us to Himself, and gave us to drink of the blessed water of life. I remember well the day He came to me in that beautiful, quiet valley, and helped also me when I thought I was forgotten by both God and man. Do you remember when He came to you?

In the case of many of us, many years have passed since that day. We have not always behaved as we should, but He has never left us. He healed our battle wounds, forgave our sin, and wiped away our tears. Today too He will be with us in grace. Where each one of us struggles by himself He will meet us, and He will gladly be with us in the day's toils and dangers in business, in the office, with the water pail, in the boat, in field or forest, or wherever men go to honest toil.

It is comforting to think of this, and it is glorious to experience it.

Grace that He found me,
Love that won me,
Grace that He bore me to His fold.

Anniversaries and Birthdays

MARCH 2

I am the door; by Me if any man enter in, he shall be saved.
John 10:9

IN the Orient it is customary that the owner of sheep incloses a small parcel of ground with a stone wall, to be a safe place for the sheep at night. That is a sheep fold. When darkness draws nigh the shepherd takes the flock of sheep home from the pasture. He goes before them, and the sheep follow him. He does not drive them, he calls them. When he arrives at the fold and the sheep have entered, the door is shut, and a night watchman goes on duty to see that ravenous beasts and thieves do not kill and steal. In the morning the shepherd returns and leads the sheep out to pasture. To him the porter openeth. The door is the way for shepherd and sheep. Robbers and beasts of prey climb up over the wall.

Jesus Himself has said that for His people He is both shepherd and door. Through Him we enter the fold and are guarded against the enemy, and with Him we go out and find pasture. Little by little, as the Scriptures are opened to us, we must be filled with admiration and thanksgiving at seeing how Jesus is our all. He hunted us up, He carried us from the wilderness into the kingdom of His grace, in the day of trouble He kept us secretly in His pavilion; in the covert of His tabernacle He hid us. He was with us through the day's trials, and was Himself the door into the Word of God, where we were surrounded by the strong and holy promises of God.

Has He not been this and much more, also for you?

But what He was, He will continue to be until we sing His praises in a blessed eternity.

> There is a gate that stands ajar,
> And through its portals gleaming
> A radiance from the cross afar,
> The Savior's love revealing.

Anniversaries and Birthdays

MARCH 3

I am the good shepherd: the good shepherd layeth down his life for the sheep. John 10:11

THE ability to be a shepherd rests in the nature of Jesus; the right to be a shepherd He has bought with His own blood. So when He goes out and seeks the lost and finds some, He is not stealing the property of others. He is looking for what belongs to Him. He knocks at the doors, shouts, and invites wherever there are men who have knowledge of Him. As a mother rejoices when one of her children is saved from death, so the Good Shepherd is glad at heart over every sinner He is able to save. There is joy in heaven over one single sinner that repents. Man must be very precious in the sight of God when it means so much that just a single one is saved. Yea, the Lord says: "To Me you are precious, you have great worth, and I love you."

"Lord, Thou hast here Thy ninety and nine;
Are they not enough for Thee?"
But the Shepherd made answer: "This of Mine
Has wandered away from Me."

I was this one, and you were this one.

Have we let Him lay us on His shoulder and carry us home?

Jesus has promised to guard against all the dangers in the world those who can truthfully answer Yes. Finally we too by His power "may enter in by the gates into the city," and never more go out of it.

"The Lord is my shepherd; I shall not want."

The Lord my shepherd is;
I shall be well supplied:
Since He is mine and I am His,
What can I want beside?

He leads me to the place
Where heavenly pasture grows;
Where living waters gently pass,
And full salvation flows.

Anniversaries and Birthdays

MARCH 4

I knew Him not; but that He should be made manifest to Israel, for this cause came I baptizing in water. John 1:31

AT bottom this is a strange word: that John must make Jesus manifest to Israel. If he had not come, and if he had not accomplished what he did, people would not have learned to know Jesus, even though He had spent His whole life among them. What then was it that John did, so that Jesus was made manifest to Israel?

He awakened the people. He spoke weighty words about a holy and righteous God, who would judge all sin and hypocrisy. The people came to see their lost estate; and the cries to wake up, stirred a desire and need for getting away from sin, and into a new life. But then John could help them no further. They were stuck. It was just then that John stretched out an arm, pointed to Jesus, and said, "Behold, the Lamb of God, that beareth the sin of the world!" Then Jesus was made manifest to them, because they were lost sinners who were looking for help.

It is to such people that Jesus is made manifest this very day, and only to them. What use have we for a Savior when we believe that we can help ourselves? Unless the demands of God are brought home to a person so that he sees his own helplessness, he will have no use for a Savior. But where sin has become alive, a living Savior is needed. It is great grace from God that one sees himself as a sinner. You who see your sin, who feel it as a plague, and who see no other way out of the difficulty than Jesus,—praise God! You are on the right way.

I come to Thee with sin and grief,
For Thou alone canst give relief,
Thy death for me, dear Lord, I plead:
O Jesus, help me in my need!

Shouldst Thou a strict account demand,
Who could, O Lord, before Thee stand?
Purge all my secret sins away:
Be Thou, O Christ, the sinner's stay!

Anniversaries and Birthdays

MARCH 5

If any man thirst, let him come unto Me and drink. John 7:37

WE well know that there is a struggle all through life for the food and drink that the body needs. But to many people it is not clear that we have a soul that needs nourishment quite as much as the body.

And yet that is true. We dare not say that it always is the desire to commit sin that urges people when they fill the theatres and dance halls and other meeting places both worse and better. It is doubtless nearer the truth to say that the motive is the inner craving for the joys of life, the soul-thirst. The hollow cry of the harlot, the drunkard and his glass, and the miser who digs for gold day and night, all tell us about the soul that thirsts.

Others try to quench this thirst in good company, good books, and good knowledge. One cannot adversely criticize this procedure; nevertheless this is not the drink with which to quench the thirst of a soul. He who knows us thoroughly, says: "If any man thirst, let him come unto Me and drink!" That is the fountain that quenches the thirst of all.

All that man seeks outside of Christ—the worst as well as the best—can never quench the thirst of the soul. Only Jesus can do that. From Him we get what we need because He gives us what we lost. He leads us back to the fountain of life, because He gives us fellowship with God.

> O Fount of grace redeeming,
> O River ever streaming
> From Jesus' holy side:
> Come Thou, Thyself bestowing
> On thirsting souls, and flowing
> Till all their wants are satisfied.

Anniversaries and Birthdays

MARCH 6

I am the vine, ye are the branches: he that abideth in Me, and I in him, the same beareth much fruit: for apart from Me ye can do nothing. John 15:5

A VINE-TREE is good for nothing except to bear fruit. Of the vine-tree the prophet Ezekiel says: "Shall wood be taken thereof to make any work? or will men take a pin of it to hang any vessel thereon?" No; either it must bear fruit, or be burned. The branches on the vine that do not bear fruit are cut off, gathered together, and cast into the fire. I have seen that done.

The people of God are in this world to bear fruit. "Herein is My Father glorified, that ye bear much fruit," says Jesus.

We may ask: What is fruit? What fruit does Jesus speak of here? Everything in our lives, which is of God, is fruit. Apart from His power we can do nothing. "The fruit of the Spirit is love, joy, peace, longsuffering, kindness, goodness, faithfulness, meekness, self-control." This fruit is given to those who abide in Christ. As in the spring the sap flows along between the bark and the wood right out to the tips of the tiniest twigs, and forms buds, leaves, flowers, and fruit, so the power from God will find its way through us, and create fruit for God, if we are in Christ.

Consequently the matter of prime importance for us Christians is to have the mind of Christ. If His life is not developed in us, we bear no fruit, and we are under the judgment. But the person who is in the Word of Jesus Christ, in His comfort, and in His cleansing discipline, he bears fruit.

Grace, every morning new,
And every night we feel
The soft, refreshing dew
That falls on Hermon's hill!
On Zion it doth sweetly fall:
The grace of One descends on all.

Anniversaries and Birthdays

MARCH 7

Nicodemus, a ruler of the Jews, the same came unto Jesus by night. John 3:1-2

THAT surely was no easy trip for the great man. But the demand for truth, and the many unsolved questions left no peace. All that he was, all that he had studied, and all that he had taught others only made his perplexity greater. We have reason to believe that more than once he had stood in a crowd of people and had listened to John Baptizer speaking. Perhaps he was present on the day that John called out, "Behold, the Lamb of God, that taketh away the sin of the world!" Everything had tended to increase the need for light and help. And so he goes to Jesus.

A wonderful night! In those quiet hours light was shed upon his life. Now everything lies before him as an open book: his own life and God's revelation, clear from the time that Moses lifted up the serpent in the wilderness, and on to Christ who must be lifted up on a cross. Not so long after this, when the cross was raised on Golgotha, and nearly all men in darkness and despondence left Jesus, Nicodemus walked quietly over there, and did according to the Word of the Lord. The mystery of the cross had solved the mystery of life.

Among us there are many who resemble Nicodemus in standing high in society, in being good men, and in longing for light. But so few of these go with Nicodemus to Jesus. That is unspeakably hard and sad.

If you are one of these, I beseech you to break down every obstacle, and to go to Him who wants to give you light, and be your Savior.

He will solve the problem of your life too.

A ruler once came to Jesus by night,
To ask Him the way of salvation and light;
The Master made answer in words true and plain:
Ye must be born again.

Anniversaries and Birthdays

MARCH 8

From that time began Jesus to show unto His disciples, that He must go unto Jerusalem, and suffer many things of the elders and chief priests and scribes. Matt. 16:21

WHAT Jesus said to the disciples that day in the way, He could not have told them before, because they were not able to bear it. But now it had to be said whether they took it or left it. With divine wisdom He reveals a part of what must happen to Him in the great conflict about our salvation.

But what Peter then thought was entirely devoid of sense and meaning, later became life's purest joy and most precious treasure both for him and for the other disciples. And is not that the way the Lord always deals with His people? Our future lies hidden in the eternal counsels of God. Everything is written in the book sealed with the seven seals that Jesus took and was able to open (Rev. 5:5-7). In His great wisdom God sees how best to guide us so that we shall be set free from sin and the world. Then as the wax seals crumple under the pressure of His Savior-hand, the impression often given is that everything is going to ruin. While we beg to be spared, it often happens that we get new blows for an answer. But what we understood most imperfectly, became later in life our most precious possession, and a chief reason for thanking God.

When finally all things lie before us as an open book in the light shed on it by eternal life, then we shall cry out: The Lord did all things well!

Give, Lord, this consummation
To all our heart's distress,
Our hands, our feet, O strengthen,
In death our spirits bless.
Thy truth and Thy protection
Forevermore we pray:
With these in heavenly glory
Shall end our certain way.

Anniversaries and Birthdays

MARCH 9

The Teacher is here, and calleth for thee. John 11:28

IT was one of His own that Jesus inquired for that day. A heavy pall of sorrow had settled on the home, not only because the brother was dead, but also because Jesus had not come when He learned of the sickness. Martha apparently did not doubt that He could help. All that she had seen done by Him during these years was more than enough to make her certain that He was able. But He did not arrive until all was over. That is the way it looked to Martha; but not to Jesus: and soon the greatest joy sprang from the deepest sorrow.

Many of the friends of Jesus down through the centuries have sent for Him—and He has not come. So everything was over for us too, and like Martha and Mary we also stood at a grave. But then one day—perhaps when we least expected it—Jesus came and inquired for us. Not that He would give back to us the loved one who had passed on, but He gave us something that cannot be expressed in words. He gave us a glimpse of the glory that waits beyond all graves. Then as He asked us too, "Believest thou this?" and we were able to answer Yes without further inquiry, we understood why He had not done as we wished, and why He had not come before.

As the heavens are higher than the earth, so are the Lord's ways higher than our ways. We are to believe that. Then we can be at peace in the midst of life's severest struggle, and then He will come and will reveal His glory to us.

Thy way is ever open;
Thou dost on naught depend;
Thine act is only blessing,
Thy path light without end.

Anniversaries and Birthdays

MARCH 10

But Christ having come a high priest of the good things to come, through the greater and more perfect tabernacle, not made with hands, that is to say, not of this creation, nor yet through the blood of goats and calves, but through his own blood, entered in once for all into the holy place, having obtained eternal redemption. Heb. 9:11-12

JESUS entered into the holy place not made with hands, and obtained for us eternal redemption.

It is a Man who enters there, into heaven itself, and accomplishes what we others should have done, but could not. In the holy place the enmity between God and us was slain, the peace was signed with the blood of God and of the Son of man, and the way unto the Father was again opened for us.

"Now once at the end of the ages hath Christ been manifested to put away sin by the sacrifice of Himself." He did not take away our sin from the presence of God when finally we repented and believed, but He had taken it away by His sacrifice. Jesus entered so fully into human life and conditions and assumed our responsibility so completely, that all that He was and did and is, that is ours. God imputes to us all that He did, as if we had done it ourselves.

"Because we thus judge, that one died for all, therefore all died." Thus speaks the Word of God. Glorious comfort for us!

Christ is the meeting place between God and men. Over Calvary the heavens are again opened for a condemned generation.

> That God has laid His anger by,
> He by His gift hath shown us;
> He gives His Son for us to die,
> In Him He now doth own us;
> These joyful tidings tell abroad,
> That Jesus Christ, the Son of God,
> From sin doth us deliver;
> Who then should not be glad today
> When Christ is born, the sinners' stay,
> Who is of grace the giver?

Anniversaries and Birthdays

MARCH 11

These things have I spoken unto you, that in Me ye may have peace. In the world ye have tribulation: but be of good cheer; I have overcome the world. John 16:33

IN reality all of our struggle is a struggle for peace. The greatest sacrifice, the worst suffering, the bloodiest war —all is a struggle for peace. Weary groans arise from the earth that is ravaged and without peace. And strangely enough: in the midst of all war there still is a note of harmony: "the whole creation groaneth and travaileth in pain together." In the air, in the sea, in the ground, from the smallest bird to the strongest beast, the eagle that soars highest in air, and organisms at the bottom of the ocean—each and all groan together.

Jesus meets this groan with His peace. Perhaps that is the reason that these groans never die. And so the creation waits and groans, with hope against hope.

Jesus says that He is our peace, that in Him we may have peace, and that He gives us His peace. Our peace with God is not built on anything of ours. Our peace with God is in Christ. Christ is our peace because He made peace with the blood of His cross. For us the deciding thing is not to experience peace, but to believe on the peace that is in Christ. If we believe that He is our peace, then it will also be granted us to experience peace. "My peace I give unto you." What is ridiculous in us is that we are determined to experience peace with God before we believe on the peace between God and us in Christ. We have tribulation in the world, and peace in Christ.

"And He came and preached peace to you that were far off, and peace to them that were nigh" (Eph. 2:17).

In Jesus I find rest and peace—
The world is full of sorrow;
His wounds are my abiding place;
Let the unknown tomorrow
Bring what it may,
There I can stay,
My faith finds all I need today,
I will not trouble borrow.

Anniversaries and Birthdays

MARCH 12

Him who knew no sin He made to be sin on our behalf; that we might become the righteousness of God in Him. II Cor. 5:21

THIS is the greatest word that God has given us about the worth of the redemptive work of Jesus. There is no other word in the Bible so difficult to get by for those who want Jesus as a Savior but not as an Atoner.

It is strange how difficult it seems to be to agree to the fact that Jesus appeared before God in our stead. We consider it reasonable and great that Jesus showed us God's love through His suffering and death; but that He was made to be sin on our behalf, so that we might become the righteousness of God in Him,—this truth many will not accept. To know nothing for our salvation save Jesus Christ and what He has done,—that evokes anger and scoffing even from many who want Jesus as their Savior. There must be something about this that deeply offends our proud nature. Our nature rebels at the thought that God has entirely left us out of account, and only taken another into consideration in our place.

But I desire to testify that this is my best comfort, and the only foundation I have to build on in life and in death. That He bore our sins in His body upon the tree when all transgressions met Him, and that He died for our sins and was raised for our justification, that is the foundation of my salvation.

Let us all grasp this in faith. Then we are building on what God has done for us.

Paschal Lamb, by God appointed,
All our sins on Thee were laid;
By almighty love anointed,
Thou hast full atonement made.
All Thy people are forgiven,
Through the virtue of Thy blood:
Opened is the gate of heaven;
Peace is made 'twixt man and God.

Anniversaries and Birthdays

MARCH 13

But Mary kept all these sayings, pondering them in her heart.
Luke 2:19

EVERYTHING that we keep in our hearts becomes a power in our lives. What the heart is enthusiastic over becomes the upholding power in all that we undertake. "Out of the abundance of the heart the mouth speaketh." The stingy person likes best to talk about money; the vain person about finery, the frivolous one about fun, and the immoral person about what is coarse and unclean. All those who want to win men, therefore seek first and last to win their hearts. Satan, sin, and the world knock at the door of your heart. Jesus knocks, too.

"Son, daughter, give me thy heart!" That is God's prayer to us. No one knows as well as He what it will mean to us, whether we let Him have our heart or not.

"Keep thy heart with all diligence;
For out of it are the issues of life."

He who is wise enough to keep the Word of God in his heart is likened unto

"...a tree planted by the streams of water,
That bringeth forth its fruit in its season,
Whose leaf also doth not wither;
And whatsoever he doeth shall prosper."

In the Word we find our salvation, our life, and our strength; there we learn life's noblest wisdom, there we find the way through life and death.

"The grass withereth, the flower fadeth, because the breath of Jehovah bloweth upon it; surely the people is grass;—but the Word of our God shall stand forever" (Isa. 40:7-8).

"For ever, O Jehovah,
Thy Word is settled in heaven" (Psalm 119:89).

Lord, Thy Word abideth,
And our footsteps guideth;
Who its truth believeth
Light and joy receiveth.

Anniversaries and Birthdays

MARCH 14

And the tempter came and said unto Him, If Thou art the Son of God, command that these stones become bread. Matt. 4:3

SINCE Jesus could not escape temptations, though He was without sin, how much more then must we, who have been ravaged by sin, be fortified to encounter tempting powers. A Christian should therefore remind himself that he walks in danger, no matter where he goes. But we are not all tempted in the same way, nor to the same sins. Because each of us has his weaknesses, Satan meets each one at the point where he can most easily bring about his fall.

Still, that is not always our worst misfortune. Our greatest misfortune is that we are so slow at learning what our weak points are: and so we often think we are strongest where we in reality are weakest, and have no power. Where we are self-confident, no one is on guard-duty, and so the enemy crosses the frontier and enters the fort without meeting any opposition. But where we consider ourselves helpless, we fear danger and pray for help from Him who has promised to strive for us.

To learn to know oneself is not only the way to wisdom, but also the source of victory. It is thus that a Christian finds the way to the power of God, and thus he may live to know that he who trusts in God is never put to shame. Then we too can help those who are tempted, because we ourselves were tempted and won.

"Who comforteth us in all our affliction, that we may be able to comfort them that are in any affliction, through the comfort wherewith we ourselves are comforted of God" (2 Cor. 1:4).

Fighting, we shall be victorious
By the blood of Christ our Lord;
On our foreheads, bright and glorious,
Shines the witness of His Word;
Spear and shield, on battlefield,
His great name: We cannot yield.

Anniversaries and Birthdays

____

____

____

____

MARCH 15

For what shall a man be profited, if he shall gain the whole world, and forfeit his life? or what shall a man give in exchange for his life? Matt. 16:26

JESUS gives man a high rating. He makes a comparison between one man and the whole creation, and says that the whole world is worth less than one human soul. To lose your soul is to lose everything, even though you could gain the whole world. So highly does Jesus price a soul!

What of man to whom so great a treasure has been given? What is his own valuation of his soul? Most people hardly remember that they have a soul; others hold that man has no soul; and of those who believe there is a soul only a little flock have learned rightly to appraise these eternal riches.

The crowd thoughtlessly tosses its one precious life right into the jaws of everything that tears the soul to pieces, that destroys and kills. Satan and ungodly people fill the world with soul-destroying trash and humbug. Art, literature, and seats of learning are saturated with a killing poison that painlessly devours souls. Come, let us go where desire draws us! That is the world's chorus-cry. Forget your soul, forget your God, forget your judgment!—and man loses his soul in this death roar.

But He who knows eternity, He who knows what a soul is worth, He who knows the meaning of the expressions, "Saved for eternity," and "Eternally lost!"—He has quite a different manner of thinking about our souls.

"Lost!"—where the word, "Come!" is never heard, where no clock strikes the hour, where no sun ever sets, and where day never breaks—"Lost!"

Man! Friend! Reflect! If you lose your soul, all is lost. Repent, and give your soul to Him who can bring full salvation to it, and can bring it in to life's eternal day.

Begone! vain world, with all thy pleasures,
And keep thy joys far from my sight;
In thee and in thy tempting treasures
My soul no longer finds delight.
The world may seek and love its own:
I love my Jesus, Him alone.

Anniversaries and Birthdays

MARCH 16

Lord, if Thou hadst been here, my brother had not died. And even now I know that, whatsoever Thou shalt ask of God, God will give Thee. John 11:21-22

THE prayer, or more correctly the message, that Martha and Mary sent to Jesus permits us to look into a deep and true friendship. When distress came to their home, the sisters thought it would suffice to let Jesus know what conditions were. It did not occur to them to ask Him to come, or to tell Him what to do. With them it was a foregone conclusion that He would both come and help.

Something great has happened when the fellowship between Jesus and us has become so deep and intimate that we can take things the way that Martha and Mary did. Then we need not scream aloud in nervous tension, nor use many touching words. Even on the saddest days we need only remind Him of our state. We can omit writing rules for Him, or even telling Him our special desires. When He learns what conditions are, He will have to do as He pleases. That is trust, that is faith, that is friendship! Screaming and bawling and loud-voiced prayer surely constitute no testimony of a thorough acquaintance, faithful friendship, and confidence in Him who does all things well. Where love and friendship are most genuine, there is least need of strong words and definite demands.

Never mind if that happens to us which we desire least of all, and everything ends in a grave. He says to you and to me as to Martha: If thou believest, thou shalt see the glory of God. Let us believe that. Then everything that happens to us will be to the glory of God, and will help both us and others to greater faith in Jesus.

Judge not the Lord by feeble sense
But trust Him for His grace;
Behind a frowning providence
He hides a smiling face.

Anniversaries and Birthdays

____

____

____

____

MARCH 17

The people that sat in darkness
Saw a great light,
And to them that sat in the region and shadow of death,
To them did light spring up. Matt. 4:16

AND the light that sprang up was Christ!
He gives light through time and eternity.

Jesus knows everything! He tells us simply and clearly the story of creation, where we came from, and where the way leads to when we leave this life. He gives us a light that is brighter than the sun on the past, the present, and the future. He gives daylight to soul, mind, and thought, He reveals our sin and need, and points the way to that Light that takes sin away, and gives eternal life. Where the road is closed against us all, He opens the door and dispels the darkness. He is the light of the world. Only He.

When now and then we succeed in remembering this: what all this is, and what God gave us in Christ Jesus, then we feel like hiding for shame because habit, thoughtlessness, and unbelief have gotten us out of our right mind. If we saw this truth as it is and as we possess it, we would rejoice day and night at a happiness and blessedness so great and boundless. While millions of people live and die in black darkness without knowing themselves, or God, or what awaits them beyond the grave, you and I can distinguish between good and evil, and know the path away from sin and death, yea, we can see life everlasting most clearly and most gloriously in the midst of death. When the sun sinks into the sea for always for those who do not know Jesus, at that hour it rises in all its glory over His friends.

"The glory of God did lighten the city, and the lamp thereof is the Lamb."

O Christ, our true and only light,
Illumine those who sit in night;
Let those afar now hear Thy voice,
And in Thy fold with us rejoice.

Anniversaries and Birthdays

____

____

____

____

MARCH 18

Jesus therefore said unto them, "Verily, verily, I say unto you, Except ye eat the flesh of the Son of man and drink His blood, ye have not life in yourselves." **John 6:53**

IT was these words that offended the people so deeply in Jesus' day, and caused many to leave Him in anger. It is this same truth that people are most offended at in our day, too, and it is because of this truth that most people turn away from Christ now also.

What does Jesus really want to tell us in these words? Where is the dagger-point in them?

I believe it is this that we must come to Him with a completely surrendered will and in all earnestness, and acknowledge to ourselves and to Him that all other ways are closed to us, and that without Him we are lost. And we must lay this lost life on Him, and have all we need in Him. Outside of Him nothing can satisfy our soul.

But should we be offended at this? Well, yes, all those who desire to build on their good works, and do not wholly surrender to Christ, they are offended. But this is life's only food and drink for all those who want to be saved at any cost, and who know nothing for salvation except Jesus Christ. God be praised that Jesus Christ is an all-sufficient Savior for us.

"And in none other is there salvation: for neither is there any other name under heaven, that is given among men, wherein we must be saved" (Acts 4:12).

Mark the sacrifice appointed!
See who bears the awful load;
'Tis the Word, the Lord's Anointed,
Son of man, and Son of God!

Anniversaries and Birthdays

MARCH 19

For what the law could not do, in that it was weak through the flesh, God, sending His own Son in the likeness of sinful flesh and for sin, condemned sin in the flesh. Rom. 8:3

THE law is God's will revealed to us in human words. There God tells us who He is, and what we shall be. He who does what the law commands, and leaves undone what it forbids, that man shall live by what he does.

But it was this that did not succeed, not because the law was weak, but because we were weak. When God tried to make new men of us by the law, He failed. It proved impossible because the building materials were not in us. We were like decayed wood and broken glass; and so He had to lay us aside. He could no longer count on us.

But in His great wisdom and love God found another way. He sent us His Son in the flesh, and on the man Jesus Christ He laid the demands of the law, and reckoned with Him for us. In Him there was material for the creation of a new man, and so He laid the sin, guilt, punishment, judgment, and death on Christ, and demanded of Him what He had a right to get from us. He condemned our sin in the flesh of Christ, and thus presented us unblamable before His face. That is what God did.

When it is a question of our salvation we have a right to turn entirely away from ourselves, and to trust in Christ alone. As perfect as God is in Himself, so perfectly is our salvation planned in Christ. That is what God did.

Redeemed, restored, forgiven
Through Jesus' precious blood,
Heirs of His home in heaven,
O praise our pardoning God!
Praise Him in tuneful measures,
Who gave His Son to die;
Praise Him whose sevenfold treasures
Enrich and sanctify!

Anniversaries and Birthdays

MARCH 20

Jesus therefore said, "Let her alone: it was that she might keep it against the day of my burying. For the poor ye have always with you; but Me ye have not always." John 12:7-8

WHAT do you suppose there really was about Mary that caused Jesus to praise her more than Martha?

The deepest things in life are not easily formed in words; but perhaps we may say that Mary found rest in Jesus, and received His Word, and then the glory of His face shined upon her. The result of this was that she offered everything she owned on Him. Not for Him but on Him. Hardly knowing what she is doing she breaks the alabaster cruse of exceeding precious ointment of pure nard. An inner vital force drove her so she felt compelled to offer up everything on Him.

I cannot in words differentiate between sacrificing for Jesus and offering on Him, but I am certain that there is a great difference. We can do much for Jesus without giving Him our all. To offer all on Him because the heart cannot do otherwise, that is the fine art of Christianity. That is when fragrance comes down from heaven from what a saved sinner gives the Savior. Highest value does not attach to what you do, but to what you are.

"For we are a sweet savor of Christ unto God, in them that are saved, and in them that perish."

May the Spirit of Jesus Christ so fill our souls, our homes, and our lives!

Sitting at the feet of Jesus,
Hearing His most blessed Word:
To be seated near my Savior
Is the choicest place on earth.

Anniversaries and Birthdays

____

____

____

____

____

____

MARCH 21

But He, when He had offered one sacrifice for sins for ever, sat down on the right hand of God; henceforth expecting till His enemies be made the footstool of His feet. Heb. 10:12-13

GOD'S right hand is His unlimited power to attain to everything and to master everything. That is the arm of omnipotence which enabled Him to bring all created things into existence with life and laws, and which makes it possible for Him to extinguish everything by the breath of His mouth, if He so wills. It is that power in God which is not bounded by time and space, the hand that holds the keys to death and the realm of the dead, the power that attains to everything and can do everything. And Jesus, our brother, governs this hand! As the stones hailed down on Stephen he saw the heavens opened to him, and he saw the Son of man standing on the right hand of God.

Now in that seat of honor we see our flesh and blood;
We then must joyful be, and never mourn again.

But in the Book we also read that He sits there waiting for His enemies. It is not clear to me what enemies He is expecting. But we do know that He awaits all those that He bought at so great a price. He is waiting for you who still are away in sin. We have reason to believe that He will wait so long as He sees a single person who can be saved.

You who believe that Jesus will come again: Remember that He is expecting to save still more people before He comes.

"And account that the longsuffering of our Lord is salvation."

Jesus wants you all:
Not one is so unworthy
That Jesus does not love Him.
He can save you here and now,
Jesus wants you all.

Anniversaries and Birthdays

MARCH 22

Even as the Father hath loved Me, I also have loved you: abide ye in My love. John 15:9

As little as our thought can comprehend the divine, eternal, and almighty One, so little can we understand how much is contained in the statement that the Father loves the Son. We can only say that His love must be as great as God Himself.

But what should appeal to us as the greatest of all great things, is that as the Father has loved Jesus, so Jesus loves His own. To be loved by Jesus as much as the Father loves Jesus,—well, that cannot be understood. Jesus is the only begotten Son of God, He is as pure and holy as God, He played in His presence before the existence of any created thing, and has never offended the Father. That is more than can be said of us. We cost Jesus His life, we resisted Him, we have been disobedient, and what is worse, we have disobeyed after we were saved. And yet He loves us as much as the Father loves Him.

We are at great pains to make advances in our personal Christianity, but we have small success, and so we collapse into despondency, legalism, toil, and doubt. Just think what would happen if we heard and followed these words of Jesus: "Abide ye in My love!" Then there would be many changes both in us and by us. You poor and tired man, come and hide in the love of Jesus Christ! Stay there with your faith, your sin, and your wounds! Lay all your burdens there too: present, future, this day, and the day you have not seen yet.

That is the best place for us all in life and in death. That is where we are to be in all eternity, too.

Jesus, Thy boundless love to me
No thought can reach, no tongue declare:
O knit my thankful heart to Thee
And reign without a rival there.
Thine wholly, Thine alone, I am,
Be Thou alone my constant flame.

Anniversaries and Birthdays

MARCH 23

The disciples went, and did even as Jesus appointed them.

Matt. 21:6

MANY things would be simpler both in doctrine and in life if we Christians followed the rule of doing what Jesus told us to do. Even what looks small becomes great when it is done for the Savior. Just untying a donkey and bringing him from the stall may be to the honor of Jesus, and to the welfare of others. The ridiculous and un-Christian idea that the Christian life should be divided into "Christian" and "secular" parts has done much damage in the kingdom of God.

The people of God are a kingdom of priests who are in His church, and stand before God's altar wherever they live and work. If the Christian life is divided into two parts, "Christian" and "secular," that breeds hypocrisy which takes the power out of true godliness. He who does not worship God in his work-clothes, does not worship Him in Sunday clothes. The altar of our sacrifice must stand where the struggle for existence goes on, where we toil, where joy and sorrow meet us, and where our life's calling bids us go.

Christ has at least as much desire to go out in a fishing boat, as to be in a cathedral. When the farmer unties his horse with prayer and thanksgiving, he does that for Jesus.

So is the kingdom of God. And such must He be who is to save and help us.

Thou man of God! Look upon everything that you have to do as public worship and as a work for Jesus. Then you will be strong and happy in all your work.

Living for Jesus a life that is true,
Striving to please Him in all that I do,
Yielding allegiance, glad-hearted and free,
This is the pathway of blessing for me.

Anniversaries and Birthdays

____

____

____

____

MARCH 24

Behold, the Lamb of God, that beareth the sin of the world!
John 1:29

SIN is the great calamity for us men, yea, for the whole creation. Sin is the cause of all the sorrow and distress in the world. If sin were banished, all evil would disappear as dew before the sun. Sin has separated us from God, and has brought upon us sorrow and sickness and death. The entire world is sunk down in blood and tears. Generations come and generations go,—but their ways and goings look so hopelessly much alike.

But in the midst of all this dark night, the heaven is opened to us in grace. God comes down to us and becomes man. Out over the sin-ravaged generation sounds the voice of God's prophet: "Behold, the Lamb of God, that beareth the sin of the world!"

A wonderful word! Can anything greater be told us, and can anything more comforting reach our ears?

What we were in duty bound to bear, the Lord laid on Christ, and He removed "the iniquity of that land in one day." When He tasted of death for every man, He took away our sin and debt, and when you and I repent and believe that we are saved in Him, then He cleanses us by faith, and God regards us in Christ as if we never had sinned.

Repentance and forgiveness of sins shall be preached in the name of Christ unto all the nations, because the Son of man has authority on earth to forgive sins. And when the believing sinner leaves his body, to be at home with the Lord, he is freed from sin forever.

In that way the Lamb of God takes away the sin of the world.

Far, far away, like bells at even pealing,
The voice of Jesus sounds o'er land and sea,
And laden souls by thousands meekly stealing,
Kind Shepherd, turn their weary steps to Thee.
Angels of Jesus, Angels of light,
Singing to welcome the pilgrims of the night.

Anniversaries and Birthdays

____

____

____

____

MARCH 25

Tell ye the daughter of Zion,
Behold, thy King cometh unto thee,
Meek, and riding upon an ass,
And upon a colt the foal of an ass.
Matt. 21:5

ON Palm Sunday the King of Zion rides on the foal of an ass, and His eyes are full of tears. He is not riding a proud war-horse at the head of a great army. On the contrary He sits mild in spirit on the back of a beast of burden. And He rides into the city, not to be crowned king in Israel's sanctuary, but to purchase us from earth to God with His blood.

Here is the Man who will embrace you with His love;
Here is the Man who will benefit you with His bloody sweat.

Such a King fits our case, One who can release "every sin-bound slave." Thus He came to us, too. He came when mother bent her knee at the cradle, He came in school, in church, in the chapel, in the woods, on the mountain, and in the valleys. He came when we left the home of our childhood with the sun of life's springtime over us to go out into a cold and sinful world. He came when night and life's storms made us restless and sick at heart. He came and wanted to save that which was lost. Thus He came to me, and to you, too.

Did you receive Him?

If you did not, receive Him today. He stands at the door and knocks now. Open the door to Him and He will save you, and in grace take you into His eternal kingdom. The greatest sin anyone can commit is to shut Jesus out.

Dear Master, Thine the glory
Of each recovered soul;
Ah! who can tell the story
Of love that made us whole?
Not ours, not ours the merit;
Be Thine alone the praise,
And ours a thankful spirit
To serve Thee all our days.

Anniversaries and Birthdays

MARCH 26

Jesus therefore six days before the passover came to Bethany, where Lazarus was, whom Jesus raised from the dead. John 12:1

FOR a Christian there is a wonderful drawing power in the name Bethany. Not the town, but a very special home in that town. Up through the whole Christian era there have always been people who have considered it the greatest thing in the world to have a home like that. When we want to give a good home the best name we know, we say, "It was a real Bethany."

What is there about this cottage that makes it seem so attractive and poetic? One cannot be in doubt about the answer: Jesus was there. He was always welcome in that home. As natural as it was for Lazarus and his sisters to receive Him, just so dear was it for Him to be there.

That kind of home is the best property one can have in this world. Success and life's joys do not consist in riches, honor and might: they consist in having peace with God, peace of soul, and peace in the home, and to be content with present possessions. Jesus gives this abundance of life's riches to all to whom He gains admission. In the life and home where Jesus is permitted to dwell, flowers from lost paradise give forth their fragrance. From such homes light and joy go out to other people.

Let it be our deepest wish and our prayer from day to day to have Jesus in heart and home.

When Jesus enters meek and lowly,
To fill the home with sweetest peace;
When hearts have felt His blessing holy,
And found from sin complete release,
Then light and calm within shall reign,
And hearts divided love again.

Anniversaries and Birthdays

MARCH 27

Having loved His own that were in the world, He loved them unto the end. John 13:1

OTHERS besides Jesus have known the day of their death, and others besides Him have met death with repose. But no one has forgotten himself out of love for others as completely as Jesus did. As calm as though nothing important was ahead, He eats His supper with them, rises from supper, pours water into a basin, takes a towel, and goes from man to man washing and wiping their feet. That is more than human: That is divine. But the love that would undertake to save us must be that great.

And as He was, so shall also we be in this world. From Him who is meek and lowly in heart we are to learn to love and to serve.

We are passing through an unclean world, and it is so easy to get our feet mudded up. When we see that our brother has become unclean, may we then remember the words of Jesus, that we are to do as He did: not make the unclean man worse, but try to remove what has defiled him. It is in such cases that it will become evident how much we have of the love of God that serves and helps others.

When you see that your brother has got dirty from sin, then do not make him more unclean with bad words, but help straighten him out. "If ye know these things, blessed are ye if ye do them." He that loves is born of God.

Our hearts let new-created be,
Our walk make pure and holy.
Help us offense and sin to flee,
And ever serve God solely,
So that our faith in Christ, our Lord,
May prove itself in deed and word
Before the world about us.

Anniversaries and Birthdays

MARCH 28

But Peter answered and said unto Him, "If all shall be offended in Thee, I will never be offended." Matt. 26:33

IT is not always wrong to have faith in oneself. He who believes that he is good for nothing in the practical affairs of this world will be a burden both to himself and to others. On such people this proverb fits: "God cannot help the person who will not help himself."

But when it is a question of victory over sin and Satan, self-confidence is a great misfortune. To believe that you are strong enough in your own might to stand against the assaults of evil, that always brings defeat to a Christian. No man has power in himself to conquer evil: only the power of God is stronger than the might of sin and Satan. Consequently he who considers his own might sufficient closes the passage way of God's power, with the result that he will be found lying wounded and bruised. But when we helpless ones appeal to God, His power is made perfect in our weakness.

Paul's whole life got a new content when he found this very secret way to victory. Then he gloried in his weaknesses, just because the power of God then rested on him. We would be spared many defeats if we would quit depending on ourselves, and if we used more time looking up to Him who gives grace to the humble.

"My God with His lovingkindness will meet me:
God will let me see my desire upon mine enemies."
(Psalm 59:10).

Savior, when we call, O hear us;
In the trying hour be near us,
Lest the foe should prove too strong:
To Thy mercy we betake us;
Never leave us, nor forsake us;
Power and grace to Thee belong.

Anniversaries and Birthdays

MARCH 29

"Father, the hour is come; glorify Thy Son, that the Son may glorify Thee." John 17:1

AS from a mountain top a general sees the enemy army streaming in over the plains toward the place of battle, thus with divine eyes Jesus sees the hour approaching when He alone shall meet the prince of darkness.

The hour is come! God took this hour into account before the foundation of the world. I believe that if He had not done that, He would not have created anything. Jesus counted on the same hour, Satan too, and men looked forward to this hour from the day that God promised to bring them back to Paradise. Old Testament believers looked forward to this hour with trust and hope, and in this hope they went home to God.

The hour is come! Hell trembles, heaven rejoices, and earth looks hopefully up to Him who presses on to attain to perfect obedience even unto death. It is in this that Jesus was obedient, that victory is found. The second Adam had to be victorious where the first Adam failed, or everything would be lost for us in all eternity. But when He cried, "Not as I will, but as Thou wilt," the victory was in the deepest sense won. It was in Gethsemane that the struggle was the hardest, but the victory was also assured there.

Through obedience and suffering the Captain of our salvation was made perfect. And now the hour is come to us too when we must either choose, or reject the perfected salvation. Blessed is the man that knows the time of his visitation and uses it aright.

A Lamb goes uncomplaining forth,
The guilt of all men bearing;
Laden with all the sins of earth,
None else the burden sharing!
Goes patient on, grows weak and faint,
To slaughter led without complaint,
That spotless life to offer;
Bears shame and stripes and wounds and death,
Anguish and mockery, and saith,
"Willing all this I suffer."

Anniversaries and Birthdays

MARCH 30

For God so loved the world, that He gave His only begotten Son, that whosoever believeth on Him should not perish, but have eternal life. John 3:16

THIS is the everlasting miracle, the sun shining over a lost and condemned race. God loves us: you, me, and all others. All those who are sinful, beaten, and half dead; all those who are proud of their sins and loud-mouthed in their hatred of God—God loves all these.

Go with Him through the Bible. Behold Him when He must open the gate for the first people away from the tree of life, and out into sin, shame, suffering, and death. The love that is as strong as death could not let them go away into a hopeless night. He promised that they might return in a new and living way. Aye, before the first spark of life flew through space, everything was settled for us in God and of God. God so loved!

No one asked Him for it. There was not yet one single creature who could send up to Him as much as a sigh for help. It was in God's own heart that there was born a compelling need to give His Son, and Himself with Him. No one but God is to have the thanksgiving and praise and honor for the salvation that was given us in Christ. Through all eternities there will be but one song for all those who are saved out of every race, and people, and nation: the song of the Lamb who purchased us unto God with His blood.

But so great as this love is, so great and gruesome will "the outer darkness" be for all those who refuse to let the light of truth into their hearts. But all those who in faith accept the gift of God, shall live even though they die.

Yea, Thou hast loved our fallen race,
And rather than condemn us,
Cast out and banished from Thy face,
Thine only Son didst send us;
Who died upon the cross, that we
Should all be saved for ever;
Hence Jesus also died for me,
My soul, forget it never.

Anniversaries and Birthdays

MARCH 31

How much more shall the blood of Christ, who through the eternal Spirit offered Himself without blemish unto God, cleanse your conscience from dead works to serve the living God?

Heb. 9:14

CHRIST brought Himself to God as an offering without blemish. Marvelous arms that bore this sacrifice, and blessed Man that permitted Himself to be laid on those arms! Through all heavens, in all creation, yea, right down in hell these words seem to resound: "Here am I, holy God, here am I. Take me as a sacrifice for all who deserve judgment, punishment, and death. Do not settle with them, but with me. Do not look at them: look at me! What Thou, eternal and holy God, must demand, judge, and punish, that demand Thou, and judge, and punish here. Here am I, here I lie upon my own arms as a sacrifice for all."

Then God took this sacrifice and made Him to be sin for us. "All we like sheep have gone astray; we have turned everyone to his own way; and Jehovah hath laid on Him the iniquity of us all."

The Savior has loosed the whole world from damnation,
O yes, on His heart every sinner He bore,

Ho, all you of restless conscience, all you who are under condemnation, come, and see, and seize the fruit of the sacrificial death of Christ. Depart from Sinai, and come to Calvary, come and bathe in the sea of life. Then your conscience will be cleansed, and you will be transferred from bondage to the glorious freedom of the children of God, from dead works to living works, from the power of Satan unto God.

Who can tell the pleasure
To belong to Jesus?
Jesus is my life-joy;
His I would be alway.

Anniversaries and Birthdays

APRIL 1

All we like sheep have gone astray; we have turned everyone to his own way; and Jehovah hath laid on Him the iniquity of us all. Isa. 53:6

A SHEEP experimenting in self-government is soon frightened, and easily goes astray. It cannot defend itself against beasts of prey, it does not seek rescue when there is danger, and cannot find the way home when once it is lost.

God says that we men are like that. We go astray like sheep. When did one ever see any other creature of God so completely lost in sin as a man? A tiger and a lion defend their mate and young, but a man can murder his wife, and a mother her child. "The ox knoweth his owner, and the ass his master's crib; but Israel doth not know, my people doth not consider."

It is to us that almighty God brings this great help: that He let His Son take our iniquities on Him. God did this when He sent His Son in the likeness of sinful flesh and for sin. And after He has purchased us unto God with His blood, He goes about hunting us up, and He takes on His shoulders and carries home all those that can be found. He keeps us as the apple of His eye, and after that He takes us to glory.

At times when this becomes vivid, so that I see it and believe it, then I marvel and then I am ashamed because I rejoice so little, and thank God so little, though He has done so much for me. How blessed when tongue and speech shall be freed from sin in eternal life! My soul, thank God today, too, in life and in work!

I will sing of my Redeemer
And His wondrous love to me;
On the cruel cross He suffered,
From the curse to set me free.

Anniversaries and Birthdays

______

______

______

______

APRIL 2

Now is My soul troubled; and what shall I say? Father, save Me from this hour. But for this cause came I unto this hour. Father, glorify Thy name. John 12:27-28

THE pressure of Satan's mighty army was so great that it almost seemed that Jesus was on the point of yielding. Before He really knows what He is doing, He cries, "Father, save Me from this hour!" But at once the air is cleared, He sees how matters stand, and He knows what is at stake. The hour is come, war is on in dead earnest. He is prepared, and He cries, "Father, glorify Thy name!"

By this victory which Jesus won over Himself, Satan was beaten, and heaven calls down that His prayer is heard. In a little while He hangs on the cross where the last battle is fought, and the victory won for all time. From the cross He will and can draw all men unto Himself. It is from the cross that Christ has the power to draw the sinner to God. Only from the cross. An electrical locomotive has no power if it is not connected with the power house. So Christ would lack the Savior-power to draw men, if He had not given His life for our sins according to the Scriptures. It is from Calvary through the crucified Jesus that the sinner is drawn to God. "And I, if I be lifted up from the earth, will draw all men unto Myself."

Here we have a firm foundation;
Here the refuge of the lost:
Christ the Rock of our salvation:
His the name of which we boast.

Lamb of God for sinners wounded!
Sacrifice to cancel guilt!
None shall ever be counfounded
Who on Thee their hope have built.

Anniversaries and Birthdays

____

____

____

____

____

APRIL 3

And He came out, and went, as His custom was, unto the mount of Olives; and the disciples also followed Him. Luke 22:39

THE words, "as His custom was," do not have a particularly evangelical sound, and many Christians are afraid of them. There is a danger, too. If habit leads us into forms without content, then habit is harmful. But when habit is the servant of a pulsating, vital content, it will lead us in the right way.

When a Christian has the habit of taking his Bible every morning and meeting God in the Word and in prayer; and when the head of the family who believes in God calls the people of the household together for devotions morning or evening, and prays for God's blessing on home and work, there will develop in those people not only a healthful national life, but also a Christian life resting on the grace of God.

Many Christians live more according to impressions than according to a sound rule of life, and so things go by chance with the life that according to its nature demands the right to grow according to fixed laws. In spirit-filled times such people live in the skies, but when hard and dry seasons come round, they collapse and wither away.

Happy the Christian who does not break the laws given for the life with God.

"He shall be like a tree planted by the streams of water,
That bringeth forth its fruit in its season.
Whose leaf also doth not wither;
And whatsoever he doeth shall prosper."

"But unto Thee, O Jehovah, have I cried;
And in the morning shall my prayer come before Thee"
(Psalm 88:13).

Thou receivest me, O Father,
As a child and heir of Thine:
Jesus, Thou who diedst, yea, rather
Ever livest, Thou art mine.
||: Thou, O Spirit, :||
Art my guide, my light divine.

Anniversaries and Birthdays

______

______

______

APRIL 4

Then cometh Jesus with them unto a place called Gethsemane, and saith unto His disciples, "Sit ye here, while I go yonder and pray." Matt. 26:36

GETHSEMANE! A quiet place with flowers and upstanding trees. There Jesus had His severest struggle. All that He is in soul and spirit, in feeling and disposition is made to be sin on our behalf. Now He lies in the crucible over hell fire. God, holy and righteous, meets Him. All that we owed was demanded of Him: the account had to be paid.

Here in this garden the matter must be settled in its deepest essence. It was in a garden that Adam was disobedient. It is in a garden that Jesus must conquer by being perfectly obedient. If He is not victorious here, He will not reach Calvary, and all is lost.

Gethsemane! Heaven looks down into this garden, and listens and trembles. With quiet strength and complete truth the words sound forth while His sweat falls to the ground like drops of blood: "Not as I will, but as Thou wilt"—"Father, glorify Thy name!"—and the victory is won.

Let Judas come now; let friends forsake Him. Judgment and death may now take Him to Golgotha. Do ye seek Me? Did I not tell you that I am He? Overcome by this bloodless victory, those rough soldiers went backward, and fell to the ground. They had not the power to seize so great and victorious a Leader: He must urge them to take Him. He hastens on to Golgotha. Erect, He stands forth, and moves on toward death, quiet as a lamb. He goes to be made perfect as the Author of our salvation.

The hour in dark Gethsemane
I never shall forget,
When Christ alone the battle fought,
In grief and bloody sweat.
Gethsemane, Gethsemane,
I must remember thee,
Where God's eternal Son I saw
In prayer on bended knee.

Anniversaries and Birthdays

____

____

____

APRIL 5

"Arise, let us be going: behold, he is at hand that betrayeth Me."
Matt. 26:46

JUDAS knew the way to the most peaceful and holy sanctuary that the world could give to our Savior. The traitor found the way to the place where Jesus prayed while "His sweat became as it were great drops of blood falling down upon the ground."

There is no place on earth where either Jesus or His people can be entirely safe. The same Satan that found the way to Gethsemane through one of the disciples of Jesus, also knows how to find the way to us where we least expect him. The worst wounds have been inflicted on us where we felt strongest and safest; and many of those that we thought were our best friends, failed us, and became adversaries. Into our prayer-chamber, too, Satan finds the way, and wants to get us to doubt Him who so often answers our prayers in a way that is different from what we thought and wished. But to meet the traitor in our own bosom, that is worst of all! When our evil nature in Christian garb gives us its false kiss, we are often led astray.

We can be entirely secure only in Jesus Christ our Lord. There we can say with Paul: "For I am persuaded that neither death nor life, nor angels, nor principalities, nor things present, nor things to come,—nor any other creature, shall be able to separate us from the love of God which is in Christ Jesus our Lord."

There you have the Rock of ages. There is the Friend who never fails you.

Love alone the law fulfilling,
Is the bond of perfectness,
Love, Who came a victim willing,
Paid our debt and brought us peace;
Therefore love and peace in union
Ever grow in sweet communion,
And through love we may abide
One with Him who for us died.

Anniversaries and Birthdays

APRIL 6

"Remove this cup from Me: howbeit not what I will, but what Thou wilt." Mark 14:36

"Father, I desire that they also whom Thou hast given Me be with Me where I am, that they may behold My glory, which Thou hast given Me: for Thou lovedst Me before the foundation of the world." John 17:24

WHEN Jesus meets face to face the demands that God makes of Him as the Savior of the world, He is led into a grievous soul-struggle. The cup that He is to receive now, is full of the dread that sin has brought upon all humanity, and He cries out in great anguish, "Remove this cup from Me!" But the words that follow, "Howbeit not what I will, but what Thou wilt," show us that He has won the victory. "Made to be sin on our behalf" meant a hell of suffering for Him, but in this suffering He wins the victory by surrendering His will entirely to God. That is complete victory. Then the Son of man is glorified, and God is glorified in Him.

The strange thing is that while Jesus has surrendered His will to God, His own will comes forth again with a quite irresistible power. "Father, I desire!" He shouts toward heaven. When I give My will to Thee, and My life for the salvation of the world, "I desire that they also whom Thou hast given Me be with Me where I am." I desire to share with Mine own all the glory that Thou gavest Me before the foundation of the world. Father! That desire I will never relinquish.

Wonderful will! If we fully understood what it contains, and believed it, we could hardly live for sheer joy.

Jesus, Thy feast we celebrate;
We show Thy death, we sing Thy name,
Till Thou return, and we shall eat
The marriage supper of the Lamb.

Anniversaries and Birthdays

APRIL 7

"My Father, if it be possible, let this cup pass away from Me: nevertheless, not as I will, but as Thou wilt." Matt. 26:39

SOME of the promises given in connection with prayer know no bounds. We may ask for whatsoever we will, and we shall receive it. In other Bible passages that also speak of prayer, bounds are set to what God can and will give us in response to our prayers. If we abide in Him, and His Word abides in us, then we may ask whatsoever we will, and it shall be done unto us. If we go away and bear fruit, and our fruit abideth, then the Father can give us all that we ask in Jesus' name.

Had not these "if's" been written into the promises of God, we might in our prayers have demanded of God anything we thought of, because He had bound Himself to give. But He knew that we would misuse so great a right, and so He put the answer to the prayer into an "if."

Some people think that when we do not get all that we pray for, the reason is always unbelief. These people should listen to the prayer that Jesus offered in His greatest agony: "Nevertheless, not as I will, but as Thou wilt." When He prayed that way, how much more should we do so.

What do we really know about what is best for us? But He who sees everything, He knows. Let Him give what He sees is best for us. That is fitting for us.

It is right and it is Christian to show Him this confidence also when we pray.

> I ask Thee for the daily strength,
> To none that ask denied,
> A mind to blend with outward life,
> While keeping at Thy side,
> Content to fill a little space,
> If Thou be glorified.

Anniversaries and Birthdays

APRIL 8

Bearing the cross for Himself. **John 19:17**

And he that doth not take his cross and follow after Me, is not worthy of Me. **Matt. 10:38**

THE cross that Jesus bore was ours; but He took it and made it His own.

No one else could have carried that burden, and in truth it was heavy enough for Him, too. He could still the tempest, heal the sick, and raise the dead from their graves, but when He bore His cross, He sank to the ground. In sorrow and anguish of soul He cried out, "My God! My God! why hast Thou forsaken Me?" This burden was verily more than a piece of wood: it was everything that made trouble between God and us. All this He bore in spirit and soul, and on His body; and then He died on a tree!

It is this cross of Jesus that has made a cross for all who will follow Him. To depart from all the sin that He bore for us, and to follow Him from day to day in things great and small, that is our cross. The cross is not sickness, poverty, and the hard life that sin lays on all men. Only those who follow Jesus walk the way of the cross.

When you deny yourself and give Christ your allegiance, when you leave the world and go to your Bible, into your prayer chamber, and when you go out among people, and walk as a child of light with a humble mind, in honor and dishonor, in evil report and good report, then you are following Jesus, and then you are bearing the cross after Him.

Jesus, I my cross have taken,
All to leave, and follow Thee;
Destitute, despised, forsaken,
Thou, from hence, my all shalt be.
Perish every fond ambition,
All I've sought, and hoped, and known,
Yet how rich is my condition!
God and heaven are still my own.

Anniversaries and Birthdays

APRIL 9

They took Jesus therefore: and He went out, bearing the cross for Himself unto the place called the place of a skull, which is called in Hebrew Golgotha: where they crucified Him. John 19:17-18

GOLGOTHA! You wonderful, holy hill! When we mention your name, a surge of deep seriousness, a quiet joy, and heartfelt thanks pass through our spirit. During thousands of years our race looked forward and longed for you: and as long as time endures men will look back to you. As the sun lights up the earth, so you with your cross are our only light.

Golgotha! There we meet God and man in one person, hanging on a tree. There God and man meet for reconciliation, there sin gets its judgment, punishment, and death; there the head of the serpent is crushed, the enmity slain, and peace signed with blood. There the heavens are opened, and opened is the way to the tree of life; there God comes to meet us as a Friend and a Father; there the throne of grace is established, so that we can draw near to the Holy One with boldness, and may receive mercy, and find grace to help us in time of need.

Golgotha! Our shelter in the evil day, our light in darkness, our solid rock in the midst of the stormy ocean, the haven for sinking ships, an anchor of the soul, and the way to eternal life through the grave.

Golgotha! The world hates you, and believes it can find the way and port without you; but we know of a certainty that when all the lights that men have lighted are gone out, then you light up the night, and lead all believers to the eternal, perfect day.

Come to Calvary's holy mountain,
Sinners, ruined by the fall;
Here a pure and healing fountain
Flows to you, to me, to all;
In a full perpetual tide,
Opened when our Savior died.

Anniversaries and Birthdays

APRIL 10

But we behold Him who hath been made a little lower than the angels, even Jesus, because of the suffering of death crowned with glory and honor, that by the grace of God He should taste of death for every man. Heb. 2:9

TO suffer death and to taste of death mean more than to die. Death may come fast and easily, but to live and to suffer in the midst of death, without being permitted to die—that is more. This was what Jesus did. Alone He lies there in the garden and cries out, "My soul is exceeding sorrowful, even unto death!" But He was not to die then, because He must taste death, in the manner that we should taste it in all eternity. And then came an angel from heaven and drove death away from Him.

Then God made Him a little lower than the angels. Then He was like a worm and not like a man, because He had to meet everything sinful and everything holy, all that God's righteousness demanded of us, and all Satan's power. In this night of death heaven and the Father were departed from Him, because He should suffer death and taste of death for all men.

To live in the midst of death, made to be sin, without being permitted to die, that must for the Holy One be hell.

The life of Jesus in this world, His meeting with sin and Satan were for Him a life in the midst of death. He reached the full measure of this suffering in the anguish of soul in Gethsemane. That is surely where the prophet sees Him when he says:

"I am poured out like water,
And all my bones are out of joint:
My heart is like wax:
It is melted within me" (Psalm 22:14).

This suffering is our salvation.

Jesus, may Thy love constrain us
That from sin we may refrain us,
In Thy griefs may deeply grieve.
Thee our best affections giving,
To Thy glory ever living,
May we in Thy glory live.

Anniversaries and Birthdays

____

____

____

APRIL 11

"... And through Him to reconcile all things unto Himself, having made peace through the blood of His cross. Col. 1:20

AT present perhaps more than at any time in the past there is in mode of thought and view of life an aversion to the teaching that the blood of Jesus is ground for atonement and the forgiveness of sin. Men tell us that a God that demands blood before He can be atoned is a remnant of paganism.

But in the Word of God we read: "Apart from shedding of blood there is no remission." Right from the first book of the Bible, where we read of Abel's blood, and to the last where the song of the Lamb peals forth, the Word of God says that our only basis of salvation is He "who purchased us unto God with His blood."

As blood is the life of the human body, so blood is the life in the Bible, too. If we take the blood out of the Bible, it is without life from God. But not only that. Those who consider themselves Christians without faith in the blood of Christ do not possess the life in God. The multitude which no man can number, those who stand saved in the presence of God, out of all races and peoples and tongues, they are all there because they have washed their robes and made them white in the blood of the Lamb.

In the degree that the word of the blood is separated from life, teaching, and faith, in the same degree the Christian life in us and about us becomes pale and dies. In place of living Christianity we get "religious unrest." Let me say to you who desire to get to heaven, that you must never let go your faith in the blood that has reconciled us to God, and that cleanses from all sin.

Sweet the moments, rich in blessing,
Which before the cross we spend;
Life and health and peace possessing,
From the sinner's dying Friend.

Truly blessed is this station,
Low before His cross to lie,
While we see divine compassion
Beaming in His gracious eye.

Anniversaries and Birthdays

APRIL 12

And he said, "Jesus, remember me when Thou comest in Thy kingdom." And He said unto him, "Verily I say unto thee, Today shalt thou be with Me in Paradise." **Luke 23:42-43**

FROM the crooked ways of the robber and the murderer, through a prison, his trail leads to death. His whole life is one single row of great, blood-red sins. And now he hangs there tied to a cross. Even if he wished to do so, he could never more as much as reach out an arm to do good. He must see that his life is wasted, and he knows full well what to expect when he now soon shall appear before the Judge of the living and of the dead.

But near by him hangs the Savior of the world. He probably knew who Jesus was. The witness he gives Him tells us about that. "His reward will be good,—but mine—I will fare ill,"—and then from a heart in agony comes this prayer, "Jesus, remember me when Thou comest in Thy kingdom!" And this man, hanging on a cross, is saved. "Verily I say unto thee," Jesus answers, "today shalt thou be with Me in Paradise."

That is being saved for Jesus' sake by grace alone.

And although we know this, there are many among us who do not dare to believe that they can be saved just as they are. So many changes must be made first. But these changes are not made, at any rate not for the better, and so they are not saved. May the word about the thief and Jesus help you, you who are toiling with yourself, so that you get to see and grasp the Savior now.

We cannot cancel the sins we have committed, neither can we make ourselves better than we are, but we can grasp the outstretched hand of Him who came to save sinners.

When Jesus comes, O blessed story!
He works a change in heart and life;
God's kingdom comes with power and glory
To young and old, to man and wife;
Through sacrament and living Word,
Faith, love, and hope are now conferred.

Anniversaries and Birthdays

____

____

____

APRIL 13

When Jesus therefore had received the vinegar, He said, "It is finished:" and He bowed His head, and gave up His spirit.

John 19:30

WHEN Jesus gave up His spirit on Golgotha, that work was finished which He had assumed for our salvation, before the world was created. Through the centuries everything has been sustained on His promise and responsibility. Before the death of Christ, too, all those who repented and believed, received in Him grace and release from their sins. He bears all things by His Word, and His promises are valid for all times and all generations. The God who appeared unto Abraham by the oaks of Mamre, and who commanded the angels to take the filthy garments from off high priest Joshua and to clothe him with new apparel, was the same as He who died for our sins according to the Scriptures. The rock that followed Israel in the wilderness was Christ. In the Old Covenant the people of God looked forward to Golgotha, and believed on Him who was to come: we of the New Covenant look back, and believe on Him who came.

The question about the difference between the promise and the finished work of salvation, we shall leave unanswered until we see Him as He is. But this is certain, that as a sun in the middle of a circle shines on all parts of the circle, so Jesus stands as Savior both in the Old Covenant and in the New. We will grasp Him in faith as our only Redeemer; we hope in Him, and are fully assured that what He has promised, He has performed; and what He now is in heaven, that is enough for our salvation.

That Lamb is Lord of death and life,
God over all forever;
The Father's Son, whom to that strife
Love doth for us deliver!

Anniversaries and Birthdays

APRIL 14

"I am the resurrection, and the life: he that believeth on Me, though he die, yet shall ye live." John 11:25

AT long last Jesus arrives at Bethany; but in human opinion altogether too late. Now He stands by a grave where death has extinguished the last hope, and He stands there and weeps together with the others. But the tears that flow from His eyes are not hopeless ones. Just as surely as He stands there as a true man and weeps over the great power of death, so surely is He the Captain of life; and so He calls a living man out of the grave where a human body was just beginning to mix with the earth.

"Lord, if Thou hadst been here, my brother had not died," said Martha to Jesus. Many people say the same thing today. But now as then Jesus answers, "If thou believest, thou shalt see the glory of God." Just after He had said this, Lazarus stood in the family group very much alive. After all, then, did not Jesus arrive in time? He who just has faith enough to wait for Him, will find that everything is right at the last. He who places his confidence in the Lord will never be put to shame.

"I am the resurrection, and the life. Whosoever liveth and believeth on Me shall never die." I confess that these words of Jesus are the most delightful music that reaches my ears. And when I can also answer Yes to His question, "Believest thou this?" I smile at the grave that may soon be mine, and that contains so many of my dear ones. Christian, lay hold on the word of Jesus about eternal life!

Jesus lives! let all rejoice!
Praise Him, ransomed ones of earth!
Praise Him in a nobler song,
Cherubim of heavenly birth!
Praise the Victor-King, whose sway
Sin, and death, and hell obey.

Anniversaries and Birthdays

____

____

____

____

APRIL 15

And if Christ hath not been raised, your faith is vain; ye are yet in your sins. I Cor. 15:17

THE fight that Jesus stepped into is not only a meeting with Satan and sin, but also a battle between life and death. No one can vanquish death who has not first conquered sin.

There is therefore an organic connection between the value of the death of Christ and His bodily resurrection. If the death of Jesus is only a revelation of God's love, then His grave is not empty. But if He took sin away by His sacrifice, if He blotted out the bond written in ordinances that was against us, if God made peace by the blood of His cross, and if He entered in once for all into the holy place and obtained eternal redemption, then Jesus is risen from the grave.

This is in complete harmony with the Word of God. "If Christ hath not been raised, ye are yet in your sins," we read. "Then they also that are fallen asleep in Christ have perished."

One cannot separate the atoning death of Jesus from His bodily resurrection. The rationalist has no Atoner and therefore no empty grave, but the Bible and the Christian faith have both. The rationalist sees an original cell that came into being somewhere, and then through millions of years gradually has been changed and developed to higher and still higher forms of life. The Christian sees a new creature, he sees a new race step forth in Christ who took sin away, and thereby obtained power over death. Apart from Him everything moves toward a grave: in Him are resurrection and life. He who finds Him has found the way out from sin and death. Eternal life is in the risen Christ.

Jesus lives! I know full well,
Naught from me His love shall sever;
Life, nor death, nor powers of hell,
Part me now from Christ forever.
God will be a sure defense:
This shall be my confidence.

Anniversaries and Birthdays

APRIL 16

And he saith unto them, "Be not amazed: ye seek Jesus, the Nazarene, who hath been crucified: He is risen; He is not here: behold, the place where they laid Him!" Mark 16:6

ON Good Friday darkness lay over the world, heavy and dismal as death. When the Prince of life gave up the spirit, darkness came.

But Easter morning dawns clear, strong, and eternal. The day of life breaks the night. The darkness must away, and the new time has arrived that never more can sink toward evening and toward death. That which now is done by Him, who from times eternal promised to be our Savior, can never crumble to dust. What He took away, and what He has won—all has gone victoriously through the temptations of Satan, through God's holy and righteous demands, and through the fires of death and of hell. The new paradise has opened its portals to the race of Adam, the tree of life stands with ripe fruit for the sons of death, and whosoever will may eat and live, eternally made free from sin.

Easter morning! Thou life-giving sun arising over an earth in the shadows of death! You gave us escape from death, you gave us life. On Easter morning a Man steps out of His grave, never more to be laid in the grave again. On Easter morning death meets his Master. Through the open grave and the living Jesus, heaven shouts to us that the Son of God took sin away by His sacrifice.

Easter morning! Thou art life's eternal day over the children of death.

Can you believe anything so great without being seized by holy joy?

He closed the yawning gates of hell;
The bars from heaven's high portals fell;
Let hymns of praise His triumphs tell.
Hallelujah!

Anniversaries and Birthdays

APRIL 17

And the angel answered and said unto the women, "Fear not ye; for I know that ye seek Jesus, who hath been crucified. He is not here; for He is risen, even as He said. Come, see the place where the Lord lay." Matt. 28:5-6

THERE are many even today who seek Jesus but do not find Him. Even though they seek Him uprightly, and consider finding Him life's greatest joy, they still do not succeed.

Why do you not find Him? Because you seek Him where He is not. You pray God that you may be saved, and that Jesus may reveal Himself to you, and when you have done that, you seek Him in your own heart. You expect to find Him there. When your life is made over, and you feel saved, blest, and happy, then you will believe that you are saved. In that manner many people lose their way and go farther and farther out into the darkness.

Jesus is in His Word. The word of the Bible is the Word of God, and our Savior is there. There we read that He "was delivered up for our trespasses, and was raised for our justification." There it says also that he who believes in Him has eternal life. We do not read that he who feels and experiences salvation in his heart, he is saved. No, it says that he who believes is saved.

Listen! If you are seeking Jesus, and desire to be saved, then believe His Word when it says that you are saved. You are not to believe only that He has saved you, but you are to believe that you are saved, that you may be a child of God as you are now. Then you will find Jesus.

Here on Thy Word in faith we lean,
There Thou shalt be forever seen;
And when our journey endeth here,
Receive us, Lord, in glory there.

Anniversaries and Birthdays

____

____

____

____

____

APRIL 18

"We have seen the Lord." But Thomas said unto them, "Except I shall see in His hands the print of the nails, and put my finger into the print of the nails, and put my hand into His side, I will not believe." **John 20:25**

IT is probable that Thomas, more than the others, had made the hope that Jesus was He who should redeem Israel, a part of his very life. When all this failed, he collapsed more than any of the others. Doubt and despondency settled down over his inner man like a suit of steel armor. He rejected hope, light, and faith.

We know that there are many people like Thomas. But what makes us marvel is that Jesus meets such people according to their own wish. God has not promised that we may experience Jesus Christ as our Savior before we believe in Him, and still He comes to Thomas and asks him to see and feel. Come, Thomas, and put your fingers in my sores. Then Thomas is compelled to believe.

There are many honest people now, too, who will not believe that they are saved before they have experienced that they are saved. Then Jesus comes and gives their souls peace, joy, and light. They feel that they are saved, and then they believe. What an ocean of Savior-love for stubborn people!

But now when Jesus has met Thomas and all the others that resemble him, a sad lament breaks forth from His heart: "Thomas! Thomas! You should have believed My Word. Have I ever failed you? Was I not worthy of your confidence?" May this sorrowful reproach not fit you and me, but rather these words: "Blessed are they that have not seen, and yet have believed."

Whene'er we contemplate the grace,
The love and condescension
Of Christ to our apostate race,
Which pass all comprehension,
Low at His feet we bend;
Own Him the sinner's friend;
Determined naught to know beside
Christ Jesus, and Him crucified.

Anniversaries and Birthdays

APRIL 19

When the doors were shut where the disciples were, for fear of the Jews, Jesus came and stood in the midst, and saith unto them, "Peace be unto you." **John 20:19**

THE defeat, the shame, the despondency, and the scoffing caused the disciples to lock themselves in. They were afraid of themselves, and they were afraid of others. Trusting that Jesus was the person He claimed to be, they joined His company and preached that He was Israel's hope. And now He is dead! They saw Him die, they saw the spear pierce His side, and they saw Joseph lay Him in a grave. This happened in rapid succession till all was lost.

For honest people such things are hard to take. They have lost their Savior and their future. Rumors that He was alive got Thomas to assure them that until he put his finger into the print of the nails and put his hand into His side, he would not believe. Another disappointment would be more than he could endure.

And then before they are aware, the living Jesus stands in the middle of the hall. He comes in to His own through a locked door, and He gives them His peace. See, here are My hands and My side! "The disciples therefore were glad, when they saw the Lord."

Have you lost Jesus? Does it seem to you that you have lost Him whom your soul loves? No, you have not lost Him. He lives, and in a little while you shall see Him greater and more glorious than ever before. Even if your door should be locked by sorrow and doubt, He will surely find the way in. He has done that so many times, and when He again appears to you, you will thank Him also for the time that He was hidden.

From God shall naught divide me,
For He is true for aye,
And on my path will guide me,
Who else should often stray;
His ever bounteous hand
By night and day is heedful,
And gives me what is needful,
Where'er I go or stand.

Anniversaries and Birthdays

____

____

____

APRIL 20

And it came to pass, while they communed and questioned together, that Jesus Himself drew near, and went with them. But their eyes were holden that they should not know Him.

Luke 24:15-16

WHEN darkness, adversity, and dreary days come upon the Christian, and everything that we consider excellent and good vanishes, then the way becomes "lonely and thorny and strait" even for a strong and courageous person. The night that then sinks down around us shuts out the view both for this life and for that which is to come. Those that we thought were our best friends disappeared when we had most use for them, and when our Savior and peace with God vanished also, well, then the traveling was heavy.

But in the Word that we are considering today, Jesus wants to tell us that in such times we are not as badly off as we think. Jesus walks with us then, too. Even if we do not see Him, He sees us, and though we do not recognize Him, He knows us. Though our eyes be closed, that does not prevent Him from helping us on those very occasions, so that we may look more deeply into God's Word and into the Savior-heart of Jesus. In that manner the darkest night becomes the brightest day.

Also in life's darkest hour
The testament of grace is sure on high:
What matters now the feeling and the going
You may always remain a child!

You who just now are living through a dark and dreary time, you who think that all is lost, you must remember that as certainly as He walked with His own formerly, so certainly does He walk with you now.

Frail children of dust, and feeble as frail,
In Thee do we trust, nor find Thee to fail.
Thy mercies how tender! how firm to the end!
Our Maker, Defender, Redeemer, and Friend!

Anniversaries and Birthdays

APRIL 21

And they constrained Him, saying, "Abide with us; for it is toward evening, and the day is now far spent." And He went in to abide with them. Luke 24:29

MOST of the promises in the Bible about answers to prayer tell us that God answers speedily. He has even promised, "Before they call, I will answer." But there are also passages that show us that He lets us wait, even if what we are praying for is according to His will. Jeremiah laments: "When I cry, and call for help, He shutteth out my prayer." The Canaanitish woman was coldly turned away again and again, although she prayed for salvation for her child. After the crushing defeat at the death of Jesus, when the disciples saw Him alive again, they had to constrain Him before He would be persuaded to abide with them.

The fact that we must wait a long time for an answer is no reason that we should quit praying. If God always answered our prayers at once we should surely attach more significance to our Christianity and our prayers than we had a right to do. When need and suffering are great, and God still lets us wait for an answer, He wants to teach us to believe, and then show us that the sole reason for all we get is His unspeakable grace.

"Why art thou cast down, O my soul?
And why art thou disquieted within me?
Hope thou in God; for I shall yet praise Him
For the help of His countenance."

"Be strong, and let your heart take courage,
All ye that hope in Jehovah."

O Jesus, I must now confess
The world hath but vexation
And anguish, sorrow, dire distress,
As is Thy declaration.
In Thee is peace
And sweet surcease;
Thy bosom is my resting-place
Where I find consolation.

Anniversaries and Birthdays

APRIL 22

Jesus therefore saith unto them, "Children, have ye aught to eat?" They answered Him, "No." . . . . Jesus saith unto them, "Come and break your fast." **John 21:5, 12**

HOW wonderfully Jesus cares for His own! He meets Mary at the grave, and wipes away her tears. He sends a special greeting to Peter who swore that he did not know Him. He walks mile upon mile with those who have forgotten the Word of God, and interprets the Scriptures to them. He stands in the middle of the room where the disciples have locked themselves in in sorrow and terror, and says, "Peace be unto you!" He goes to the beach before sunrise, gathers faggots, builds a fire, and prepares food for His friends. He calls to them from the beach and asks them come to Him for breakfast. Is it not a wonderful sight to behold the risen and glorified Savior occupied with such things? Can you see this without feeling glad and thankful?

I am sure that these words reach many who know what it means to get into both temporal and spiritual darkness. Formerly there was light and goodness everywhere: now all seems to be gone. You have lost Jesus, and with Him both faith and peace. You are not successful in your daily work either: every way of escape is blocked.

Listen! You who believe that all hope is gone: See how He took care of His own in times past! He does the same now, too. Our Savior cannot help those who help themselves; nor can He give anything to those who have already had enough to eat. But them of low degree He hath filled with good things, and He hath given help to the helpless.

I need Thee, blessed Jesus,
For I am very poor;
A stranger and a pilgrim,
I have no earthly store.
I need the love of Jesus
To cheer me on my way,
To guide my doubting footsteps,
To be my strength and stay.

Anniversaries and Birthdays

____

____

____

APRIL 23

But when day was now breaking, Jesus stood on the beach: yet the disciples knew not that it was Jesus. . . . That disciple therefore whom Jesus loved saith unto Peter, "It is the Lord."

John 21:4, 7

SEVERAL disciples were in the same fishing crew the night when Jesus came to them at daybreak, but only John recognized Him.

I have often wondered what the reason might be for this. Let me tell it as it has seemed to me. Peter and the others who did not recognize Jesus had their minds full of all the reverses they had encountered. Their whole soul was so entirely taken captive by sorrow, complaint, and doubt that the picture of Jesus lay hidden in that darkness. They were so completely taken up with their disappointment that they neither saw nor thought of anything else. But John had not forgotten Jesus. He saw Him clearly with his inner eye. He could not forget the One he loved and had lost. So when he heard the voice, and saw Him on the beach, he recognized Him as the One who lived in his thought and mind.

Those whose minds are full of everything except Jesus cannot easily hear His voice or recognize Him when He comes and wants to help. Our ability to see the Lord and to recognize Him is weakened by having our minds filled with matter that is foreign to God. But he who in life's struggle can keep his heart and thoughts in Jesus Christ, he will hear His voice, and he will recognize Him both in sorrow and in all the bustle of the world.

It is well to hear and see our Savior through everything that meets us.

> Come, holy sun of heavenly love,
> Send down thy radiance from above;
> And to our inmost hearts convey
> The Holy Spirit's cloudless ray.
>
> May faith, deep rooted in the soul,
> The flesh subdue, the mind control:
> May guile depart, and discord cease,
> And all within be joy and peace.

Anniversaries and Birthdays

____

____

____

APRIL 24

And Simon answered and said, "Master, we toiled all night, and took nothing: but at Thy word I will let down the nets." Luke 5:5

PETER'S sad complaint that morning is well known among us Christians of this day. So little seems successful, and so much fails.

Father and mother struggle not only a whole night but through a whole lifetime that their children may be saved, and yet they are living away from God. The Christian teacher wears himself out in the school room, trying hard to help the little ones to Jesus, but the work seems to be in vain. The little flock of believers in town and country try to gather people about the Word, but no one is converted. The missionary sits worn out in the midst of a strange people who give him scorn and stripes as pay for all the sacrifices he has made that the name of Christ may be known. The Christian nurse prayed for sick people who forgot it all when they got well. The Christian preacher sits tired and discouraged when evening comes, because he sees no fruit of his labors.

You discouraged servant of Jesus Christ, do not lose heart! No one who serves the Savior with an honest purpose shall lack fruits. "Thy work shall be rewarded." He that doeth good shall reap in due season if he faint not. When eternity's morning dawns we shall be permitted to see that the Lord has blessed our work.

"They that sow in tears shall reap in joy."

O Jesus, Thou hast promised
To all who follow Thee
That where Thou art in glory
There shall Thy servant be;
And, Jesus, I have promised
To serve Thee to the end;
O give me grace to follow,
My Master and my Friend!

Anniversaries and Birthdays

APRIL 25

So when they had broken their fast, Jesus saith to Simon Peter, "Simon, son of John, lovest thou Me more than these?" John 21:15

MANY things had come up between Peter and Jesus in just a few years before this question is put to Peter. Time and again he has offended, and occasionally he has sinned greatly, but the end of the whole matter is that he gets a special greeting from Jesus on Easter morning. The angel who sits on the grave asks the women to bring the message to Peter. Now the erring Peter and the forgiving Savior meet again, and the question is asked, "Lovest thou Me?"

Today this question is directed to you and me. Jesus expects an answer from us, too. What can we answer? Do you love Jesus? The most natural thing for many of us is to answer with a tear, and this wish: I would so gladly love you, but, but—it is pretty poor, pretty small.

Let me name some signs whereby love is known. Perhaps you then can answer more readily. You like to be with the person you love; for him or her you open your heart without compulsion, yea, you cannot help doing so. Of its own free will love opens the door to life's secret rooms. You gladly do something for the person that you love. You listen to his wishes, and then go where you think he will prize your services. If you are living thus with Him and for Him, then you love Him.

Teach me all Thy steps to trace,
Strong to follow in Thy grace;
Learning how to love from Thee,
Loving Him who first loved me.

Anniversaries and Birthdays

____

____

____

____

____

____

APRIL 26

"Verily, verily, I say unto you, If a man keep My Word, he shall never see death." John 8:51

THE hope of eternal life is the morning star that sheds its light on a world full of graves. If the light of this star should be extinguished, and if we should know of a certainty that the death of the body meant the end of everything, then being a man would be the greatest misfortune, and life on earth would be entirely without meaning.

But listen, discouraged man! Lift your soul toward the land where the sun never sets, where there is no grave, where death is hardly a memory, where sorrow and longing are drowned in peace and eternal life. Try to let your heart grasp the truth that this future awaits you. Then you have in your own hand the key to all the puzzles of life, then you have strength to endure, no matter how heavy the burden, and then you have light in the hour of death. Then you also possess the Artist who composes the melody for eternity's song, and who can give peace and quiet to every heart-string. As the cataract makes its song in the falls, so shall suffering, longing, and faith teach you the song that never dies.

My Lord and my God! The more I meditate on Thy words, the more I am laid hold on by Thee. My faith is renewed, wings are given to my hope, and joyously do I look forward to the day when I shall be permitted to behold Thy face and hear Thy voice. Then I shall kneel and kiss the hand that led me through both life and death. At times I feel my heart-strings quiver, seized by heavenly powers; and if my mouth were entirely in order I should sing Thy praises day and night. But help me over the boundary; the song and the melody lie ready in my breast, and are only waiting for a tongue that sings in a clean mouth.

Onward we go, for still we hear them singing,
"Come, weary souls, for Jesus bids you come;"
And through the dark, its echoes sweetly ringing,
The music of the gospel leads us home.
Angels of Jesus, Angels of light,
Singing to welcome the pilgrims of the night.

Anniversaries and Birthdays

APRIL 27

And you did He make alive, when ye were dead through your trespasses and sins. Eph. 2:1

GOD has done this for us by Jesus Christ our Lord. Thus He again opened the door for us to eternal day. For us who were dead in trespasses and sins, for us who turned everyone to his own way, for us everything was laid on Him. He who knew no sin was made to be sin on our behalf. He who did not know the fruit of death, He tasted of death for all men; and for us eternal death was exchanged for eternal life. When He put death under His feet, we received life. He "raised us up with Him, and made us to sit with Him in the heavenly places in Christ."

As Adam gave us death, Christ gave us life. As Adam gave us hell, Christ gave us heaven. "For as in Adam all die, so also in Christ shall all be made alive." And all this we can get without money and without price, simply by turning and believing on the name of the Son of God. "For this is the will of My Father, that everyone that beholdeth the Son, and believeth on Him, should have eternal life; and that I should raise him up at the last day."

Wherefore, all you who want to save your lives, come to Him! Come soon! Come now! Come to Him who casts no one out, but who cleanses from sin, and makes alive the hearts of the contrite. Why will you go into eternal death, when you stand near the open door of life? Do not offer the excuse that you cannot be saved. Be honest and tell facts as they are: you can be saved if you want to be saved.

Just as I am, though tossed about
With many a conflict, many a doubt,
Fightings and fears within, without,
O Lamb of God, I come, I come.

Anniversaries and Birthdays

APRIL 28

Wherefore, holy brethren, partakers of a heavenly calling, consider the Apostle and High Priest of our confession, even Jesus. Heb. 3:1

HOLY brethren! That is a beautiful name for saved sinners, a name that seems to fit rather poorly us who are so lacking in holiness. But He who saved us and called us with a holy calling, has Himself given us this name. Let us rejoice in this name, honor it, and not forget our nobility. It is right that we acknowledge that we are sinners; but it is also right to remember what God in His grace has made us.

What do you suppose was the purpose of the author of the letter to the Hebrews in using these words, "Wherefore, holy brethren, . . ."? Oh, the Jewish Christians were moving away from Christ and back to the Old Covenant dispensation. "The shadow of the true" had impaired their sight, so that they did not behold the glory in the face of Jesus Christ, and so he exhorts them, as a mother her child, not to be hardened by the deceitfulness of sin: "Holy brethren, behold Jesus, and hold fast the beginning of your confidence firm unto the end."

How many factors want to coax and allure us also away from Christ! Many who once laid hold on Jesus in faith, and had the life with God in their hearts, now have left nothing but the shadow of the good things. Church and pastor, altar and pulpit, chapel and Christian talk have taken the place of the glory in the face of Jesus Christ. That danger is near, very near to all of us. And it is shockingly great. He who loses Christ, loses all. To your last day you must overcome everything that would turn your heart from Christ.

O let me feel Thee near me—
The world is ever near;
I see the sights that dazzle,
The tempting sounds I hear.
My foes are ever near me,
Around me and within;
But, Jesus, draw Thou nearer,
And shield my soul from sin.

Anniversaries and Birthdays

APRIL 29

What then shall we say to these things? If God is for us, who is against us? **Rom. 8:31**

THIS word cannot mean that when God is for us, nothing can be against us. Quite the opposite. It is just when we try to follow Jesus that opposition wakes up. Asaph complained when he saw the prosperity of the wicked, and that the godly fared ill, and that fits today, too. Neither does Paul conceal the fact that he had to pass through a world that was against him just because he was a Christian. Anything that helps us slip through the world easily is not a Christian virtue.

. But what does our text mean? I believe it means that when God is for us, He makes everything that we encounter work for our good, and to the advantage of others. That is the way it worked in the case of Joseph, of Daniel, of Paul, and of all the others who had God for them in all that they encountered in life. And if we think things over calmly, what do we find that we have experienced in our own life? Was it not just what went against us that caused us to cry for help, and that also caused us to experience the grace of God?

The main point with a Christian is not how much or how little is against him, but whether God is for him. "To them that love God all things work together" for the best.

"For the mountains may depart, and the hills be removed: but My lovingkindness shall not depart from thee, neither shall My covenant of peace be removed, saith Jehovah that hath mercy on thee" (Isa. 54:10).

If God Himself be for me,
I may a host defy,
For when I pray, before me
My foes confounded fly:
If Christ, the head, befriend me.
If God be my support,
The mischief they intend me
Shall quickly come to naught.

Anniversaries and Birthdays

APRIL 30

Let us therefore draw near with boldness unto the throne of grace, that we may receive mercy, and may find grace to help us in time of need. Heb. 4:16

IT is when need knocks at our door that we may knock at the door of grace. No matter how self-evident this may seem, it is nevertheless just then that we have our greatest doubts that we will be welcome. We have gone to that door so many times before: dare we go once more? Is not that sinning on grace?

What makes you feel sad and heavy is that you think there is so little fruit to show for all that you get. With all the grace that you have received to this day, you should be a different kind of person. Your grade is poor on patience, love, and Christian disposition. Your life does not measure up to what you should be as a Christian. Your victories are few, and often you get nowhere. This causes you to doubt, and makes you discouraged.

If this is your condition, you are surely in the right in all that you accuse yourself of. He who is not ashamed of his own folly, is of all people worst off. But our sin and shame should not constitute a reason for doubting Him who sits on the throne of grace and who has promised us "mercy and grace to help us in time of need."

Wherefore draw near with boldness unto the throne of grace, all you tired and worn Christians! There is your place: it has been given you by God Himself. Sinai is too steep for you, and your knees are too weak; but at Golgotha everything that you need is given to you without money and without price. Lay hold on grace today also as you did the first time, and you shall become strong in the Lord.

Rich Thy mercy— strangely good!
O how oft have I offended!
But, through Thy redeeming blood
All my fear of wrath is ended:
Yes, I now can witness give:
Jesus sinners does receive!

Anniversaries and Birthdays

MAY 1

"A little while, and ye behold Me no more; and again a little while, and ye shall see Me." **John 16:16**

A CHRISTIAN cannot live in this world exclusively in light, prosperity, and good days. If any one of us should be so "unfortunate" as to encounter nothing in this life except what we call "good fortune," he would be badly off. Those who must fight their way through opposition, storms, and darkness have the happiest and most healthful Christian life, and their condition is most conducive to growth and fruit-bearing.

Therefore God has not promised His people only good days. On the contrary, He has said that we must enter into the kingdom of God through many tribulations. When darkness envelops us on the way that we are compelled to take, then we realize how helpless we are; but it is also then that the Lord is our light. When the burden gets too heavy, we must get someone else to carry it for us. He who does not feel his helplessness needs no help.

When Jesus hides we understand most clearly what we have lost by His absence; and when He reveals Himself anew we learn to thank Him a little better than before. A Christian has no reason to lose courage if a dark cloud hides the sun of his life. The sun is not gone: a cloud has hid it from view. In a little while we shall see it again.

That is God's way with His people.

Thy way and all thy sorrows
Give thou into His hand,
His gracious care unfailing,
Who doth the heavens command;
Their course and path He giveth
To clouds and air and wind:
A way thy feet may follow
He too for thee will find.

Anniversaries and Birthdays

MAY 2

For we are His workmanship, created in Christ Jesus for good works, which God afore prepared that we should walk in them.
Eph. 2:10

THE salvation that God gave us in Christ consists not only in this that sin was atoned and the debt paid, but also in this that all that we had failed to do because of our mistakes and omissions, He did for us in His perfect human life. He has in word and deed, in mind and spirit fulfilled all righteousness.

It was not for His own sake that He as a child and as a youth grew in grace and knowledge, that He obeyed His parents, and did His work through a whole life. It was all for us.

The whole life of Jesus as man stands forth as a new creation. He is the new man of God, the second Adam. Therefore all good works are ready for us in Him. They are there for us in the same way that the forgiveness of sins, life, and peace that we must have, are in Him.

So if Christ comes to dwell in us by faith, we will get from Him the one as well as the other, also His good works. The peace that fills our life is of Christ and shows itself in life: so it is also regarding good works. Only what is of God will endure before God. As pipes carry the water, so are we pipes or conductors for all the good that is done by us, and which is of God. That these works which issue through us are attributed to us, is only a new testimony to God's love.

It is when we see ourselves as instruments of God in all we do, that we are able to give Him the honor. Then we become happy in the great miracle of this life: to be permitted to be servants of Jesus Christ.

And this our joyful theme shall be
When, called to see our Savior,
We join the glorious company
Around His throne forever;
Then we in highest strain
Shall praise the Lamb once slain,
Who hath redeemed us by His blood,
And made us kings and priests to God.

Anniversaries and Birthdays

____

____

____

MAY 3

"What wilt thou that I should do unto thee?" **Luke 18:41**

JESUS directs this question to a praying man. It is a question that hardly seemed necessary. When a man comes and prays, "Have mercy on me!" one would think that Jesus knew what the man wanted.

But let us suppose that Jesus comes to us who are praying now and asks, "What wilt thou that I should do unto thee?" I wonder what we would answer. We, too, pray so often, "Lord Jesus, help me!" but if pressed for a definite answer, we perhaps would not always know just what we wanted. It is easy to fill a prayer with thoughtless words, and thus fall right into the danger that Jesus warns us against: "And in praying use not vain repetitions, as the Gentiles do: for they think that they shall be heard for their much speaking."

Let us ask ourselves when we appear before God in prayer: What do I want now? What do I really need? Like David, to present your case before God, and then wait: that is truly a Christian prayer. All this effeminate, nervous, and jaded attitude that pervades our time is carrying us in among the Pharisees and Gentiles when we pray.

It is God's will that we be awake on this point, too, so that we draw near unto God with a true heart. It may happen then that our words are few, but the heart will be more inclined to open itself in real need, and with a longing for an answer.

"Ye shall seek Me, and find Me, when ye shall search for Me with all your heart" (Jer. 29:13).

Lord, teach us to pray!

O Jesus, Lamb of God alone,
Who didst for all our sins atone,
Be merciful, I Thee implore,
Have mercy, Lord, for evermore!

Anniversaries and Birthdays

___

___

___

___

MAY 4

We who have fled for refuge to lay hold of the hope set before us: which we have as an anchor of the soul, a hope both sure and stedfast and entering into that which is within the veil.

Heb. 6:18-19

IN the Christian life there are two forces to bring us through the world, and into life eternal. These two forces are faith and hope. The essence of the life with God is love. It is this that faith grasps, and that hope sees before it in perfect glory. When the victory finally is won and we have reached the goal of our faith, then both faith and hope have finished their work, while love is as eternal as God.

When hope and faith shall pass away,
And love shall last for aye.

Hope is the Christian's aeroplane. In that he rises above and away from this world, from combat and wounds. Hope enters within the veil where Christ is, and there it is as an anchor of the soul. It crosses the last line of defense, to the place where victory is won, and from there it gives the militant Christian faith and new power.

As birds of passage in the southlands feel drawn toward the north when spring comes, so hope invites and lifts the Christian away from this world; and as wings carry the bird over the earth, so hope carries the Christian toward heaven.

The Christian carries in his bosom a well grounded certainty that he can expect something unspeakably good.

Apostles, prophets, martyrs,
And all the sacred throng,
Who wear the spotless raiment,
Who raise the ceaseless song;
For these, passed on before us,
Savior, we Thee adore,
And, walking in their footsteps,
Would serve Thee more and more.

Anniversaries and Birthdays

MAY 5

He must increase, but I must decrease. **John 3:30**

ALL our attempts to become good before we believe that we are saved for Jesus' sake, always end in defeat for us when sincere. Wherever we try to move forward we find the way closed. Everything turns out just the opposite of what we think, wish, and struggle to gain. Trying to free ourselves we get still more enmeshed, and when we want to move upward, we go down hill.

Not until the Spirit of God gets our eyes turned away from ourselves, and to Him who saved that which was lost, do we find the solution. When we saw Christ as our all before God, the hour of salvation and peace had come. In that moment for the first time, we got a glimpse into this word: "He must increase, but I must decrease."

We are not only to win life, but also to live it. In our conversion we learned that the gate is narrow: now we are also to learn that the way is straitened. That learning, too, is "bitter and sour as death for our nature," but that is the way on which we must move forward. Without knowing it or wishing it we Christians, too, are in danger of increasing where we ought to decrease. Therefore God must lead us into new difficulties, so that we again are unable to move, where we must go forward. We who could so boldly help others, cannot help ourselves now.

In that way God helps us away from self-confidence, and forward to a clearer view of Him who must be our all. To Him who has loved us and loosed us from our sins with His blood, be the glory and the dominion in all eternity.

For ever here my rest shall be,
Close to Thy bleeding side;
This all my hope and all my plea:
For me the Savior died.

Anniversaries and Birthdays

MAY 6

"Blessed are they that hunger and thirst after righteousness: for they shall be filled." Matt. 5:7

NO life can nourish itself. Wherever we find forms of life, whether in the air or in the earth, in nature or in spirit, the same rule prevails: life must get nourishment from something outside itself.

The same law holds good in the Christian life. The life we received from God cannot successfully go to itself for nourishment and power. A Christian who possesses healthful life in God must therefore continually reach out two empty hands toward the source from which his life sprang. Where this hunger for life ceases, there is great danger. But it is hard for us to learn that this must be so, and because we do not understand life's true nature, we continue to complain about that which we should praise God for.

The fountain of life is not in ourselves, it is not even in our life with God, but in God, in Christ and His grace. So what appears to us to be poverty and misfortune, namely, that we are always poor, hungry, and thirsty, that is our good fortune. The person who does not feel drawn to the regions of grace, and to the fountain of life with his empty water pot, that person is unsaved. He dwells where death is king, and his life in God has either become sick or is extinct.

If you cannot find comfort or help in yourself, praise God and rejoice in Him who not only gives you life, but also gives nourishment and new power to your life. The fountain of life is in Him, and in His light we shall see light.

No word is sung more sweet than this;
No name is heard more full of bliss;
No thought brings sweeter comfort nigh
Than Jesus, Son of God most high.

Anniversaries and Birthdays

MAY 7

Wait for Jehovah:
Be strong, and let thy heart take courage;
Yea, wait thou for Jehovah. Psalm 27:14

NO one has any reason to wait for Jehovah when it is a question of salvation. God's Savior-heart will be no more open tomorrow than it is today. No one who comes today will be shown away. If you think that it will be easier some other time, though your soul longs for peace now, then remember that this is one of Satan's tricks to keep you from being saved. Today is the day of your salvation, today you may have the forgiveness of sins and grace. Accept grace today, and you are saved.

But if you have come into the fellowship of God, then you have also enrolled in God's school to be trained to become a better Christian. Then this Word of God sounds forth to you: "Wait for Jehovah!" Then the Savior sometimes decides to lead His people into spiritual darkness, and to put them into the crucible and the refiner's fire. Then we pray and get no answer, we knock and the door is not opened. We may be misjudged, people may lie about us, but neither God nor man seems to do anything to cause justice to be rendered to us. That is the time to wait for Jehovah; we may gather purified gold from the oven of tribulation, if we wait for Him. When He again reveals Himself to the soul, we see that in this period of waiting He has given us something unspeakably great. But we will not see that until afterward.

"Therefore turn thou to thy God: keep kindness and justice, and wait for thy God continually" (Hosea 12:6).

Let but my fainting heart be blest
With Thy sweet Spirit for its guest,
My God, to Thee I leave the rest,—
"Thy will be done!"

Anniversaries and Birthdays

MAY 8

They that wait for Jehovah shall renew their strength; they shall mount up with wings as eagles; they shall run, and not be weary; they shall walk, and not faint. Isa. 40:31

THE person who is discouraged and doubts has no strength; but trust and hope put courage in the soul. Even he who is deepest down in "the slough of despond," rises with new courage and holy joy when hope awakens.

When we look at ourselves and at the world we live in, everything becomes dark and impossible; but if we look into God's Book we always find a way out. Hope carries man past the darkest shadows, and the whole world's oppression vanishes away and becomes a lever to lift up toward grace and power him who does not lose his faith in God.

If we go through life complaining and discouraged, that brings no honor to God, no happiness to ourselves, and no help to others. But to wipe tears away and wash his face, that is fitting for him who has Jesus as his Savior and God as his Father. And if we then will examine the way we have traveled, we will find that every one of the milestones without exception bears the inscription: "Hitherto hath Jehovah helped us." Should that not tell us that He will be with us today, and in days to come?

So, you discouraged Christian, spread your wings once more! Before you know it, you will again mount up like a young eagle and sail high above life's sorrows, and strong and joyous you will thank God for everything in the name of Jesus.

He that hopes in the Lord shall renew his strength.

How pleasant is our lot, how good
And blest beyond expression;
For, having cleansed us by His blood,
He bears us with compassion,
Applies His healing power
To us, each day and hour;
Yea, we in Him redemption have,
In death itself and in the grave.

Anniversaries and Birthdays

MAY 9

Comfort ye, comfort ye my people, saith your God. Speak ye comfortably to Jerusalem; and cry unto her, that her warfare is accomplished, that her iniquity is pardoned, that she hath received of Jehovah's hand double for all her sins. Isa. 40:1-2

CONDITIONS of life for God's people on this earth are not always bright. He who denies this has not learned to know either the world or himself. God has told us that the way a Christian must walk is straitened. Fear of dangers, fear of being left behind, responsibility for the salvation of others, a feeling of shame at not being what one could and should be, and many other things often make a Christian discouraged and fearful. It is at such times that one laments as did Christians before us: "The Lord has deserted me; the Lord has forgotten me."

But God has taken into account that such times would come to us, and therefore He has put His divine comfort into His Word. Hearken to a little of what He has to say to us: "Can a woman forget her sucking child, that she should not have compassion on the son of her womb? yea, these may forget, yet will not I forget thee. Behold, I have graven thee upon the palms of My hands; thy walls are continually before Me."... Our warfare is accomplished, our iniquity is pardoned, we have received of Jehovah's hand double for all our sins.

If I forget thee, O Zion,
Let my right hand forget her skill,
So says the Lord our God.
No, ne'er shall I forget that Zion is my bride;
As dear child of my bosom I her will safely hide!
I else then must forget the wounds in My own hand,
My cross, My blood, My anguish, and all My painful grief.
No, Zion is my joy most chief!

Anniversaries and Birthdays

MAY 10

I will give thanks unto Thee, O Jehovah; for though Thou wast angry with me, Thine anger is turned away, and Thou comfortest me. Isa. 12:1

IT would not be good for us always to see the Lord as a loving and gracious God. We would then easily cease fearing ourselves, and we would forget that our God is a consuming fire. When we see that God is holy and angry, we also get to see how pitiful and how completely lost we are; and if He may not smite us, neither can He heal us. The Lord wounds and He heals, He kills and He makes alive.

When we see the Lord as our righteous Judge and ourselves as unholy and sinful men, then we must either yield or be crushed. Happy is he who yields—for him the Lord's anger will become the source of the highest joy. This is true, not because it is good to see the Lord's anger, but because a light shines out of that holy fire into our inner man that causes us to cry: "Woe is me, I am a sinful man!" When the Lord hears that cry His anger is turned away, and He gives comfort.

Such is the Lord's way with His own. If we are to reach the goal that He has set before us, He must lead us in this way. Let us all bow before the holy wrath of God, for then we shall also receive His gracious comfort.

From the depth of nature's blindness,
From the hardening power of sin,
From all malice and unkindness,
From the pride that lurks within,
By Thy mercy,
O deliver us, good Lord!

Anniversaries and Birthdays

MAY 11

He that spared not His own Son, but delivered Him up for us all, how shall He not also with Him freely give us all things?

Romans 8:32

IT is both remarkable and sad to see how we Christians can be anxious and fearful about little things in life.

We believe that God thought of us in His grace before the creation of the world, and we believe that He gave His life for us. We also believe that we have the forgiveness of sins in His name, and that He has made us His children. But in spite of the fact that we believe all these great things that God has done for us, yea, the greatest of all that is great, we nevertheless continue to carry our everyday burdens in life.

We believe that God is our Savior, but we do not have confidence in Him as our Father. We believe that He opens heaven for a lost sinner, but we doubt that He will help us in our daily life. "How are I and mine going to fare?" father groans. "Who is going to take care of my children when I can do no more?" mother laments. The day that we never have seen, and that we perhaps never shall see, that day we are carrying on our shoulders as a heavy burden, and we grieve and lament about that which God has promised to take care of for us. Yea, He has even said that we shall be anxious for nothing, but shall cast all our cares upon Him, because He careth for us.

It is appropriate for us who are Christians to trust Him who is our Father. He who gave us His Son, should He not also give us everything else that we need?

If thou but suffer God to guide thee,
And hope in Him through all thy ways,
He'll give thee strength whate'er betide thee,
And bear thee through the evil days;
Who trusts in God's unchanging love
Builds on the rock that naught can move.

Anniversaries and Birthdays

MAY 12

I waited patiently for Jehovah;
And He inclined unto me, and heard my cry.
Psalm 40:1

THAT we do not have time to wait for the Lord is not always proof of faith and true godliness. It may be because we distrust God, and because of our selfish nature that we want the answer to our prayers in a hurry. Abraham had to wait a long time even though God's promises to him could not be misunderstood. Evil will befall the child that gets all it wants as soon as it asks for it. In that manner many have been spoiled for life. It is not only receiving that is an art: it is a much greater art to use aright what one receives. While the Lord lets us wait, He tries to teach us to use aright what we have, and at the same time He prepares us to receive more.

Wait and be silent in prayer and faith,
That will give your soul surcease.

At this point many will answer thus: "During almost all my life I have been praying for something that I know is according to the will of God, and I am still looking for the answer." Here is my reply: There are manv things that you and I do not understand but which the Lord takes into consideration. For that reason you shall not doubt that your prayer is according to the will of God, neither shall you doubt that He will answer. You shall be certain that the answer will come in the Lord's own time with happiness for you and help for others.

Many of us older people can now see that it would have been a bad thing for us if we had gotten all we asked for, in the way we wished, even though we prayed for things that were according to the will of God.

O Israel, wait for the Lord!

Then hope, my feeble spirit,
And be thou undismayed:
God helps in every trial,
And makes thee unafraid.

Await God's time with pleasure,
Then shall thine eyes behold
The sun of joy and gladness
His brightest beams unfold.

Anniversaries and Birthdays

____

____

____

MAY 13

Art Thou He that cometh, or look we for another? Matt. 11:3

JOHN is in jail.

His work had been broken off while he was still in the full power of manhood, with courage to live, and with a will to tell the truth to a godless people. The dark prison cell and his hard fate have eaten awav his strength, and the sleepless nights have fostered doubts: Did I mistake my calling? Did I speak falsehood when I cried out, "Behold the Lamb of God, that taketh away the sin of the world!" Everything is confused, and doubt gnaws and corrodes within him.

Our intellect-worshipping and soul-sick generation is ravaged by doubt. Many of God's best witnesses, too, who for a time in their lives brought people the message of Jesus Christ in spirit and in truth, are now doubters—with courage broken and wounded soul. "Is what I have said true? Was I really converted? Am I a Christian, or have I never been a Christian?"

How are we to get out of so dark a night?

I know only one way out. That one I have tried, and I can testify from my own experience that it is good. What is that way out of the difficulty? It is to bring your doubt to Jesus and tell Him openly how matters stand. Say that you have doubts, and tell Him what you doubt. Then He will remove your doubt. We cannot drive doubt away by thinking or arguing, but Jesus takes it away if He gets the chance. How it is done I do not know: I only know that He does it.

> Stood we alone in our own might,
> Our striving would be losing;
> For us the one true Man doth fight,
> The Man of God's own choosing.
> Who is this chosen One?
> 'Tis Jesus Christ, the Son,
> The Lord of hosts, 'tis He
> Who wins the victory
> In every field of battle.

Anniversaries and Birthdays

____

____

____

MAY 14

Rejoice in the Lord always: again I will say, Rejoice! Phil. 4:4

TO rejoice in the Lord is not always the same as to feel happy. To be sure, the Word of God exhorts us to rejoice always, and it tells us that joy makes us strong, but it also says that those who mourn and always fear are blessed. To rejoice in the Lord always must therefore be something different from just feeling happy.

Not even the fact that you are enduring sorrow, adversity, and conflict proves that you have lost your joy in the Lord. It may often be that the jov in the Lord is most perfect, deep, and strong when one is enduring the greatest sorrow. The person that I love is the one that I go to when I am in the greatest distress, and exactly at such times does one learn to rejoice most in faithful friendships.

A Christian always gets closest to the heart of God when life is most grievous; and it is especially at such times that he learns to love Him whose door is open to those that seek Him when in distress. Therefore a Christian can rejoice in the Lord in all of life's vicissitudes. We can be jubilant with our mouths, while the heart loves the world. But many, many times it has happened that where sorrow is a guest the joy in the Lord is greatest.

Sorrowful yet always rejoicing—that is the secret of life which a Christian has found.

> Shall I not then be filled with gladness,
> Shall I not praise Thee evermore?
> And triumph o'er all fears and sadness,
> E'en when my cup of woes runs o'er?
> Though heaven and earth may pass away,
> I know Thy Word stands fast for aye.

Anniversaries and Birthdays

MAY 15

Keep thy heart with all diligence;
For out of it are the issues of life. Prov. 4:23

THE heart is the center of life and of vital power. When the heart is injured, there is always great danger. We can lose arms and legs and sight and still save our lives; but if we lose our heart, there is an end of life.

It is therefore important to take care of the heart also from a purely bodily point of view. He whose heart has been damaged, be it ever so little, will continually carry his life in his hands. But what the Word here exhorts us to take care of is the new heart that we got when we were born of God. When we gave God our heart, a new man of God was created in us. There Christ dwells by faith, and there we have the Spirit as seal and earnest until we receive the inheritance from God. It is this new heart that we are to take care of above everything else.

But how shall we take care of this heart? Can we do it?

To me the answer comes through these words: Watch over your thoughts, passions, disposition, words, your whole life! If you have become unclean, then cleanse your soul in obedience to the truth so that nothing offensive to God remains in the heart. The heart is our holy of holies, and only God must be there. If what is sinful and earthly is permitted peacefully to settle down there, the heart will suffer harm.

"Create in me a clean heart, O God;
And renew a right spirit within me."

My Jesus, let my heart receive
So great a taste for Thee:
That day and night Thou mayest be
A priceless Gift to me.

Anniversaries and Birthdays

MAY 16

Remember also thy Creator in the days of thy youth, before the evil days come. Eccl. 12:1

HE who no longer is young can best see what the time of youth is, and what it has to give a person. The waning day often calls back memories of the break of morn.

The years of youth are beautiful. They are full of hope, poetry, and the desire to know life by experience. But they are also full of responsibility and danger. In youth the foundation is laid for our entire future. It is in youth that most people make their choices both for time and for eternity. One of the best pictures of what youth-life contains is a spring morning in one of our beautiful valleys when the sun rises over the mountain tops. The waterfall and the river are sounding a deep bass, the snow is melting, the hillsides are becoming green, life is bursting forth from the blackest loam, the flowers are unfolding, and a thousand tongues of birds are singing. The farmer plows, spreading fertilizer on the fields, harrows, and sows the grain. It is sowing time and growing time for evil and for good.

The time of youth is spring in our life. Then we have the good days of life, because then we are to choose the direction that our life will take. Therefore there is no time in life so fitting for seeking God, as the years of youth. It is spring, there are decisions, it is seedtime, it is the time of growth and unfolding. That is the time that life sends down its roots.

It is wonderfully great to hear the Savior's call just at the sunrise of life. Who can tell the blessedness of those who accept the call of Christ in their youth!

Savior, while my heart is tender,
I would yield that heart to Thee;
All my powers to Thee surrender,
Thine and only Thine to be.
Take me now, Lord Jesus, take me,
Let my youthful heart be Thine,
Thy devoted servant make me,
Fill my soul with love divine.

Anniversaries and Birthdays

MAY 17

And Israel said unto Joseph, "Behold, I die: but God will be with you and bring you again unto the land of your fathers." Gen. 48:21

THROUGH all times people have loved their fatherland. And this love was never deeper and purer than in those who had to dwell in a foreign land. When the Israelites were in Babylon they hung their harps on the willows and wept with longing for the home land. The same thing happens today when one must live separated from his people and fatherland.

National boundaries, language, relationships, racial heritage, neighbors, school, house of prayer, church, and cemetery—all of these and much more bind people together into one single big family. As God has promised to bless and protect people in their homes, when they work together in love, so He will also bless and protect the people of a nation when they hold together and live in faith and godliness.

It is surely no Christian virtue to be indifferent to the welfare of one's fatherland. "And seek the peace of the city whither I have caused you to be carried away captive, and pray unto Jehovah for it; for in the peace thereof shall ye have peace" (Jer. 29:7). God said that to those Israelites who were compelled to live in Babylon. How much more will He say to us that we must work and pray for our people and country. We must pray for the president, for the government, and for all those who are in positions of authority over us, so that we may live in peace, decorum, and godliness. The Word of God says that to you and me.

May we feel our responsibility toward fatherland and people so that we in work and in prayer bear them up toward God, including all from palace to lowest hut. God wills that.

God bless our native land!
Firm may she ever stand,
Through storm and night;
When the wild tempests rave,
Ruler of wind and wave,
Do Thou our country save
By Thy great might.

Anniversaries and Birthdays

MAY 18

In whom, having also believed, ye were sealed with the Holy Spirit of promise, which is an earnest of our inheritance, unto the redemption of God's own possession, unto the praise of His glory. Eph. 1:13-14

HE who has become a child of God by faith in Christ, has thereby also become an heir of God and a joint-heir with Christ. Everything that God has will be divided between Christ and His saved people. He who is not ashamed to be called our brother, He will also divide the inheritance with us.

But we shall not get this inheritance while we are here. God has arranged it so that His people must pass through the world by faith. On the way through the desert to Canaan we must every day gather the manna of grace in an empty container. We cannot lay it up in store for the next day: God has only promised that if a new day dawns, grace will also be new. Not until we enter our right fatherland will the inheritance be ours.

However God will not let us go through the world entirely empty-handed. He has set His seal on us, and thus stamped us as His own possession; He has given us His Spirit as a pledge of the inheritance we shall receive. When this stamp is on us, no one can snatch us away from God, and with this earnest we are sure of receiving the inheritance.

We do not understand much of this now, but we have an inkling that something unspeakably great is laid up and awaits us. Consequently, what is of vital importance to us is that we do not lose the seal and the earnest. Our prayer must therefore always be: "Lord, take not Thy Holy Spirit from me!"

Jerusalem, thou city fair and high,
Would God I were in thee!
My longing heart fain, fain to thee would fly,
It will not stay with me;
Far over vale and mountain,
Far over field and plain,
It hastes to seek its fountain,
And quit this world of pain.

Anniversaries and Birthdays

MAY 19

And straightway Jesus, perceiving in Himself that the power proceeding from Him had gone forth, turned Him about in the crowd, and said, "Who touched My garments?" Mark 5:30

IN the midst of the great throng where one pushes and jostles the other, a sick woman manages to work her way to Jesus. She had spent all that she had to get her health back, but only grew worse. Now she goes to Jesus. In childlike faith she touches His garments, and at once she is well.

That is a miracle. But it is just as great a miracle that Jesus perceived in Himself that the power proceeding from Him had gone forth. In this there is great comfort for us, too, That gives us reason to believe that everything that we receive from Jesus when we in faith touch Him, we receive with His full knowledge; not only because He is all-knowing, but because He gives us a part of Himself, something that He perceives is taken from His own person. All the millions of men who in a spiritual sense have touched Him have received some of His power.

Is not that comfort? In that way all the people of God become a part of Jesus. He who is so rich must Himself be eternal life, and the person who receives this life from Him shall never die. Is it strange then that all eternity shall be filled with the song about Him who purchased us unto God with His blood, and who came and dwelt in our hearts?

Let us then together with this woman touch Him in faith.

Then though on earth I suffer
Much trial, well I know
I merit ways still rougher,
And 'tis to heaven I go;
For Christ I know and love,
To Him I now am hasting,
And gladness everlasting
With Him this heart shall prove.

Anniversaries and Birthdays

MAY 20

For we walk by faith, not by sight. **II Cor. 5:7**

THE Christian's pilgrimage through the world to his home with God is a walk by faith. No one of us has seen heaven, God, or Jesus Christ. To us, too, it may be said: "Whom not having seen ye love."

Our faith is the foot that stands on the Word of God, the hand that grasps Christ and His cross, that takes the sword to fight the good fight, and holds fast to the invisible One as though we saw Him. If a Christian quits believing, he has nothing to stand on, nothing to hold fast to, and possesses no goal of life. Without faith it is impossible to please God, and without faith it is also impossible to experience God. We walk by faith, not by sight. That means: We must go all the way through this life in faith.

Paul, too, had to believe even though he had been in the third heaven and had seen and heard unspeakable things there. When he stands at the end of life he says rejoicingly: "I have kept the faith!" He considers that to be unspeakably great.

Let us thank God for everything that we may experience in the fellowship of Jesus Christ, but let us not thank Him least because He permitted us to believe, and let us never quit praying Him to preserve us in the Word and in faith until our death. Many are imprisoned for eternity because they quit believing. May that never happen to any of us!

I know the work is only Thine,
The gift of faith is all divine;
But if on Thee we call,
Thou wilt the benefit bestow,
And give us hearts to feel and know
That Thou hast died for all.

Anniversaries and Birthdays

MAY 21

And the prince of Jehovah's host said unto Joshua, "Put off thy shoe from off thy foot; for the place whereon thou standest is holy." And Joshua did so. Joshua 5:15

HELPLESS and alone Joshua stood before Jericho. Strong walls rose up just where he must go forward. Similarly the Christian also comes face to face with difficulties and problems that he must solve, but cannot. If then we resemble Joshua in praying the Lord for help, we ought to remember what the prince of Jehovah's host said to him: "Put off thy shoe from off thy foot."

If I am to tell you what this word means to me, I must say it thus: Lay bare your soul before God, hide nothing from Him of all that you see and know and that is on your heart. If there is something special that you are struggling with, something too great to overcome, then tell Him; mention the enemies by name. Tell Him where you are being defeated, and in what respect you are accomplishing nothing either with yourself or with others. Bring your whole life, the outer as well as the inner into the light of day before Him. Then you are putting off your shoe from off your foot. Thus you must stand on a holy place.

Then the Lord will show you the way to victorv. If you obey the Lord's command in this manner, you shall see the strongest walls fall before you. Then the Lord fights for us. "For the eyes of Jehovah run to and fro throughout the whole earth, to show Himself strong in the behalf of them whose heart is perfect toward Him."

Leave all to His direction:
In wisdom He doth reign:
Thy wonder far exceeding,
He will His course maintain:
So He as Him beseemeth
His wonder-working skill,
Shall put away the sorrows,
That now thy spirit fill.

Anniversaries and Birthdays

MAY 22

Nathanael saith unto Him, "Whence knowest Thou me?" Jesus answered and said unto him, "Before Philip called thee, when thou wast under the fig tree, I saw thee." John 1:48

NATHANAEL thought that he was both hidden and forgotten where he sat, but just then Jesus saw him. He did not get to know, while he still sat under the fig tree, that Jesus saw him, but he found it out later.

If we look at this occurrence from an inner and spiritual point of view, we know that what Nathanael experienced, has happened to many. Sin and sorrow and doubt had settled down over the soul, everything inclosed us as a dark night, and we thought we were forgotten by both God and men. But then Jesus saw also us. We did not know it, but we learned it later, and now when we look back to that time, we marvel that we did not see Him then.

Now, too, many sit alone, and think they are forsaken by both God and men. An unsuccessful life with sin added to sin has brought you to the conclusion that you are dismissed and forgotten by all. But that is not true: the Savior sees you right where you are now. Even if you do not see Him, He sees you. Surely the Lord is not far from each one of us. David says:

"If I take the wings of the morning,
And dwell in the uttermost parts of the sea;
Even there shall Thy hand lead me,
And Thy right hand shall hold me."

That is what we ought to believe about God. Then we, too, shall see Him who saw Nathanael under the fig tree.

"Fear not, I am with thee, oh, be not dismayed,
For I am thy God, and will still give thee aid;
I'll strengthen thee, help thee, and cause thee to stand
Upheld by My righteous, omnipotent hand."

Anniversaries and Birthdays

MAY 23

Happy is the man that feareth alway;
But he that hardeneth his heart shall fall into mischief.
Prov. 28:14

A CHRISTIAN shall not only be secure and joyous: he shall also fear and be cautious. The Bible does not deem only those blessed who always rejoice, but also those who always fear.

When the question is about God as our Savior and Father we always have reason to be secure and calm. What He in His Word has promised us can never fail; therefore we can with complete assurance and blessed tranquillity put everything in His hand. But when we are up for consideration, both as men and as Christians, we always have reason for distrust and fear. Our nature houses strong and hidden forces which in cooperation with Satan always seek to direct us astray. Not only that we are tempted to that which all men call sin, but also that we wish to credit ourselves, in our account book, with what God in grace gave us, and thus magnify ourselves at the expense of God's benefits.

A Christian must never rely on himself, not even on his spiritual awakening, conversion, and faith; no, not even on the grace in his heart. There is a law in the kingdom of God that never can be broken, namely, that he who relies least on his own power, finds his strength in the Lord. Only he who, distrusting self, relies on the Lord, shall never be put to shame.

"Oh fear Jehovah, ye His saints;
For there is no want to them that fear Him"
(Psalm 34:9).

Faith finds in Christ whate'er we need
To save or strengthen us indeed.
Receives the grace He sends us down,
And makes us share His cross and crown.

Anniversaries and Birthdays

MAY 24

And the centurion answered and said, "Lord, I am not worthy that Thou shouldest come under my roof; but only say the word, and my servant shall be healed." Matt. 8:8

IT is a great art, though simple, to go through life on the Word of God. It was this art that Abraham had learned when he went out to a land that he knew not, and held fast to the promise, hoping against hope when everything looked impossible. At the command of God, Moses stretched his hand out over the sea, and a way was made for Israel. On God's Word Peter walked out on a stormy sea, the robber passed from the cross to Paradise, and the centurion went home and found his boy, who had been deathly ill, quite well again. It was by faith in God that the Philippian jailor was saved with all his house, and that the Canaanitish woman got her daughter set free from the power of Satan.

What could be safer to build our life on than the Word of God? Nevertheless it is so much easier for us to rely on a mere man. God has assured us that what Jesus has done for our salvation is perfect enough, but yet we doubt, and we ask our deceitful heart whether this be true. God has promised to be our Father, and that "all these things shall be added unto" those who seek His kingdom first; but in spite of that we pass our days full of care and anxiety for food, clothing, and our future. Come, Christians, let us awake and be ashamed of our lack of confidence in God and His Word. He keeps His promises: let us believe that.

In Thee we trust, in Thee alone;
For Thou forsakest not Thine own;
To all the meek Thy strength is given,
Who by Thy cross ascend to heaven.

Anniversaries and Birthdays

MAY 25

For I am persuaded, that neither death, nor life, nor angels, nor principalities, nor things present, nor things to come, nor powers, nor height, nor depth, nor any other creature, shall be able to separate us from the love of God, which is in Christ Jesus our Lord. Romans 8:38-39

THE redemption that appeared, finished in Christ, on Easter morning, is just as perfect as God Himself. The hand that grasps the sinner who is clinging to the cross is stronger than all, and no one shall snatch us out of that hand. It is there that the weakest becomes the strongest, the anxious one becomes secure, and the sorrowing glad.

As the anchor digs deeper into the sand, and takes a stronger hold as the storm increases in fury, so the child of God nestles most closely to the Savior in the day that need and danger are greatest. He who relies on himself is always in danger, but he who trusts the Lord is never put to shame.

So let storms howl about us, let all the forces of evil pursue us, let sickness, poverty, dishonor, ridicule, and shame be our most faithful attendants—no one can harm him who is in the Lord's hand. There darkness becomes light round about us, there the fire purifies the gold, there the storm drives us toward the land of life.

"Trust in Jehovah with all thy heart,
And lean not upon thine own understanding" (Prov. 3:5).

"They that trust in Jehovah
Are as mount Zion, which cannot be moved, but abideth forever.
As the mountains are round about Jerusalem,
So Jehovah is round about His people
From this time forth and for evermore" (Psalm 125:1-2).

On Him be thy reliance,
If thou would'st prosper well:
To make thy work enduring
Thy mind on Him must dwell,
God yieldeth naught to sorrow
And self-tormenting care:
Naught, naught with Him availeth,
No power save that of prayer.

Anniversaries and Birthdays

MAY 26

But if any of you lacketh wisdom, let him ask of God, who giveth to all liberally and upbraideth not; and it shall be given him.

James 1:5

WE men are poorly supplied with wisdom. One can often see an animal behaving more sensibly and wisely than a man. We see but a short space ahead—and often we think, speak, and live like fools. And in the midst of our folly we think that we are wise; yea, many consider themselves wiser than God.

Hear what a wise man of olden days has said: "He that careth not for wisdom is a fool, but his ways are right in his own eyes. He is occupied with folly, he does not desire to be wise, but only desires to show forth what dwells in him, and he walks in darkness. But blessed is the man who has found wisdom, and who getteth understanding. Wisdom is better than pearls, and of all treasures none can compare with this." Thus the wise man Solomon spoke.

Wisdom makes us truth-loving, mild in our judgments, peace-loving, and happy. Where life has left deep wounds, wisdom brings the jar of ointment, and shows the right way to those who went astray. Job says:

"Behold, the fear of the Lord, that is wisdom;
And to depart from evil is understanding."

That was doubtless the reason that David prayed, "Lord, teach me wisdom in the depth of my heart."

No one but God can give us this costly gift. Therefore also the fear of the Lord is the source of wisdom. Should we not then pray God to give us this beautiful treasure, since He giveth and upbraideth not, and makes the simple wise?

Thou art the truth: Thy Word alone
Sound wisdom can impart:
Thou only canst inform the mind,
And purify the heart.

Anniversaries and Birthdays

MAY 27

Humble yourselves therefore under the mighty hand of God, that He may exalt you in due time. I Peter 5:6

THE deepest corruption in human life, the root of all sin, is pride. The humble spirit voids the root sin of power because it opens the way so that the grace of God can reach to our inmost being. The Christian who loses the humble mind, also loses the power of God. Only the humble person is made strong by the grace in Christ.

What then shall we do so that this heavenly flower may thrive in our life?

I think we will succeed when we sincerely appear before God with this prayer: "Show me, Lord, what there is in me and about me that shuts out the humble mind. And when Thou hast showed me that, give me, too, the power to acknowledge to myself and to Thee that this is my sin." This is surely the right way. But here, too, pride is present to close the way. He who is victorious here is on the right way.

The secret of our victory does not consist primarily in overcoming evil, but in delivering up the sin itself to God. He who does that has humbled himself under God, and is under grace. It is then that the beautiful heaven-flower called humility grows and appears in our daily life.

May the demand for this beautiful Christian virtue become great in us.

"Pride goeth before destruction,
And a haughty spirit before a fall.
Better it is to be of a lowly spirit with the poor,
Than to divide the spoil with the proud" (Prov. 16:18-19).

Lord, we Thy presence seek;
May ours this blessing be:
Give us a pure and lowly heart,
A temple meet for Thee.

Anniversaries and Birthdays

MAY 28

For the love of Christ constraineth us; because we thus judge, that one died for all, therefore all died. II Cor. 5:14

THE essence of God is love, and the essence of Christianity is love, too. He gives His children the same nature that He Himself has.

Love is deposited in our hearts by faith and by the Holy Spirit. It does not originate with us in the sense that we loved God first. It was He who loved us and gave His Son as an atonement for our sins. That is our great good fortune! If that had not been the plan, we should never have arrived at loving with the love that is of God. But he who gets his eye on this fair treasure and accepts it, he learns to love God. He that loves is born of God.

Our great task as Christians is to get more of this love into our lives. All our efforts to advance in sanctification will eventuate in a whited sepulchre, unless we are led more deeply into the love of Christ. Paul says that the way to this growth passes through Golgotha. When in the spirit he stands there the truth becomes vivid to him that One died for all, and that therefore all died. The love that he sees there, lays hold on him so strongly that he gives his whole life to Him who died for us all. He desires no longer to live unto himself, but for Him who died and rose again for us.

God grant us more of the love that we meet on Calvary! Then our entire life will be borne of joy and serving love.

E'er since by faith I saw the stream
Thy flowing wounds supply,
Redeeming love has been my theme,
And shall be till I die.

Anniversaries and Birthdays

MAY 29

Blessed are the peacemakers: for they shall be called sons of God.
Matt. 5:9

IT is a hard fate to be compelled to pass one's life among crooked and quarrelsome people. There is hardly anything that so wears away one's happiness and zest of living as being together with people that love strife, and who seem to live for the purpose of setting one person up against another. If in addition to all this, they have mouths that are as religious as their hearts are full of evil, then the misfortune is still greater, if not for themselves, then surely for others.

But as perverse and evil people bring unhappiness and strife into a home, among relatives, and into a neighborhood, and create a hell on earth, so peace-loving people bring paradise with them. Even in the hardest and most adverse conditions happiness and courage will win when people love peace. The longer we live, the more highly we prize people who bring peace with them. When "good neighbors" are counted as belonging to daily bread, these are verily not empty words. It strengthens both body and soul to live among people who love peace. Jesus Himself says that they shall be called children of God.

May He who is peace and who gives peace make us children of peace and servants of peace among men.

Where peace rules heart and home Satan does not thrive. There the God of peace dwells.

> To Thee, O dear, dear Savior!
> My spirit turns for rest,
> My peace is in Thy favor,
> My pillow on Thy breast;
> Though all the world deceive me,
> I know that I am Thine.
> And Thou wilt never leave me,
> O blessed Savior mine.

Anniversaries and Birthdays

MAY 30

Come ye after Me, and I will make you fishers of men. Matt. 4:19

MANY Christians feel it as life's heaviest burden to seem to get so little done for God. Mother and the servant girl wash and cook, day after day, year in and year out, in some cases almost a lifetime, and when day is done they see no results of their toil. The clerk measures and weighs, the office worker writes and keeps accounts, the factory worker attends a machine, and the farmer toils in field and forest.

What results for God are there out of all this?

Let us hear what Jesus says: "Come ye after Me, and I will make you fishers of men." Let us concede that these words contain something that applies especially to the twelve. It is still entirely true that every Christian who follows Jesus becomes a fisher of men, no matter what position in life he occupies. In the kingdom of God the question is not about what work we have, but about our disposition. If we live and work in the spirit of Jesus, then we follow Jesus, and then He makes us fishers of men: that never fails. It is un-Christian to think that only a missionary, a pastor, or a preacher can bring people to God. There are, alas, altogether too many of these who never follow Jesus, while the working man testifies about His Savior in all that he is and does.

If you and I follow Jesus in this way, we will invite others to Jesus by our life and work. Take that comfort with you today, and you will be happy.

> Let every thought, and work, and word,
> To Thee be ever given:
> Then life shall be Thy service, Lord,
> And death the gate of heaven!

Anniversaries and Birthdays

MAY 31

Now we believe, not because of thy speaking: for we have heard for ourselves, and know that this is indeed the Savior of the world. John 4:42

NOW, too, there are many who believe only because there are others who have said it; not because they have met Christ and experienced the salvation in Him. Children believe because father and mother believe, and because they learned it in school. What kind of faith is this? It is right and good as far as it goes, and we ought to be thankful so long as people have this faith. It is worse when children and youth scoff at and deny what we have found to be our life's most precious possession. The Christian's task is to try to bring to Christ those who still believe only because of what others have said.

There are Christians who tear to pieces and condemn everything that is not completely finished all at once. They do not seem to understand the value there is in possessing the knowledge and the faith that we must have in order to come to Jesus. It was that faith that brought the people of Sychar out to Jesus, and made it possible for them to know Him as their Savior by experience. We ought not tear to pieces what is good, even if it is not complete enough. But we who have found what the others have not, we must help them to attain to what we have.

You who are reading or hearing this and know in your heart that you have not yet found Christ: Come now! There have been so many who like you thought that they would come; but they postponed it too long, and arrived too late. That may happen to you, too, if you do not come today.

"He that will, let him take the water of life freely."

My merry heart is springing,
And knows not how to pine;
'Tis full of joy and singing,
And radiancy divine;
The sun whose smiles so cheer me
Is Jesus Christ alone:
To have Him always near me
Is heaven itself begun.

Anniversaries and Birthdays

JUNE 1

Who being the effulgence of His glory, and the very image of His substance, and upholding all things by the Word of His power, when He had made purification of sins, sat down on the right hand of the Majesty on high. Heb. 1:3

JESUS CHRIST the Son of God upholds all things by the Word of His power. All things.

This is almost too much for us to believe. Still it must be so. "The Word was with God and the Word was God." It was that eternal and almighty Word that appeared before God in our place when the first people had brought ruin on everything. If He had not taken the universe on His shoulders, everything would have been destroyed.

Christ is the living power in the universe.

Once you and I, too, were sinking under the burden. Sin was too heavy for us, and the judgment in our conscience made us tremble before a holy God. But then one day a word came to us from the mouth of the Savior, and that was strong and great enough to lift us away from the burden of sin, up to God, made free and glad. A Christian should never forget that miracle.

Many times since that day we have again been on the point of going under. We forgot God's Word and lost strength and hope. But He who had promised to be with His own always, again brought a Word that carried us over a new abyss; and to this day His Word has been strong enough to sustain us. We are also fully assured that it is strong enough to carry us through death.

Heaven and earth, and sea and air,
Still their Maker's praise declare;
Thou, my soul, as loudly sing,
To thy God thy praises bring.

See how God this rolling globe
Swathes with beauty as a robe;
Forests, fields, and living things,
Each its Master's glory sings.

Anniversaries and Birthdays

JUNE 2

And be not drunken with wine, wherein is riot, but be filled with the Spirit. Eph. 5:18

EVERYONE who has been given faith in Jesus, has received the Holy Spirit who "Himself bears witness with our spirit, that we are children of God." No man can say, "Jesus is Lord," but in the Holy Spirit. "If any man hath not the Spirit of Christ, he is none of His." For in one Spirit we were all baptized to be one body.

But just as certainly as this is true, so certainly must we acknowledge that many Christians have little room for God's Spirit in heart and life, and therefore the apostle exhorts us to be filled with the Spirit. Our Word today also clearly shows us this. When Christian people exist on so low a plane that they get drunk on wine, it must be time to awaken them out of sleep, and to remind them that such a life does not become them who are to be led by the Spirit of God.

Consequently, to be filled with the Spirit is not the same as being unable to receive more of God's Spirit. A child gradually understands more and more as it grows up. Thus the Christian receives more of the Spirit as he gradually grows in the grace and knowledge of Christ.

But just as impossible as it is for us to get enough of the knowledge of Christ in this world, so impossible is it for us to get enough of the Spirit of God once and for all. Therefore a Christian should always accept the Word of exhortation, "Be filled with the Spirit," and pray God that He in His grace will give us more of His Spirit.

Shine in our hearts, Thou blessed Light,
Teach us Jesus Christ to know aright,
That we all may surely,
In His grace confiding,
Be with Him securely
Evermore abiding.
O have mercy, Lord!

Anniversaries and Birthdays

____

____

____

____

JUNE 3

And I will pray the Father, and He shall give you another Comforter, that He may be with you forever. John 14:16

IN what wonderfully great and gracious fashion God has ordered everything for us men. The more we try to explore the love of God, the more we realize that when we received Christ, we received everything with Him. God elected us in Him before the world was, and He Himself came down to us, and having been made perfect by the things which He suffered, He became the Captain of our salvation. When the victory was won, He went to heaven as our Advocate, and everything that has to do with us must come through Him. Neither can Satan get by Christ, when he accuses God's people. Jesus ever lives to make intercession for us.

But this is not all. We have also received "another Comforter," who will be among us here on earth. He will find us and awaken us, so that we see that we need salvation; He will bring us to Christ and reveal Him to our inner eye. He shall teach us all truth, and remind us of all that Christ has said. He shall be our seal and the earnest of our inheritance until the day of our redemption, when we shall receive the inheritance ourselves. On our pilgrimage through this world He shows us our sins, disciplines us, gives us hunger for grace, and leads us to Christ anew. There the soul is cleansed, there He comforts us, heals our sores, sets the conscience free, and when evening comes, He gives us light to cross the border to Jesus Christ our Lord.

Thou Fountain whence all wisdom flows,
Which God on pious hearts bestows,
Grant us Thy consolation,
That in our pure faith's unity
We faithful witnesses may be
Of grace that brings salvation.
Hear us, cheer us by Thy teaching;
Let our preaching and our labor
Praise Thee, Lord, and bless our neighbor.

Anniversaries and Birthdays

JUNE 4

Quench not the Spirit. **I Thess. 5:19**

THE Spirit's fire in heart and life may be quenched both rapidly and easily. If we are not on our guard we may soon be among those who are dead while they live, regardless of how holy and burning in the spirit we once were.

The Spirit of God has promised to guide us into all truth, also the truth about ourselves. When the Spirit throws His light into our nature, and we see the evil disposition, the perverse will, and the sinful thoughts that want to rule, if then we do not take up the battle against this inner hurt, we may quench the Spirit. Where the inner discipline and cleansing cease, there God's Spirit loses His foothold, and cannot work. Then we become blind to our own folly, and can get so far into the darkness that we do not see our sin either in heart or in works.

It is deep down in the heart that the foundation must be laid for all true Christian life. It must be laid there by the Spirit who punishes us for our sins, and leads us to the fountain in "the house of David" that cleanses from sin and from uncleanness. But it is here, too, that it is so easy for us to grieve the Holy Spirit, and to extinguish the bridal torch that we bear. Then darkness surrounds us.

We can never shout too loud to each other about being careful here. All those who are earnestly striving for a holy life, know how great this inner danger is. Let us watch over ourselves so that we do not quench the Spirit.

> One secret thought
> With evil fraught,
> Which in the heart was cherished,
> Havoc of God's grace hath wrought,
> And the soul hath perished.

Anniversaries and Birthdays

JUNE 5

Seeing ye have purified your souls in your obedience to the truth unto unfeigned love of the brethren, love one another from the heart fervently. **I Peter 1:22**

THIS short but mighty word of exhortation leads us into one of the deepest and most serious realms of our Christian life. The hottest battles are fought here. Many have fallen away from God because they forgot to purify their souls.

All who struggle to live uprightly with God know how easy it is to forget the purification from sin. Everything unclean that is about us and in us, and that we meet day and night has a strong tendency to dull the sensibilities for what is clean and holy. Then we are tempted to compare ourselves with other Christians instead of with God, and with that we are in the midst of the danger—and do not see it ourselves. The angel of the church in Laodicea was not only wretched, miserable, poor, blind, and naked, but the greatest calamity was that he did not know it. This is where our greatest danger is found too: we may become blind to our own impurity.

We know the truth, and if we walk the way that is shown us there, we will find the path to "the fountain in the house of David." Let us bring to that fountain everything unclean that has settled on our inner life. Cleanse away in the sea of grace pride, love of the world, hatred, evil words, and everything else that is unclean. It is this that Satan above all things wants us to omit. But blessed is he who keeps himself clean!

Each soul astray
From Christ, the way,
Should keep God's people humble;
Jesus warns, "O watch and pray,
Lest ye fall and stumble."

Anniversaries and Birthdays

JUNE 6

My soul longeth, yea, even fainteth for the courts of Jehovah;
My heart and my flesh cry out unto the living God. Psalm 84:2

LONGING is a sign of a true Christian life. As we are gradually set free from sin and from love to the world, the need of God becomes stronger in us. Christian Scriver says that a Christian's longing is divided into three branches: In faith he longs to be *in* Christ; in love he longs to live *for* Christ; and in hope he longs to depart and to be *with* Christ.

All these three sides of the Christian life are very prominent in Paul. He pressed on that he might lay hold on Christ; he did not hold his life of any account that he might accomplish the ministry which he had received from the Lord Jesus; and he longed to depart.

This quiet need of getting more of the mind of Christ is surely that which we recognize most easily in our Christian life. I suppose it is this need that especially gets us on our knees, and that calls forth most tears and prayers from the depths of the heart. What wonderful, exalted joy one experiences when peace rules in the heart and longing draws one toward Christ.

May no Christian ever lose this longing, and may also the longing to serve Him, and to see Him as He is, become a greater power in our lives. Then we will also be stronger and richer in love and hope.

Nearer, my God, to Thee,
Nearer to Thee!
E'en though it be a cross
That raiseth me;
Still all my song shall be,
Nearer, my God, to Thee,
Nearer, my God, to Thee,
Nearer to Thee.

Anniversaries and Birthdays

JUNE 7

And having shod your feet with the preparation of the gospel of peace. Eph. 6:15

HE who desires to fight the good fight must have peace with God in a good conscience. Not until the peace of Jesus Christ dwells in the heart can we move about in peace. It is the Spirit that dwells in the Gospel which creates calm in the heart, and which distinguishes a soldier of Jesus from all other soldiers.

A Christian must overcome evil with good. The people of God must never fight for the sake of a fight: that kind of fight does not belong in the kingdom of God. When father and mother punish their child more in anger than in love, and when the preacher is cold and cutting in his delivery of the Word of God, then their feet are not shod with the gospel of peace.

To be mighty in the truth is not always the same as to be truth-loving. The sword that the old warriors used had to be so elastic that point and grip might meet, but at the same time so strong that it sprang back and was as straight as before, as soon as the pressure ceased. The Gospel must give the Christian such a sword; then we will fight not only for the Gospel, but in the Gospel. Paul wept with a chain on his foot and a sword in his hand. Those were tears from a fighter who loved peace.

Happy is the Christian who in all his warfare has his feet shod with the gospel of peace. He will be victorious in all his battles.

These are they who have contended
For their Savior's honor long,
Wrestling on till life was ended,
Following not the sinful throng;
These, who well the fight sustained,
Triumph by the Lamb have gained.

Anniversaries and Birthdays

____

____

____

____

____

JUNE 8

Blessed are the pure in heart: for they shall see God. Matt. 5:8

TO be pure in heart cannot be the same as being without sin, or never doing wrong. If that were the case no one in this world would have a pure heart.

But what is it to have a pure heart?

First and foremost it is something inside of us that feels sick and hurt at everything unholy and unclean, and which therefore cannot live without confessing everything to God just as it is. A pure heart is that within us which cannot endure one single sin resting on conscience unconfessed and unforgiven; but must open the door so that light may flood all that is crooked and sinful, and must openly lay bare every sore to Him who has promised to heal all sores.

Then we draw near to God with a true heart, then we are of the truth, then we shall hear the Savior-voice of Jesus Christ. Then we walk in the light, and the blood of Jesus Christ cleanses from all sin. Then the pure are purified, and then we see God.

It is the hidden sin that makes the heart impure, and that casts a shadow between us and God.

And this danger lurks at the door of us Christians every single day. To live in the truth and to walk in the light, as God is in the light, that is the way that leads up to God. Here is the straitened way, of which Jesus says: "Few are they that find it." Have you found it?

"Create in me a clean heart, O God;
And renew a stedfast spirit within me" (Psalm 51:10).

Grant us, dear Lord, our cross to bear
Till at Thy feet we lay it down,
Win through Thy blood our pardon there,
And through the cross attain the crown.

Anniversaries and Birthdays

JUNE 9

"Take My yoke upon you, and learn of Me; for I am meek and lowly in heart: and ye shall find rest unto your souls." Matt. 11:29

A YOKE is a piece of wood that fits on a person's shoulders and is used in carrying something on each side. This yoke is well known in the Orient, and also in some Occidental countries.

Here Jesus tells us of something that He calls His yoke, something that He will give us to use when carrying burdens. He adds that His yoke is easy, and tells at once what it is: "I am meek and lowly in heart." It is His mild and gentle disposition that He will give us to bear our burdens with, those too that He lays upon us. We may be assured that with the mind of Christ we can easily bear all that life commands us to bear. Pride and a cold and obstinate mind rob us of the power to conquer evil, and they steal life's supporting power. The mild, gentle disposition is able to carry the very heaviest load without complaint.

He who has the mind of Jesus Christ becomes "strong in the Lord, and in the strength of His might."

That is the mind that was given us when we were born again, and as the years go by we must try to give an increasingly large place to that mind in heart and life. Then we shall bear all our burdens easily, to our own happiness and to the honor of Him who gave us His gentle, mild disposition.

"Come unto Me, ye fainting,
And I will give you life."
O cheering voice of Jesus,
Which comes to aid our strife;
The foe is stern and eager,
The fight is fierce and long;
But Thou hast made us mighty,
And stronger than the strong.

Anniversaries and Birthdays

JUNE 10

"I thank Him that enabled me, even Christ Jesus our Lord, for that He counted me faithful, appointing me to His service."
I Tim. 1:12

THAT is the way Paul looks at his life and at his work. The Lord appointed him to the service, counted him faithful, and made him strong. He was only an instrument that God had chosen and had made capable in His work, and therefore the Lord was indeed everything to him.

It was this same view that David had of his life when he sang, "The Lord is my shepherd, He leads me, He restores my soul, He guides me in the paths of righteousness for His name's sake."

Thus we too should look at our life and our work.

When so many things go wrong in the struggle for existence and in the Christian work, the reason usually is that we put ourselves in the place where the Lord alone must rule and have all the responsibility. Because we have not attained to this genuine Christian view, our ego, our will, our responsibility, and our honor, all crowd in to the realm where the Lord alone shall have both the honor and the responsibility. If we looked on our life and work as a service to which God had appointed us, and for which He had given us faith and strength, much of what we now consider a burden would be transformed to a song of praise, because we had discovered God's plan for our life.

It has been said that in the school that God keeps for His children there are three classes. In the first we get only far enough to learn, "I and Jesus." In the second it is "Jesus and I"; and in the third, "Jesus only." The third class is the hardest one to get through. Many fail there. May you and I attain to passing the examination in this class!

Blessed is he who in truth can say: Jesus only!

> Then in a nobler, sweeter song,
> I'll sing Thy power to save,
> When this poor, lisping, stammering tongue
> Lies silent in the grave.

Anniversaries and Birthdays

JUNE 11

Return unto thy rest, O my soul;
For Jehovah hath dealt bountifully with thee. Ps. 116:7

IT is easy to lose one's peace of soul. Satan does all that he can to take peace away from earth and from the hearts of men. He finds pleasure in tormenting the saints of God, and begrudges himself all rest when only he can make trouble. His arrows are both sharp and poisonous, and he feels no pity for the person that he wounds. Then if we by nature are quick-tempered and sensitive, it may easily happen that also a Christian will resemble a ship without a rudder on a stormy sea.

He who does not want to lose his rest in God must be on his guard.

Another thing that can get the soul out of balance is what we call an unsuccessful life. We did not attain to the goal that we had set for our life in this world, and what we thought would give us happiness brought us loss, shame, and dishonor. And then our confidence in God weakened. Perhaps the composer of our Psalm had got entangled in something of this sort. But now he sees everything from a different angle; he sees that it was not a misfortune; it was: "Jehovah hath dealt bountifully with thee." And so he asks his soul to return unto its rest in God.

This, in any event, is certain, that many who today have lost their rest in God, would recover it if they looked at their lives from this angle of vision: The Lord has dealt bountifully with you. A distorted view of life and distrust of God rob the soul of peace. Would you find rest again? Hold fast to the fact that the Lord does all things well.

In Thine arms I rest me,
Foes who would molest me
Cannot reach me here;
Though the earth be shaking,
Every heart be quaking,
Jesus calms my fear;
Fires may flash and thunder crash,
Yea, and sin and hell assail me,
Jesus will not fail me.

Anniversaries and Birthdays

JUNE 12

They that sow in tears shall reap in joy. **Psalm 126:5**

THE mind that God gave us when He accepted us into His grace, created in us a feeling of responsibility for our fellow men, and a desire to lead them to Christ. Then when the Christian sees how unsuccessful he has been in this work, his heart often becomes sore and full of doubt. Especially will upright preachers, and parents who see their own children leading a wild life, feel bad.

To confess faith in Him who has all power, and who has promised to hear our prayers, and at the same time to see how unsuccessful we are, may cause the strongest man to tremble, and may bring doubt to the most earnest believer. Let me say to you who are groaning under this heavy burden: Try to give this little Word room in your heart: "They that sow in tears shall reap in joy." That is what it says! You see the Word speaks of seed and tears. God says that some day a good harvest shall come forth from these.

So let your tears fall on the seed. When harvest time comes. God will show that He keeps His Word, also in regard to your work in His kingdom. "In due season we shall reap, if we faint not."

Going forth with weeping, sowing for the Master,
Though the loss sustained our spirit often grieves;
When our weeping's over, He will bid us welcome,
We shall come, rejoicing, bringing in the sheaves.

Anniversaries and Birthdays

JUNE 13

But Naaman was wroth, and went away, and said, "Behold, I thought, He will surely come out to me, and stand, and call on the name of Jehovah his God, and wave his hand over the place, and recover the leper." . . . "Behold now, I know that there is no God in all the earth, but in Israel." II Kings 5:11, 15

NAAMAN'S journey to the prophet in Samaria to be cured of his leprosy is an example that speaks to us about all those who seek God, but do not attain to assurance of their salvation.

Naaman used his understanding where he should have used his faith, and went away in a rage, unhelped. But his servants prevailed on him to go down and dip himself in the Jordan, "according to the saying of the man of God," and then he received by faith what he had sought in vain with his intellect. Now he no longer says, "I thought," but he sings out, "I know!"

Many are seeking God but never arrive at assurance of salvation because they put intellect in the place that faith should have, and experience in place of what is prepared for us in Christ. Seeker after God, listen! Step down into the river of grace with all your sores and sins, and believe the Word that says that He forgives sin! You must not believe this because you understand it, but because God has said it.

Exactly as you are you must believe that you are saved by what Jesus has done. You shall not first experience faith, feel glad, and then believe. What Jesus has done is enough for you: believe that. Then you receive peace, and go on your way rejoicing.

Faith in the conscience worketh peace,
And bids the mourner's weeping cease;
By faith the children's place we claim,
And give all honor to one Name.

Anniversaries and Birthdays

____

____

____

____

____

JUNE 14

Ho, every one that thirsteth, come ye to the waters, and he that hath no money; come ye, buy, and eat; yea, come, buy wine and milk without money and without price. Isa. 55:1

THAT wearisome restlessness and that deep longing in the hearts of men for something that they have not, God calls hunger and thirst. It is this soul-hunger that drives people to run after money, honor, power, and pleasure, and this is in part the reason that so many run riot in sin and shame. Many believe they would be happy if they only had more of earthly prosperity, and if they could live as their passions dictate. This false assumption is so deep-rooted in us that seductive forces are able to drive the multitude into eternal unhappiness.

When God sees us faring forth on this hopeless way, He calls to us in heartfelt compassion, and asks us to turn and come to Him. He tells us clearly and definitely that He has food that satisfies, and a drink that quenches thirst, and He says that we may have it all for nothing.

One should think that everyone would accept this invitation. Why do they not come?

This passage says something to the effect that we must buy, even though we are to get it all for nothing. Must we buy that which costs nothing? It costs to come. Especially does it cost to accept something for nothing. We must pay by turning away from everything and everybody, and by accepting what God gives as of grace alone.

He who does this receives everything for nothing. He drinks from the fountain of life, and is saved.

Come in sorrow and contrition,
Wounded, impotent, and blind;
Here the guilty free remission,
Here the troubled peace may find:
Health this fountain will restore;
He that drinks shall thirst no more.

Anniversaries and Birthdays

JUNE 15

God, be Thou merciful to me a sinner! Luke 18:13

IT is sin that has separated us from God, and that has brought calamity onto everything. Where sin is not found, the wall of partition between God and us is absent. Through His Word God has shown us the road that leads away from sin and into life. It passes by way of Calvary and through the grave. There Christ nailed to the cross the bond that was against us, and there He was raised for our justification. In this miracle of life, salvation and grace are given to us all.

But just as perfectly as all this is arranged for us apart from us, just so certainly must we come to Christ as lost sinners and admit that it was our debt that made Him guilty before God. The road away from sin passes through a confession: we confess who we are and what we have done. The person who together with the publican in the temple will appear before God, and say, "God, be Thou merciful to me a sinner!" that person will be saved. Then God declares this sinner to be righteous, because his heart is then opened to the justifying grace of God.

As Jesus gave Himself wholly on account of our sins, so we must give Him all our sin. Then the blood of Christ has not only paid our sin and guilt before God, then it is also receipted in our life-book, and the heart is cleansed by faith. Then these two life melodies unite in one mighty harmony: "By Himself He made purification of our sins," —and: "If we confess our sins, He is faithful and righteous to forgive us our sins, and to cleanse us from all unrighteousness."

In this manner the path leads away from sin, and to God.

Thou art the way: to Thee alone
From sin and death we flee:
And he who would the Father seek,
Must seek Him, Lord, by Thee.

Anniversaries and Birthdays

JUNE 16

And Peter answered, and said unto Jesus, "Lord, it is good for us to be here: if Thou wilt, I will make here three tabernacles; one for Thee, and one for Moses, and one for Elijah." Matt. 17:4

WE are eager to be where happiness and joy greet us with their brightness. To be permitted to walk away and up from sin and sorrow and strife, and to rest in the light that radiates from the face of Jesus Christ, that is tasting the peace that passeth all understanding. It is this joy that God has intended for His people, and which they also experience more or less, now as formerly.

And it is there that we would like to settle down, just like Peter. And why may not a Christian do that? It is just this that our Savior has promised us, and that we struggle to attain and possess. Does God prefer to see His people bent under suffering, wearily bearing a cross on a narrow way?

Oh, I think we would be allowed to stay on Mount Tabor if only we could bear it: but we cannot bear it. In a short time we would settle down to be at peace with ourselves, and think ourselves better than we are. What we would experience would seem greater to us than Jesus. Instead of walking in faith in Christ, we would build on that which tasted so good to us. Our happiness on Mount Tabor would then become our greatest misfortune. Therefore we are not permitted to dwell there. We get a command to go down into the valley again, so that we may become tired of the world's slavery, but all the more inclined to walk in the way of life.

A Christian must not become a saint in his own eyes. Our goal is to receive a great Savior and win eternal life through faith in Him.

See from His head, His hands, His feet
Sorrow and love flow mingled down!
Did e'er such love and sorrow meet,
Or thorns compose so rich a crown?

Anniversaries and Birthdays

JUNE 17

And straightway He constrained His disciples to enter into the boat, and to go before Him unto the other side to Bethsaida, while He Himself sendeth the multitude away. Mark 6:45

JESUS had solved the food problem by a miracle, and the people desired to make Him king. The disciples, too, saw a bright future before them. They surely thought the day was near when people would see that to follow Jesus paid also in a financial way. He must save them from this heresy, and so He sends them out into darkness and storm.

When believing people begin to entertain the idea that there is financial gain in being a Christian, danger is near. It is true that "godliness is profitable for all things," but if we think that financial gain is wages for Christian virtue, we are badly mistaken. And if we misunderstand God's blessings in that way. He is able now too to send His own on a way they would be the last to choose. Not because He likes to see us toiling in privation and poverty, but because He wants to teach us that to be a Christian is something that is unspeakably much greater than to own goods and gold.

Hard times including an economic depression are often difficult to get through. But all those who in faith and patience accept them as a message from God, will always receive more in such times than they lose. What we never would have learned or experienced in good days, we received when we saw the Savior again in the midst of storm and darkness. When He got aboard our boat, and the sea became still, we knew better than before who He was, and what it is to be a Christian. "The kingdom of God is not eating and drinking, but righteousness and peace and joy in the Holy Spirit."

Through each perplexing path of life
Our wandering footsteps guide.
Give us each day our daily bread,
And raiment fit provide.

O spread Thy sheltering wings around,
Till all our wanderings cease.
And at our Father's loved abode,
Our souls arrive in peace!

Anniversaries and Birthdays

JUNE 18

Being confident of this very thing, that He who began a good work in you will perfect it until the day of Jesus Christ. Phil. 1:6

THE thought often comes to the Christian that God must be tired of him.

The goal that is set before us is to grow up unto Christ, and it is just this that a Christian most of all desires. To this end he contends, weeps, and prays. But when his success seems so small, and he even appears to be going down grade rather than up toward the heights, then comes doubt. Many of us have struggled through a long life and begged God for grace every day. Should it not be reasonable to believe that we sometime might get far enough so we could say, "Now I have got past evil"? But in place of that, we must beg anew and pray the same prayer again and again. Can that be right? Would conditions be such if everything was as it ought to be?—That is the way thoughts and doubt work.

In such times we should remember something else, too: He who sought us and found us when we were running wild, He who did not tire of us when we mocked both Him and the salvation He offered, should He forsake us now when we are trying hard to win? He well knew how we were before He called us.

No, He will not give us up! He has determined that heaven shall be full of such helpless, poor fellows as you and me. He called us according to His own purpose and by the grace that is in Christ, not because we are so excellent and good.

So we may be entirely confident that He will perfect the good work also in us to the praise of His glory.

He all His foes shall quell,
Shall all our sins destroy;
And every bosom swell
With pure seraphic joy:
Lift up your heart, lift up your voice,
Rejoice, again I say, rejoice.

Anniversaries and Birthdays

JUNE 19

"Say to them that are of a fearful heart, 'Be strong, fear not: behold, your God will come with vengeance, with the recompense of God; He will come and save you.'" Isa. 35:4

ALSO a Christian knows what it is to have a heart full of fear and anxiety. Life's straightened way so often makes him tremble and fear, and the many things that violently enter into our life and that may come both unexpectedly and awkwardly cause his heart to beat in restlessness and fear. But what makes most uneasiness in the heart of an honest Christian are the wounds that sin inflicts on our soul and those cold forces of death that often seem ready to quench the fervency of our spirit.

In such times it is easy to slip into the business of works. And when Sinai is nearer to us than Calvary, the heart always becomes fearful, and judgment hangs over us; for it is only grace that makes men free. But in this Word God wants to say to all these weak and trembling souls that His heart beats with a desire to give comfort more than any mother-heart longs to free her frightened child from fear. God says: Fear not, be strong!

Hear this, you fearful heart! Be confident that what He promises, He will perform. He will quiet the fears of all those who rest on His Word. "Fear not, for I am with thee," says the Lord.

"No weapon that is formed against thee shall prosper; and every tongue that shall rise against thee in judgment thou shalt condemn. This is the heritage of the servants of Jehovah, and their righteousness which is of Me, saith Jehovah" (Isa. 54:17).

Lead me to green pastures, lead me
By the true and living way;
Shield me from each strong temptation
That might lead my heart astray;
And if e'er my feet should turn,
For each error let me mourn.

Anniversaries and Birthdays

JUNE 20

There is none like unto God, O Jeshurun,
Who rideth upon the heavens for thy help,
And in His excellency on the skies. Deut. 33:26

TO continue on through a long life brings with it changing conditions also for a Christian. Occasionally it looks as if everything has become oath-bound to make life one continual bitter strife. The smart from one blow has hardly ceased before the next is received, and the fact that one storm subsides is only a warning that another is brewing. God is far, very far away, it appears; the best friends fail, and Satan gets leave to attack the poor fellow who seemed to have troubles more than enough already. The road from Egypt to Canaan occasionally becomes both hard and long even today. Our drinking water is bitter, serpents are allowed to bite us, and the sun scorches the tired wayfarer.

But nevertheless by little and little as the years pass and we get nearer to the Promised Land, everything begins to appear to us more and more as a miracle of grace. We see that an invisible hand always has followed us, a hand that was as loving as it was strong. As Moses could say at the end of life, "There is none like unto God," so we also may say this after him, albeit haltingly. Only very gradually, but yet surely, do we see that God had a hand in everything that happened to us in life. When we went astray God hunted us up again, when we sinned He warned us, when we confessed He forgave us, when we were perplexed He whispered the words into our souls that led us in the right way; when we were discouraged and fearful He comforted us. When the call comes to start on the last journey He will be at our side and will carry us home.

"There is none like unto God." His name be praised always.

He rules on high, His throne shall never
Like earthly empires pass away,
His kingdom stands and grows forever,
Till all creation owns His sway.
The world may seek and love its own:
I love my Jesus, Him alone.

Anniversaries and Birthdays

JUNE 21

So teach us to number our days,
That we may get us a heart of wisdom. Psalm 90:12

IT is not right to forget days that have passed. Contrariwise we ought to remember the times that are no more, the roads we traveled, and what we have lived through. The sins we committed and that God has forgiven, we should not drag around, but we should remember the many times that God has been gracious to us, and how He has guided and followed us among hidden reefs in storm and darkness.

I think it is especially profitable to look back on life after one is somewhat advanced in years. Which is not saying that youth should neglect an occasional examination of the years that have fled, but he who is older sees more clearly and is able to pass a fairer judgment. In autumn the air is clearest and cleanest not only in nature but also in human life. And the blessedness of this backward look is that much of what we encountered, and which we at that time considered punishment and misfortune, we now see was full of God's Father-care. Where we thought ourselves rejected by God, there His love and grace now shine upon us. We also see that that which cost us the most in struggle and tears, gave us also life's greatest riches.

The Christian harvests this wisdom for his heart when he lets God teach him to number his days. And it is such people that become more and more thankful the longer they live. But in that case it is good to be old, too.

> But I will tell, while I am living,
> His goodness forth with every breath,
> And greet each morning with thanksgiving,
> Until my heart is still in death.
> Nay, when at last my lips grow cold,
> His praise shall in my sighs be told.

Anniversaries and Birthdays

____

____

____

____

____

JUNE 22

It is better to take refuge in Jehovah
Than to put confidence in man. Psalm 118:8

EVEN the best and longest friendship between men may fail. In cases where we thought we could rely most fully on each other the end many a time was distrust, separation, and deep wounds. If love for self and the world gets the upper hand the most delicate ties of friendship may be broken before we know it.

When thoughts go back to days that have passed, many of us will likely be reminded of much unfaithfulness and many broken promises, perhaps by both ourselves and others. To trust in oneself or other men is like building on sand. The more fully we assimilate this grievous truth the fewer deep wounds will we get when we encounter unfaithfulness and broken promises.

But then life has also taught us—at any rate us Christians—that God does not break a friendship or a word. He has never failed us, least of all when we were in a tight pinch. When everything looked dark and impossible He stood faithfully at our side and often managed to get the best results out of the worst materials. When all others forsook us, He stayed by us closer than ever; and when everything seemed headed for the abyss He took us up higher.

That is the way the Lord has treated us always, and in this way He will treat us till our dying day. So let us try to have confidence in Him. He who trusts in the Lord will never be put to shame.

"O my God, in Thee have I trusted,
Let me not be put to shame;
Let not mine enemies triumph over me" (Psalm 25:2).

No one is so safe from danger,
As God's little children band:
Not the little swallow nesting,
Not the child in mother's hand.

Anniversaries and Birthdays

JUNE 23

"I have been crucified with Christ; and it is no longer I that live, but Christ liveth in me: and that life which I now live in the flesh I live in faith, the faith which is in the Son of God, who loved me, and gave Himself up for me." Gal. 2:20

THE first thing that this verse tells us is that the redemptive work of Christ is ours as completely as though we had accomplished it ourselves. God's Word gives us the unspeakably great comfort that when One died for all, then all died in Him. Thus are we crucified with Christ.

But this which so completely is ours, is nevertheless outside of us. It is in Christ. If this which is ours in Christ is to become our personal possession, we must give ourselves wholly to Him. We must deliver up to Him for death all the sin and shame that He bore for us. In that manner, too, we must be crucified with Christ.

Evil may yet torment, wound, and defeat us; but it cannot rule over us so that we live in sinful lusts. We have got into a twofold situation: at the same time that we are dead, the sin that is in us shall die. "Ye are dead. Put to death therefore!" say the Scriptures. That which is condemned to death must be kept fastened to the cross with Christ. Our life no longer consists in following sin and obeying its desires: our life is in Christ, and in Him we fight against all evil, and we die daily. It is no longer "I"—that is to say, the evil in us—that has the right of life, and is allowed to live in us: it is Christ. By faith we insist that He is our all, and this right was given us of God.

Now I have found the ground wherein
Sure my soul's anchor may remain—
The wounds of Jesus, for my sin
Before the world's foundation slain;
Whose mercy shall unshaken stay,
When heaven and earth are fled away.

Anniversaries and Birthdays

JUNE 24

Making known unto us the mystery of His will, according to His good pleasure which He purposed in Him unto a dispensation of the fulness of the times, to sum up all things in Christ, the things in the heavens, and the things upon the earth. Eph. 1:9-10

WHEN I read this Word something grips me and awakens in me a desire to give thanks and to worship. What riches to be allowed to look into that which God has purposed, namely, to sum up all things in Christ, and in addition to be permitted to believe that one is and shall be a member of this great company!

The more I try to delve into the Word of God, the more I am convinced that the living pulse-beat in the Bible, in time and eternity, is Christ. He has accompanied His people through all times, He came and was made like one of us, He redeemed us all with His blood, He took the book out of the hand of Him that sitteth on the throne, and He shall open the book. He has created all things, purchased all, inherited all, bears all, and everything shall be united in Him, both things in the heavens and the things upon the earth.

Alas, I am able to say so little about Him, but I can at least ask everyone to accept Him as the only Savior. I am convinced beyond all doubt that he who relies on Him will never be put to shame. Ho, all you fools that reject His atoning death, and doubt that His grave is empty! What will you do with yourselves when through all eternity He is the sun that never sets, and the central point about which everything revolves? Put away your imaginary wisdom, and bend the knee before Him who gave Himself in death for us, so that we might live with Him.

I will praise my dear Redeemer,
His triumphant pow'r I'll tell,
How the victory He giveth
Over sin and death and hell.

Anniversaries and Birthdays

JUNE 25

And when the Lord saw her, He had compassion on her, and said unto her, "Weep not." Luke 7:13

WE can never reconcile ourselves to the serious truth that some day we must die. We object and struggle as hard as we can to get away, though we well know that at last everything will end in a grave. Strong and confident of victory, Death steps inside every man's door, unmoved by both tears and prayers. Unmerciful and cold he takes life away, and bids us carry each other to the grave.

But one day a Man stepped up to the side of death and bade him go away, and the mother got her child back from the realm of the dead. Jesus did not do this because He wanted no one to die from that time on. Sin must be abolished before death can lose its power. To abolish death before sin is abolished would be to make a hell of this earth. But He wanted to show us who He is, what He can do, and what will happen when sin shall be no more. That is the reason that He raised the dead man from the bier, and that He called Lazarus out of the grave.

The way that the Captain of life had to follow was to remove sin by His own sacrifice, and to raise Himself from the grave as a sign that He is Lord over death. The way that we must take is to turn and be born again. Then the seed of eternal life is planted in our spirit, and the words heard in heaven and in earth are these: "He that believeth in Christ, though he die yet shall he live." And we know that the day will come when death is no more, when all graves shall be opened, and all tears wiped away.

Weep not—lo! my Savior there,
Mercy to my soul revealing;
I, too, have obtained a share
In His heart's deep wounds so healing,
Whence the holy fountain streamed
Which this sinful world redeemed.

Anniversaries and Birthdays

JUNE 26

Wherefore it behooved Him in all things to be made like unto His brethren, that He might become a merciful and faithful high priest in things pertaining to God, to make propitiation for the sins of the people. Heb. 2:17

IT is a great comfort for us to know that Jesus was made like unto us in all things. He has walked through the world as a real man. As a child and as a youth He helped His father and mother, and all the time till He was about thirty years of age He was a manual laborer.

Sometimes I think I can see Him in my mind's eye as He moves about in Nazareth. At the close of the day's toil He takes a walk outside of the little mountain village. While sitting on a stone, He sees the sun set. He folds His hands in thanksgiving and prayer, and then He goes home again, to His simple bed, and rests till another day dawns.

Just think, if all those who toil the livelong day through a whole life, would remember this! And if all those who despise bodily labor would remember that Jesus has made worship of all honest work! Then Christian people at any rate would not be ashamed of working clothes and calloused hands. Such clothes and such hands bear the imprint of the nobility of Jesus.

The most healthful blood in the world flows in the veins of Christian working people.

Wherefore let us begin each new working day with thanksgiving and joy. We go to work together with our Savior. In that comfort there is strength for work, too.

If thou hast given Him thine heart,
The place of honor set apart
For Him each night and morrow;
Then He the storms of life will calm,
Will bring for every wound a balm,
And change to joy thy sorrow.

Anniversaries and Birthdays

JUNE 27

For everyone that exalteth himself shall be humbled; but he that humbleth himself shall be exalted. Luke 18:14

A HUMBLE mind is the most beautiful flower that can take root in the garden of our hearts. Of all Christian virtues this has most of the fragrance of heaven.

But a Christian is so often tempted to go to market with false wares. An artificial flower may resemble the genuine quite incredibly in appearance, but it has no aroma; there is no fragrance from it.

We know the words of Jesus about sitting down in the lowest place. Outwardly we may so often do this without being truly humble. If we have some hope of being praised for moving, pride and vanity will gladly go to the foot of the table. To change places is not the same as having your mind changed.

A characteristic of a humble person is that he can gladly serve and suffer where no one sees him. He does not knock at other people's doors for pity and praise. The seat of highest honor may be given him, and still he may act as though nothing great had happened to him. He may step down again and be scorned and dishonored and yet be the same. If he has wronged someone he asks for forgiveness, and he forgives those who sin against him. He is glad to visit the poor and the obscure, and he has the courage to fear God among the great and the godless. Wherever he goes he reminds his fellow men, also without words, of a better world than the one we are living in. He loves what is good and honors God in word and life, and is never without the grace of God.

Yea, were every tree endowed with speech,
And every leaflet singing,
They never with praise His worth could reach,
Though earth with their praise were ringing.
Who fully could praise the Light of life
Who light to our souls is bringing?

Anniversaries and Birthdays

JUNE 28

Let not sin therefore reign in your mortal body, that ye should obey the lusts thereof. Rom. 6:12

THE opinion that a Christian is without sin is fundamentally false. Both Bible and life tell us that the doctrine of sinlessness is through and through a heresy. On this earth one single Person has lived who was without sin; but He showed us, too, that He was far above all others in everything. God would not be very holy and heaven would not be very attractive if the saved over there were not on a higher plane than the saved here.

To believe that you are without sin in this world is to make yourself too big and God too small. The difference between a Christian and a non-Christian does not consist in this that one is sinless and the other sinful: the difference rests on the fact that one knows nothing for his salvation save Jesus Christ and Him crucified, and that he grasps Him as his only salvation. If he lets go of Christ all will go wrong no matter how long he has clung to Him. But the unsaved sinner turns away from Christ, and for that reason he is lost; but not because he in other respects is a greater sinner than others.

When we cling to Jesus and live in grace, then God gives us power against sin so we need not obey it. We are made strong and are victorious by the grace in Christ. The more helpless and impotent a Christian feels, the more room grace gets in his heart. Christ is our redemption, Christ is our strength.

Just as I am, poor, wretched, blind;
Sight, riches, healing of the mind,
Yea, all I need, in Thee to find,
O Lamb of God, I come, I come.

Anniversaries and Birthdays

JUNE 29

Wherewith shall a young man cleanse his way?
By taking heed thereto according to Thy Word.
Psalm 119:9

HE who gets through the years of youth without being polluted by sin, has won a victory and has a life-joy that he hardly can prize highly enough. But if a sin gets power over us in the years of our youth, it has a terrible power to stick to us later in life.

If we think it over we will often find that the sin that ruled over us in the years of our youth, came back with strong and tempting power to the Christian also when he was older. Many have been conquered by the sins of their youth after they had become both old and gray. It is not only the good seed that takes deep roots downward in the spring: evil is able to do the same. The idea that many a youth has, that it does not make much difference how he lives in his younger years, is a lie from Satan that has brought many into eternal unhappiness. But the youth who heeds the Word of God, wins riches that cannot be told in words. He finds life's highest joy, and with the full assurance that God is with him he can go out into an evil and sinful world, because it is written: "For the eyes of Jehovah run to and fro throughout the whole earth, to show Himself strong in the behalf of them whose heart is perfect toward Him."

"He that loveth pureness of heart,
For the grace of his lips the king will be his friend"
(Prov. 22:11).

How shall the young secure their hearts
And guard their lives from sin?
Thy Word the choicest rules imparts
To keep the conscience clean.

'Tis, like the sun, a heavenly light,
That guides us all the day;
And through the dangers of the night
A lamp to lead our way.

Anniversaries and Birthdays

JUNE 30

When He shall come to be glorified in His saints, and to be marvelled at in all them that believed (because our testimony unto you was believed) in that day. II Thess. 1:10

HOW often a Christian rejoices that he soon shall see and possess all that which God has promised them that believe! When hope permits us to look through the mists into the heavenly country the soul feels drawn to God. To be allowed to meet the Savior Himself, to hear His voice, to take His hand, and to thank Him,—just to think about all this is release and great joy.

But when in this Word it says that "in that day" our Savior shall be glorified in all His saints and marveled at in all them that believe, then even faith almost has an attack of dizziness. Who can it be that sees Christ marvelous and glorified in the saved?

I wonder if it is not God. Christ has finished the greatest miracle, whose equal not even God has seen. All the heavens are full of perfect peonle, and this multitude that no man can number were all lost and condemned sinners. And now they stand before His face holy and without blemish. All this Christ has done. His unsearchable riches have found expression in this masterly work, and God sees His glory in all this perfect life—in us. Then when also the angels see this, they have an inkling of the existence of something they do not possess, and perhaps they lay their harps aside for a while and listen to the songs from the choir of the saved.

Swing high your palms, lift up your song,
Yea, make it myriad voices strong:
Eternally shall praise to Thee,
God, and the Lamb belong!

Anniversaries and Birthdays

JULY 1

For the earnest expectation of the creation waiteth for the revealing of the sons of God. Rom. 8:19

NO matter where we turn, whether in the life of people, of animals, or of plants; in the air or on the earth, on sea or land, we hear cries of deathly fatigue from creatures making war on themselves. In terror of its enemies even the strongest beast of prey trembles like a sparrow. But in the midst of all this struggle, where one seeks the life of the other, there is one rallying point, one inviolate place where all stand together. In the midst of all the howling discord there is one single harmonious note: We "groan together." From the fish down in the deepest sea up to the eagle that sails high above all mountains, from the pale spear of grass drooping in autumn and up to the best Christian—all and everything are longing and yearning... A wonderful, a gripping thought.

Is there then any hope for this one attuned groan of us all? Jesus says, Yes. And it must be this shining star that prevents the groans from dying out. In our Bible it is expressed clearly and concisely: "But, according to His promise, we look for new heavens and a new earth, wherein dwelleth righteousness." Then creation will groan no more, because then the bondage will be at an end. When the people of God in one united company have attained to the goal of their faith, then the hour of redemption will strike also for the creation. "And He that sitteth on the throne said, Behold, I make all things new!" As birds of passage always long for the North when spring comes, so the whole creation waits for the day when all things shall be made new. And the day will come!

O Paradise, O Paradise,
We shall not wait for long;
E'en now the loving ear may catch
Faint fragments of thy song;
Where loyal hearts and true
Stand ever in the light,
All rapture through and through,
In God's most holy sight.

Anniversaries and Birthdays

JULY 2

Let love of the brethren continue. Heb. 13:1

LOVE cannot be born and fostered by commandment, and yet Jesus says that we *must* love each other. The kingdom of God in the old covenant was built on the ordinances of the law. In the new covenant the kingdom is built on the law of the Spirit of life: on a new nature created by God in our hearts. Therefore Christianity is love, just as God is love. But while love is appearing in the Christian as law sprung from life, this life itself is not outside all danger. Love's task is not just to have pleasant feelings, and then to receive the same feelings from others. If we desire to love in that way only, then our love is doomed to death. If love is to thrive and grow it must serve, make sacrifices, suffer, and forgive.

It costs! But it cost God and Jesus, too. No one has loved as God has, and no one has made sacrifices as great as His.

How would husband and wife get along—even if they loved each other ever so much and so purely to begin with—if they did not learn love's blessed art of serving and forgiving?

You and I too must as Christians get into this suffering, serving, and forgiving love. There are many Christians that it costs a good deal to love. They are so unlike us in character and in their outlook on life. Many have sharp edges, too, are unreliable and fickle. We are to love these, too. Therefore it reads: "Let love of the brethren continue."

It may be that in the group of Christians where you belong, there are some that it is difficult to love. Wherefore pray to God that you may have the love that serves and forgives.

Come, children, let us onward go!
We travel hand in hand;
Each in his brother finds his joy
In this wild stranger land.

As children let us be,
Nor by the way fall out,
The angels guard us round about,
And help us brotherly.

Anniversaries and Birthdays

JULY 3

And in the morning, a great while before day, He rose up and went out, and departed into a desert place, and there prayed.

Mark 1:35

GOD'S door and God's heart are always open to those who pray. Our heavenly Father never gets tired of listening to our lament, our groans, and our prayers. Nevertheless there are times that are especially appropriate for prayer. The morning is the best time of day for the person who desires to pray.

Leaves and flowers fold up in the evening when night and chill come on, but they open again as soon as day breaks. In the same manner our soul opens itself in the first hour of morning. He who then first meets God in prayer, receives most of the power that a man needs to go through the day in a manner befitting a Christian. God will indeed always give us what we need—with Him there is neither night nor cold—but we are not always equally willing to receive what He wishes to give. Therefore we ought to use the acceptable time.

David knew that the morning hour should be his prayer hour, and so he tells us:

"For unto Thee do I pray.
O Jehovah, in the morning shalt Thou hear my voice;
In the morning will I order my prayer unto Thee, and will keep watch."

He who undertook to save us, and who went through the world as a true, sinless man, He also knew that the morning hour in prayer gave the greatest power for the day's struggle.

We must try to overcome everything that would hinder us in seeking the kingdom of God first also in this way.

Take time to be holy,
The world rushes on;
Spend much time in secret,
With Jesus alone;

By looking to Jesus,
Like Him thou shalt be;
Thy friends in thy conduct
His likeness shall see.

Anniversaries and Birthdays

JULY 4

Let your loins be girded about and your lamps burning. Luke 12:35

IN the Orient people wear dresses, preferably such as are long and roomy. They testify to riches and high standing in society.

This apparel is a hindrance for people both in work and in walking. If one is to undertake some work, or walk some distance he must fasten up the dress with a belt around his waist. Only then is one able to work and to walk.

Now Jesus uses the dress and the belt as an illustration of how a Christian should be in this world. In this way He wants to tell us that we must work, and at the same time be ready to depart on short notice at any time. In case the call to the journey should come at night we must also have our lamps burning.

He who so well knows our nature, and who knows what power the world has to draw also us Christians, He reminds us so graciously of the danger, and shows us the way of safety.

Let us be on our guard today and keep an eye with the many things that would put out the lamp, and loosen the belt from our loins. The Christian who enters upon the duties of the day in working clothes, and in traveling dress, with lamps burning and with a belt about his waist,—to him neither death nor the Bridegroom will come unexpectedly. Therefore Jesus also says to us: "Be ye yourselves like unto men looking for their lord, when he shall return from the marriage feast; that, when he cometh and knocketh, they may straightway open unto him. Blessed are those servants, whom the lord when he cometh shall find watching" (Luke 12:36-37).

The riches of His grace
In fellowship are given
To Zion's chosen race,
The citizens of heaven;
He fills them with His choicest store,
He gives them life for evermore.

Anniversaries and Birthdays

JULY 5

"I, even I, am He that blotteth out thy transgressions for Mine own sake; and I will not remember thy sins." **Isa. 43:25**

IT is for His own sake that God blots out our transgressions and forgets the sins we have committed.

It is not always easy for us to hold fast to this. Without fully understanding it we get into the delusion of ascribing a part of the cause of our salvation to ourselves. That is the reason it is so much easier for one to believe that he is saved, and to be certain of sonship with God when he feels the good in him, than when he feels the evil. When thoughts and disposition draw toward God, when the feelings are fair and spiritual, and everything seems to help to carry us upward toward God and the good, then it is easy to believe that we are saved. But when the time comes when the good seems to be entirely absent and we feel unspiritual and sinful, when evil desires and nasty thoughts do not leave us in peace even in the prayer chamber, then anxiety, fear, and doubt come on.

Why do these disturbed sensations come then? Because we believe more in what we are or are not in ourselves as Christians, than we believe in what God has done for us. We believe more in God's gracious work in us, than we believe in Christ for us.

If we would more fully get away from ourselves and yield to what Christ is, then we should stand on the foundation that endures eternally when heaven and earth pass away. Let us stand there!

Show me now a Father's love,
And His tender patience,
Heal my wounded soul, remove
These too sore temptations;
I am weak,
Father, speak
Thou of peace and gladness,
Comfort Thou my sadness.

Anniversaries and Birthdays

JULY 6

Now our Lord Jesus Christ Himself, and God our Father who loved us and gave us eternal comfort and good hope through grace, comfort your hearts and establish them in every good work and word. II Thess. 2:16-17

LET us try to win inner peace so that these mighty words can find the way to our hearts.

Jesus Christ and God our Father love you and me. This alone should be more than enough to drive away everything that is sad and dark. But besides this that He loves us, He has also given us eternal comfort and good hope through grace. The comfort is eternal! As it was yesterday, so it is today, and can be no otherwise tomorrow either. He who rules over everything, and who owns this ocean of unspeakable gladness, "with whom can be no variation, neither shadow that is cast by turning," He has of grace given us everything that He possesses. He does not take anything of ours into consideration: He considers His love and grace alone.

Should not this comfort be great enough to remove from us all burdens and dark thoughts? Should anything more be necessary to enable us to be radiantly happy on our brief life's journey?

Discouraged Christian! Lift your eyes, look up higher! Lay hold on the Word about God's love and grace. This look into God's eternal grace, and up to the hope of glory with God shall loose the burden from off your shoulders and give you strength for every good work and word. He will give you this grace today.

Each moment draw from earth away
My heart that lowly waits Thy call!
Speak to my inmost soul, and say:
I am thy love, thy God, thy all!
To feel Thy power, to hear Thy voice,
To taste Thy love, be all my choice!

Anniversaries and Birthdays

JULY 7

"He that is faithful in a very little is faithful also in much: and he that is unrighteous in a very little is unrighteous also in much."

Luke 16:10

THE word about faithfulness and unfaithfulness, and the fruit that grows on these two attributes, runs like a river of life and a river of death through the entire Bible. This same river also flows through the life of humanity: in house and hovel, in bank and on stock exchange, in community and in state. Like an iron law the blessing and the curse proceed from faithfulness and unfaithfulness through our whole life, both the human and the Christian.

When our workday is over and payday comes, God will say to those who have been faithful: "Thou hast been faithful over a few things, I will set thee over many things; enter thou into the joy of thy lord." But to the unfaithful he says: "Thou wicked and slothful servant; . . . And cast ye out the unprofitable servant into the outer darkness: there shall be the weeping and the gnashing of teeth." Unfaithfulness closes the road for us both temporally and spiritually. "If therefore ye have not been faithful in the unrighteous mammon, who will commit to your trust the true riches?"

If we expect ever to own anything ourselves, we must first be faithful in the work we have to do for others. If we are careless with the property of others, we will also be careless with our own. It is of primary importance to learn to be faithful in little things. If one is wasteful when he has only a little food, he will fill the garbage can with food when he has an abundance. It is a chief art in life to be diligent, reliable, unassuming, thrifty, and generous. But he who learns this art has found the way to God's blessing on both his property and his work.

Lord, now make me quiet;
Quiet for Thee alone:
Glad that in the small things
I may give myself.

Anniversaries and Birthdays

JULY 8

For when by reason of the time ye ought to be teachers, ye have need again that some one teach you the rudiments of the first principles of the oracles of God; and are become such as have need of milk, and not of solid food. Heb. 5:12

A CHRISTIAN who always remains in his spiritual childhood has ceased to grow.

If we do not develop a taste for something different from what the Word here calls "milk," our inner man will stop growing. But we must not misunderstand what is said about "milk." To grow from infant food to solid food does not mean to lose the childlike faith, or to quit living with God as we did at first. The way to trained attitudes is just to continue to live in a childlike relation to God. As we received Jesus, in that manner must we continue in Him. He who grows away from hatred for sin, from the prayer chamber, and from need for grace, he stops his own Christian development.

Neither is a taste for solid food the same as having memorized the Bible and understanding all Christian doctrines. It is to have spiritual wisdom and clearness of vision so that we can distinguish between evil and good, between truth and falsehood, between genuine Christianity and that which claims to be Christian but is not. It is to be rooted in love, so we "know the love of Christ which passeth knowledge."

Here the Word distinguishes between knowledge about God and being acquainted with God. We Christians of today know much about Christ: may we also be intimately acquainted with Him! Then we would make sound Christian growth and be tried in the Word of righteousness.

Then we grow in the grace and knowledge of Christ.

Take, my soul, thy full salvation;
Rise o'er sin, and fear, and care;
Joy to find in every station,
Something still to do or bear.
Think what Spirit dwells within thee,
What a Father's smile is thine,
What a Savior died to win thee;
Child of heaven, shouldst thou repine?

Anniversaries and Birthdays

JULY 9

Happy art thou, O Israel:
Who is like unto thee, a people saved by Jehovah,
The shield of thy help,
And the sword of thy excellency! Deut. 33:29

IF a person sees his life from the right angle of vision he will always have reason to be free-hearted, happy, and thankful. The God in whose presence the worldly man trembles for fear is the Christian's best friend. When others must bear their sorrows and their wounds under judgment and fear of that which is to come, then a child of God goes to God as to his Savior and Father. Here his wounds are healed, his sin forgiven, the judgment taken away, and pain quieted.

In the conflict the Christian has the promises of God round about him stronger than steel, and can use the Word of God as a sword against his enemies. He is the shield of our help and the sword of our excellency. We can lay all our burdens on Him because He has said: "Cast all your anxiety upon me, because I care for you." Nothing that concerns us is too small for Him to take care of. His omnipotence and eternal wisdom are borne by a love stronger than death, and all this love He has given as a sacrifice for us. Considering this, can we not say, Blessed is the man whose Savior is the Lord? That must be a mighty shield and a strong sword.

So let us confidingly lay everything in His hand. In years that passed He kept all His promises, and He will do so hereafter also.

Thou canst be merciful while just,—
This is my hope's foundation;
On Thy redeeming grace I trust,
Grant me, then, Thy salvation.
Shielded by Thee, I stand secure;
Thy Word is firm, Thy promise sure,
And I rely upon Thee.

Anniversaries and Birthdays

JULY 10

For in that He Himself hath suffered being tempted, He is able to succor them that are tempted. Heb. 2:12

IT is unspeakably great that God gave us Jesus as the Atoner for our sins, and it is also unspeakably great that He walks among us and desires to save that which was lost. But is it less great that in His life on earth He has tried what we must try, and that He therefore can help us when we suffer and are tempted?

When our Savior sees tears in our eyes, He remembers the reason for His own tears. And when Satan tempts us so that it seems we are walking between fire and sword, then our Savior looks at us with a heart full of sympathy. From the depths of His human nature there arises a power which He has won in His lifetime, and His heart calls to us: "I understand you, struggling brother and sister! I too have been in the same conflict that you are in now." When our souls tremble because heaven is closed against us and because Father hides His face from us, and we fear eternal perdition, then our sad groans reach Him, and again He shouts to us: "To Me also heaven was closed when the sweat fell as blood on the ground, and the cross stood enveloped in darkness."

To see our Savior from this side also, brings great power to all the children of God who must suffer. Seen thus He suits us so wonderfully well in our daily life. Try to see Him thus today.

> And if I ever go astray,
> My wayward soul He turneth,
> To save the lost, to guide the way,
> For this He ever yearneth;
> He leadeth me, my soul to bless,
> In His own path of righteousness
> For His name's sake and glory.

Anniversaries and Birthdays

JULY 11

The everlasting God, Jehovah, the Creator of the ends of the earth, fainteth not, neither is weary; there is no searching of His understanding. He giveth power to the faint; and to him that hath no might he increaseth strength. Isa. 40:28-29

FOR God no "day is dying in the west," and no shadow tells that night is drawing on. He does not become tired, and He needs no rest. He keeps watch when everyone sleeps, and He sees where all are in darkness. David says of himself:

"Surely the darkness shall overwhelm me,
And the light about me shall be night."

But of God he says:

"Even the darkness hideth not from Thee,
But the night shineth as the day:
The darkness and the light are both alike to Thee.
For Thou didst form my inward parts:
Thou didst cover me in my mother's womb."

God is like that. No one knows where His strength comes from, and His years have no end. He dwells not only in high and holy places, but also with the sinner who is bowed down and contrite in spirit. "He gives power to the faint; and to him that has no might he increases strength." He is not ashamed to be called our brother, and by suffering He was made perfect as the Captain of our salvation. All that He in His love rules over, He uses to invite the lost to come home again, and to maintain His own in the conflict. "There is joy in heaven over one sinner that repents."

This God is our God eternally and always. Come unto Him all ye that labor and are heavy laden! With Him there is rest for our souls.

Our hearts o'erflow with gladness,
For we have learned Thy power and grace.
We may not sink in sadness,
We stand, in Christ, before Thy face.

Anniversaries and Birthdays

____

____

____

JULY 12

For our wrestling is not against flesh and blood, but against the principalities, against the powers, against the world-rulers of this darkness, against the spiritual hosts of wickedness in the heavenly places. Eph. 6:12

ACCORDING to this Word the heavenly places are a residence of spiritual powers. As God sends His angels out, so Satan sends his out. The angels of God are sent out to do battle for us, and the spiritual hosts of Satan to fight against us. These invisible powers live and work round about us and over us. They strive for lordship over nations and over every individual man, but first and last the battle is about the people of God.

The Christian's wrestling is therefore not man against man with steel and lead. The battle is between spiritual powers. Wherever a child of God is, he must be prepared to meet the spiritual hosts of wickedness. They tempt us to hatred, anger, and evil words. They set passions on fire, and incite one person against another.

It is not only the sin in us that leads astray. To be sure the enemy inside the fort is dangerous, but the enemy that slips into our souls from without is still more dangerous. The Word of God tells us that when Satan and his forces are bound and cast into the abyss, then the good will triumph on earth, even though human nature remains the same.

The Christian, who desires to get through the world well, must be on his guard against the spiritual hosts of wickedness in the heavenly places.

> I walk in danger all the way;
> The thought shall never leave me,
> That Satan, who has marked his prey,
> Is plotting to deceive me.
> This foe with hidden snares
> May seize me unawares
> If e'er I fail to watch and pray:
> I walk in danger all the way.

Anniversaries and Birthdays

JULY 13

Christ shall appear a second time, apart from sin, to them that wait for Him, unto salvation. **Heb. 9:28**

JESUS has said that He shall come to the earth again, and lead His people to the heavenly glory that He had with the Father before the world was. His second coming is foretold quite as clearly as His first coming was. The prospects seemed poor then, too. Generation after generation waited through thousands of years, and He did not come. Many gave up; others scoffed at those who waited. Just the same He came at the time appointed.

God's people have now waited long for His return. From the very day that He departed, they have looked for Him, but He has not come yet. Now, too, there are many who have quit expecting Him, and many mock those who believe that He will come. But in spite of all this, all true Christians expect Jesus to return and take His bride. Though all may not have the same longing, all wait in faith, and that is the main point. Therefore also all His people shall be permitted to meet Him in the air. As the iron filings in the scrap heap are lifted when the magnet gets close enough, so will all those who are born of God be lifted up from this earth when Jesus comes and gathers His people home.

Let us watch and wait. That gives power against sin and worldliness, and instills holy joy into the soul.

O happy day, and yet far happier hour,
When wilt thou come at last?
When fearless to my Father's love and power
Whose promise standeth fast,
My soul I gladly render,
For surely will His hand
Lead her with guidance tender
To heaven, her fatherland.

Anniversaries and Birthdays

JULY 14

O Jerusalem, Jerusalem, that killeth the prophets and stoneth them that are sent unto her! how often would I have gathered thy children together, even as a hen gathereth her chickens under her wings, and ye would not! Matt. 23:37

THE key to our heart lies in our own hand. The Savior stands on the outside and knocks. The responsibility rests with us for opening the door, or leaving it closed. He puts His ear close up to the door and awaits our Yes. To date He has not crashed a single door, nor will He ever do that. We are privileged to choose our own future: no one is going to be forced into heaven. It surely would not be heaven for us if we were forced to enter.

If with some earnestness you will consider that it is almighty God who asks permission to save you, and that you proudly answer No, then you will find the reason for the fire that is never quenched and the worm that never dies. You will soon have a caller who does not bother to knock at the door. His name is Death. He will break the door open and bring you out before Him who shall judge the living and the dead. To meet him on your own responsibility is the same as going into perdition.

But you and I, too, who once opened the door for the Savior, we also must remember that we have many secret rooms into which Jesus has not been admitted. That person is wise who opens when he hears Him knock. He will put on the new man, he will be sanctified in spirit, soul, and body and will perfect his sanctification in godliness. Then we shall sup with Him and He with us.

Behold, He at the door is calling,
O heed, my soul, what He doth say;
Deny Him not—O thought appalling—
And turn Him not from thee away.
My soul gives answer deep within:
Thou blessed of the Lord, come in.

Anniversaries and Birthdays

JULY 15

I am Jehovah, that is my name; and my glory will I not give to another. **Isa. 42:8**

GOD'S purpose and goal is that the whole creation shall honor Him. He cannot give His glory to another, and everything that does not attain to this goal of life glides into eternal death.

When the angels and the heavenly hosts ushered in the new era on earth with their song, they said, "Glory to God in the highest!" There our joy is found, and there is God's glory. When Christ shall have carried His work of salvation forward to the goal of perfectness, then this refrain will sound through all eternity: Glory be to God!

Our misfortune consists exactly in seeking our own honor. He who is hungry for honors becomes small and spoiled; but he who honors God in all things, he attains to life's highest joy, and stands as a shining example for all.

But this that God wants all the honor, is not that an expression of ambition? Can the Person who demands all honor for Himself alone be the perfect One? Does He not rather appear to be the opposite, namely, One who wants to be considered great at the expense of our poverty?

That God demands all honor is not an expression of imperiousness. He cannot do otherwise, if He is God. The demand springs from His being, it is a perfect law of life, a law for the highest joy. As the drop of water becomes one with the sea when it falls into it, and as all the many forces and colors are gathered in the sun into one single power of life and light, thus all things are to be summed up in God. In this manner He shall be honored in all things as naturally as the heart beats in one's breast, and as the bird sings in the spring sun. It is there that life and glory will be found for us through all eternity.

We are honored in God by His being honored by us. Everything shall say: His glory is great.

O Lord, our hearts awaken, To know and love Thee more,
In faith to stand unshaken, In Spirit to adore,
That we still heavenward hasting, Yet here Thy joy foretasting,
May reap its fulness there.

Anniversaries and Birthdays

____

____

____

JULY 16

But flee youthful lusts, and follow after righteousness, faith, love, peace, with them that call on the Lord out of a pure heart.

II Tim. 2:22

SO long as we are young, one of our weakest points is that we do not think very far ahead. When father and mother ask their children to beware of dangers, the answer comes back so self-sufficient and proud: "Oh, I'll take care of myself." If one draws back from danger it looks as though one is a coward, and so one stands where he ought to flee—with the result that he is left lying beaten and wounded.

Often more courage is needed to flee than to remain in the place. Jesus avoided danger many times. When they wanted to kill Him in Judea, He went to Galilee. When a woman tempted him to sin, Joseph ran out of the house; and the manly courage he showed then opened the way for him to become one of the greatest men of that time. If David had done likewise he would have saved himself from many evil days.

Very many have lost their peace and destroyed their future because they did not have the courage to flee from danger. It is a wise youth that flees youthful lusts. He who laughs at those who flee, will some day have to weep. I want to cry out to all the young people that these words reach: Run away from cards, and liquor, from immoral company, from unholy and vulgar talk, and from everything that leads away from God. What difference does it make if others make fun of you and call you a coward? Do you not know that it is the coward who makes fun of others? Your path away from evil will not lead you into the night. You go forward toward faith, righteousness, and love. You meet your God, your Savior, eternal life, and God's high heaven.

O gentle Jesus, make this heart of mine,
So full of sin,
As holy, harmless, undefiled, as Thine,
And dwell therein;
Then, God my Father, I, like Thee, shall know,
And grow in wisdom as in strength I grow.

Anniversaries and Birthdays

JULY 17

Ye are the salt of the earth. . . . Ye are the light of the world.

Matt. 5:13-14

GOD'S people compose the salt stream in the sea of humanity, the renewing power in folk-life, and the light-house that sends its rays out into the dark night of the world. Without this light all people would be in darkness, and without this salt everything would move toward dissolution and death.

Let us note that Jesus says we are salt and light. We are so inclined to change this "are" to "shall be." But Jesus does not say that. He says we "are." When we have changed "are" to "shall be" we use this word as an accusation against the people of God and for judgment on them, because they are not salt and light. But Jesus has given us that also for comfort.

As surely as the sun sends forth light and heat, and salt smarts in open, healthy sores, so surely are the people of God the salt of the earth and the light of the world. Jesus said that, and life down through the centuries has shown that He spoke truly. Through the influence that Christians have in home and neighborhood, in the life of working people, in business and politics, by making known the will of God in teaching and life wherever they are, they become the salt stream in the life of the people and a light-giving sun for men.

This great honor must give us the joy in our bosom that we do not live in vain, and it shall also call us to a greater feeling of responsibility and to live a more holy life.

"Cast thy bread upon the waters; for thou shalt find it after many days."

Praise to the Lord, the Almighty, the King of creation!
O my soul, praise Him, for He is thy health and salvation!
All ye who hear,
Now to His temple draw near,
Join me in glad adoration.

Anniversaries and Birthdays

JULY 18

It is good that the heart be established by grace. Heb. 13:9

IT is good that a man should hope and quietly wait for the salvation of Jehovah.
It is good for a man that he bear the yoke in his youth.
Let him sit alone and keep silence, because He hath laid it upon him.
Let him put his mouth in the dust, if so be there may be hope.

This does not seem to be good. To get everything we have wished for, to live in well-being and good days, that is what we think is good. When some young people do not have to work, and get everything they want from rich parents, then other young people who must toil, carry loads, and work for a living, think that their case is evil, and that of the others, good.

But God says it is good for a man that he bear the yoke in his youth. The best inheritance that one takes with him from his home is: to have learned to work; to be satisfied with little; and to believe in God. The world has got its best men and women from such homes. Consult the Bible, look into the history of the world, and you will find that this is true. Jesus did not choose His disciples among the rich in Israel, but among fishermen and working-men.

Never be jealous of the youth into whose hands roses are placed, but rejoice to learn the art of leading a life full of work, opposition, and victory. Let the rose appear among thorns, then the sun will shine in an eye wet with tears. While others are dancing their way into the night of death, the grace of God bears you into life. To be privileged to open your heart to Him who Himself fought His way through life, and to be allowed silently and confidingly to lay your burdens on Him, that is good. Then you shall not only have the good fortune of tasting the joy of conflict and victory, but shall also have the chance to help many of those who follow on the road that you walked ahead of them.

Keep us on Thy strength relying, In Thy name the foe defying;
Till Thy coming brings us peace.
O how sweet the thought, and cheering,
In the day of Thine appearing Trouble shall for ever cease.

Anniversaries and Birthdays

JULY 19

Behold, how good and pleasant it is
For brethren to dwell together in unity! Psalm 133:1

IT has never been God's intention that a Christian should live his life in God alone in this world. Therefore He has built a home for us where we shall dwell together: the communion of saints. It is there we will find one of the clearest testimonies that we are the children of God.

In this fellowship one is to help the other, and our Father and Savior has said that the blessing shall dwell there, yea, life for evermore. There we shall be "builded together for a habitation of God in the Spirit."

A Christian who shuts himself out of this holy home may easily lose his own soul. He can hardly keep himself warm alone: the world is so cold for us. We also have enemies that we can conquer only by sticking together. And if any one of us leave this home because he finds so many faults in his brothers and sisters, it may be that the greatest fault is his own. At a distance from the others, suspicion and an evil disposition grow and develop; but in the communion of saints love will cover a multitude of sins.

Let us thank God who gave us this holy brotherhood on earth, and let us sacrifice much that we may hold together there. We need each other so sorely.

> Through the night of doubt and sorrow
> Onward goes the pilgrim band,
> Singing songs of expectation,
> Marching to the Promised Land.
> Clear before us, through the darkness,
> Gleams and burns the guiding light.
> Brother clasps the hand of brother,
> Stepping fearless through the night.

Anniversaries and Birthdays

JULY 20

Faithful is the saying, and worthy of all acceptation, that Christ Jesus came into the world to save sinners; of whom I am chief.

I Tim. 1:15

IN a way it is strange to think of Paul standing with one foot in the grave and saying this about himself. If he had said that he once was the greatest sinner, one could have considered the statement more reasonable. But that he says this now, with a long Christian life behind him—he who was one of the holiest men of earth—that sounds remarkable to many.

But thus it reads, and he has said it himself. And why should it not be so? All who in truth are holy, and who see themselves face to face with God, always come more and more to the same conclusion as Paul. In the fellowship of God we get to see deeper down into the abyss of sin that dwells in our nature, but we also see farther into the depths of the grace that God has given us in Christ. He who considers nothing in his life as sin except what every man might lay his hand on, he has too high an opinion of self, and too low an opinion of God. But he who lays God's yard-stick on his life, on thoughts, desires, and disposition, how can he fail to become a great sinner in his own eyes?

But when at the same time he appropriates Christ as his all before God, then he praises Him who saves sinners.

If we were more upright in looking both at ourselves and at Christ, we would be more humble, happy, and thankful Christians.

O depth of mercy, can it be
That gate was left ajar for me?
Canst Thou still love my wayward soul?
Then take me, Lord, and make me whole.

Anniversaries and Birthdays

JULY 21

Take heed to thyself, and to thy teaching. Continue in these things; for in doing this thou shalt save both thyself and them that hear thee. **I Tim. 4:16**

OUR nature suffers from the great defect that it is difficult for us to see the evil in ourselves. We do not get our eyes on the flaws in our character and what is sinful in our life. But we can see very clearly the follies and faults of others. We are expert at seeing the sins of others, but very poor at seeing our own.

It was this distorted vision that was righted when we as lost sinners found peace with God. Then we saw ourselves as the least, and esteemed others better than ourselves. But Satan never tires of trying to rob us of this great gift of grace; because he knows that if we lose the ability to see right, our Christianity is soon lost.

He who forgets to take heed to himself, loses his feeling of sinfulness, the humble disposition, and the power that grace gives. Then it is easy to slide back into the former state: to see folly in others but not in oneself. Then evil again becomes dominant in us and about us.

What great grace it is to have correct vision, so that we see the faults of our own character, and may always remain under the discipline of grace for sins of heart and of works. May we consider no sacrifice too great in our endeavor to have and to hold this vision inwardly toward ourselves, and upward to God.

> Dear Name! the rock on which I build,
> My shield and hiding-place,
> My never-failing treasury, filled
> With boundless stores of grace.

Anniversaries and Birthdays

JULY 22

And the apostles gather themselves together unto Jesus; and they told Him all things, whatsoever they had done, and whatsoever they had taught. And He saith unto them, "Come ye yourselves apart into a desert place, and rest awhile." Mark 6:30-31

JESUS has commanded His people not only to go with Him to work: He has also said that we shall go with Him and rest.

It is true that many of us are heavy of foot when we are to go with Jesus to work. But if it is a Christian art to work for our Savior, it is no less an art to go apart with Him and rest. It is not at all God's will that we shall work all the time. He who forgets to rest, will soon be incapable of work.

The nervous chase in the work of God's kingdom wears on us more than we think. We have no peace either in our homes with our own family, or in the prayer chamber with God. It would surely be of much greater value for the work that God gave us, if we oftener found the way to rest together with our Savior. We must notice that it was when the apostles came and told about all that they had done, that Jesus said: "Now you must go and rest." And in our day it surely is time that we go apart with Jesus when we begin to tell others about what we have done. If it appears to us as though we in this way desire to honor God, we will find when alone with Jesus that we praised ourselves most.

When He again has purified the heart, we see how much dross adhered to the gold. Therefore: Remember to rest together with Jesus, you who are working for Him.

O Bread of life from heaven,
To weary pilgrims given,
O Manna from above:
The souls that hunger feed Thou,
The hearts that seek Thee lead Thou,
With Thy most sweet and tender love.

Anniversaries and Birthdays

JULY 23

And He said unto them, "Go ye into all the world, and preach the gospel to the whole creation." **Mark 16:15**

"And lo, I am with you always, even unto the end of the world." **Matt. 28:20**

MANY, who insist on being called Christians, consider it quite ridiculous to sacrifice young people and money on missionary work among the heathen.

But such a view is entirely un-Christian. The last words of Jesus to His own here on earth are as clear as they are strong. He says we are to go into all the world, and preach the gospel to the whole creation. He who has all power in heaven and on earth will be with His messengers always. It is by virtue of His omnipotence that He can give both the command and the promise.

The Christian who in spite of this is indifferent to missionary work has entered upon a devious and a dangerous way.

It has been said that the love that does not carry us across the ocean has a broken pinion. It has also been said that it is human to love one's own, but divine to love the world; also that the Christian society that ceases to send the gospel to the heathen, will soon cease to be evangelical.

As a mother cries for help when she sees her child in danger of death, so Jesus cries to us to bring the Word of life to a dying generation. Have you heard Jesus call to you to go? Blessed are you that heard and went! Jesus is with you always.

Sing to the Lord a glorious song,
Sing to His name, His love forth tell;
Sing on, heaven's host, His praise prolong;
Sing, ye who now on earth do dwell:
Worthy the Lamb for sinners slain;
From angels, praise; and thanks from men;
Worthy the Lamb, enthroned to reign,
Glory and power! Amen! Amen!

Anniversaries and Birthdays

___

___

___

___

JULY 24

"For the mountains may depart, and the hills be removed; but My lovingkindness shall not depart from thee, neither shall My covenant of peace be removed," saith Jehovah that hath mercy on thee.
Isa. 54:10

THESE are strong words, great and strong as God Himself, and they stand as fast as the eternity of God. This one word alone should be more than enough to lift all burdens from the shoulders of Christians. It is not often that we see mountains depart and hills remove; but though this should happen, we have something greater than mountains to stand on. The promises of God are more secure than mountains.

Let us believe that this is true. We need it so much. Life is full of powers that create unrest, discouragement, doubt, and judgment. Mother weeps because the children are unruly and turn away from God; and father indulges in self-accusation because he did not do his duty. Christian young people sit dejected and look as despairingly at the future as though they were without God and without hope in the world. He who loses his faith in what God has promised drifts into bondage and impotence; but those who hazard their lives on God's Word, are made free and victorious Christians.

So get up, you discouraged Christian, and place your foot again on the Word that will stand when heaven and earth pass away. He who never failed you in days that are gone, He is able to bear your burdens and solve your riddles also in days to come. He who trusts in the Lord is never put to shame.

Built of living stones, cemented
By the Spirit's unity,
Based on prophets and apostles,
Firm in faith and stayed on Thee,
May Thy Church, O Lord incarnate,
Grow in grace, in peace, in love;
Emblem of the heavenly Zion,
The Jerusalem above.

Anniversaries and Birthdays

JULY 25

Therefore He brought down their heart with labor;
They fell down, and there was none to help.
Then they cried unto Jehovah in their trouble,
And He saved them out of their distresses. Psalm 107:12-13

THIS Word helps us find the answer to many things in life that look puzzling to most people. Why shall burdens so heavy be laid on my weak back? Why shall sin have so great power over me? These great questions and sad sighs come from many people on whom sin and suffering have inflicted deep wounds.

In our Word today we read that God uses suffering to bring our hearts down; and when we stumble we learn that the world has no help for a sinner. Out of the experience of suffering and helplessness the cry rises to God, and then the time has come when He can be our Savior. We may tell people as long as we wish that grace is as free as the air—no one will accept grace until he sees that he is helpless. It is only when sin and suffering have overcome us that God's power to save can be revealed on us.

"Iniquities prevail against me;
As for transgressions, Thou wilt forgive them."

It is great grace for one to be privileged to see that he is a helpless sinner. He who sees his sin, and cries out for salvation, will be helped.

"For the people shall dwell in Zion at Jerusalem; thou shalt weep no more; He will surely be gracious unto thee at the voice of thy cry; when He shall hear, He will answer thee" (Isa. 30:19).

O very Man and very God,
Who hast redeemed us with Thy blood;
From death eternal set us free,
And make us one with God in Thee.

Anniversaries and Birthdays

JULY 26

They have all turned aside, they are together become unprofitable; There is none that doeth good, no, not so much as one. Rom. 3:12
And the blood of Jesus His Son cleanseth us from all sin.
I John 1:7

THIS testimonial is hard for us to accept. We must acknowledge that it is grievous to subscribe to so hard a judgment.

It is difficult for us to admit that we are so thoroughly bad, but it is true nevertheless. In the light from God our life is like a smouldering ruin, like smoking flax, and like a bruised reed. We are dead in trespasses and sins; evil has permeated our inmost being. Evil lays its polluting hand on everything that we think, say, and do. Jealousy, hatred, and selfishness are dominant in the inmost sources of life, both in the individual, and on up to the loftiest point in the nation's life. The highest knowledge the world has attained to is used to make weapons of murder, and if only we can push forward, we trample others down. God's judgment on us is that we are lost, and condemned to eternal death.

But He who knows our frame, and who saw our need, He it was that gave us the help. He who goes as a lost sinner to Jesus Christ receives the forgiveness of sins; because the blood of Jesus cleanses from all sin. All heavens shall be filled with saved sinners only, and these will through all eternity praise Him for salvation. Sinner, do not doubt! Jesus came to seek and to save that which was lost.

Thy grace first made me feel my sin,
It taught me to believe;
Then in believing, peace I found,
And now I live, I live.

Anniversaries and Birthdays

JULY 27

Wherefore do ye spend money for that which is not bread? and your labor for that which satisfieth not? hearken diligently unto Me, and eat ye that which is good, and let your soul delight itself in fatness. Isa. 55:2

EVERYONE who uprightly seeks peace with God and assurance that he is saved, is of the opinion that he must become different from what he is, before he dare believe that he is saved. In the work that we take up to improve ourselves we always get stuck.

It is this toil that God asks us to quit. Instead of spending money and getting no returns we are to hearken diligently to Him, and what we hear will give our soul the power of life. Farther on in the chapter God says that if we hear, He will give us the same grace that He gave David. Let us then hear some of the words that were given to David, and let us take them as words from God to us.

When David had sinned, and confessed his sin, God said to him: "I have put away thy sin; thou shalt not die." David believed those words, grace was shown him, and he was saved. When you and I have sinned, and have confessed to God, He speaks the same words to us. Let us listen to those words and accept them, then we too shall receive grace. Then we, too, are saved. God has made the way to peace and certainty of salvation as plain and free as that for us.

"Come now, and let us reason together, saith Jehovah: though your sins be as scarlet, they shall be as white as snow; though they be red like crimson, they shall be as wool" (Isa. 1:18).

Moses' law no longer rules us,
Christ's free Spirit gently schools us;
Ended now our captive thrall;
He who God obeys in all,
Through his Savior's death and merit,
Now enjoys adoption's spirit;
Hallelujah! Hallelujah!

Anniversaries and Birthdays

JULY 28

We are ambassadors therefore on behalf of Christ, as though God were entreating by us: we beseech you on behalf of Christ, Be ye reconciled to God. II Cor. 5:20

IF we are to be saved, the salvation which is ready for us in Christ must be transferred to us. It is not enough that there is a prepared salvation outside of us; we must make it our personal possession. We can be certain that what Christ wrought is enough for our salvation: we are reconciled to God by the death of Christ. But we who are reconciled, must permit ourselves to be reconciled. That is to say: We must go to Christ and accept the salvation that is prepared for us in Him.

If we will not do that, we will never be saved. Therefore God has sent His Word and His witnesses to us, who ask us to come to Christ. He took the evidence of your debt and guilt and marked it "Paid" with His own blood in God's holy place; but you must also let Him write "Paid" in the book that you carry in your own bosom, and let Him cleanse your heart by faith. He who does not as a lost sinner go to Christ, and acknowledge that he is guilty of the death of Christ, and he who does not in faith open his heart to the Savior, he must be condemned.

Christ has taken upon Himself our responsibility for sin before God: but you and I bear the responsibility of accepting Christ. We ourselves must decide whether we wish to be saved, or to be lost.

Come to Him and be saved, you who have turned your back on Him. Him that cometh He will in no wise cast out.

"I have no pleasure in the death of him that dieth, saith the Lord Jehovah: wherefore turn yourselves, and live."

Thou child of truth, how blessed!
A conqueror soon shalt be,
With songs of glad thanksgiving
A crown awaiteth thee.
To thee the palm triumphal
By God's own hand is giv'n,
Thine, to His name who saved thee,
To sing the songs of heaven.

Anniversaries and Birthdays

JULY 29

Lord, what Thou didst command is done, and yet there is room.
Luke 14:22

IN many ways it is dark and dreary for us people of this present time. Many forces are at work to carry us into straitened and hard circumstances. Nations are turning away from God and are getting into the night of a pagan wisdom. But though dark clouds gather above us, we can now as formerly cry out, "Yet there is room!"

God has not yet taken His Spirit from us: this Power for life is still working in the people. People still desire to hear the Word of sin and grace, and there are still many who long for peace with God. The grace of God is still upon us, so that many of those who are longing and seeking, find peace.

Still there's help to get,
Weary souls, cry out!
God may still be reached,
Open yet is heaven.

No penitent sinner has reason to despair, and no servant of the Lord has a right to give up the work in the kingdom of God. The angel with the sharp sickle, who is to gather the clusters of the wild vine of the earth, is still bound. All who want to save their lives can do so, for salvation's door stands wide open, and the Lord of lords calls now as before to "souls distressed." Let us thank Him who withholds judgment because He desires to save all who can be saved.

"Yet there is room!" Hear that and come!

But then we must not forget that this "Yet" tells us that the day will come when there no longer is room.

O seek the Lord today!
Today He hath salvation.
Approach Him while He may
Still hear thy supplication.

Repent and seek His grace,
His call to thee doth sound;
O turn to Him thy face
While yet He may be found.

Anniversaries and Birthdays

JULY 30

"Come, see a Man who told me all things that ever I did: can this be the Christ?" **John 4:29**

IT is right to believe and teach that God's holy and righteous demands shall drive us to an acknowledgment of our sins. Apart from law, sin is dead. It was only when the commandment came that sin revived.

But though this be ever so true, we still must not forget, that also when we meet Jesus face to face can we see our sin. In Him the demands of the Law are printed in living colors in a perfect life. The spiritually blind woman of Samaria, who met Jesus at the well, cried out, "Come, see a Man who told me all things that ever I did!" That Man was not Moses. It was Christ. When Peter met Him on the beach he got to see his sin more than ever before. It is as though we hear Peter saying: "I am a poor stick, in a pinch I run away. Do not bother about me! Let me go! You will not be able to make anything worth while out of me anyway. Go! Lord Jesus, depart from me! Go!"

That feeling of shame and despair may still come upon a disciple of Jesus when he sees his sin and unfaithfulness in the light that shines from the love of Jesus Christ. But, No; then the Savior does not leave the sinner. That is just the right time for work for Him who came to call sinners to repentance.

How difficult for a Christian too to remember that it is sinners that Jesus saves. We are continually inclined to glide back to the false view that it is "respectable" people that Jesus saves.

He saves sinners! Sinners!

> Now we may gather with our King;
> E'en in the lowliest dwelling;
> Praises to Him we there may bring,
> His wondrous mercy forth telling;
> Jesus His grace to us accords,
> Spirit and life are all His words,
> His truth doth hallow the temple.

Anniversaries and Birthdays

JULY 31

For He will deliver the needy when he crieth,
And the poor, that hath no helper. Psalm 72:12

THE Word of God delivers hard and telling blows to the proud and self-sufficient, but it speaks in a mild and comforting voice to the neglected and the wretched. I hardly believe there is a single word in the whole Bible which is rough on those who see that they are small and poor. Like an eternal, rippling fountain, grace and comfort stream forth from the Father-heart and the Savior-heart of God for all who recognize that they are helpless and lost.

When Saul was small in his own eyes, God made him king over His people; but when he thought he was great, he fell on his own sword.

The rich He hath sent empty away, but the hungry He hath filled with good things. He gives power to the faint, and to him that has no might He increases strength. He saves the miserable, and brings down the haughty eyes. Rejoice, ye heavens! Shout for joy, ye lower parts of the earth! For the Lord hath comforted His people and has had mercy on the afflicted.

This is the Lord's Word. It is no good fortune for us—as we so often are tempted to believe—to get what we want, and to be satisfied with ourselves. Our good fortune is to feel that we are helpless, poor, and impotent, and then in all our poverty to go to Him who came to help the helpless.

"*I know that Jehovah will maintain the cause of the afflicted,*
And justice for the needy" (Psalm 140:12).
"*For Thou wilt save the afflicted people;*
But the haughty eyes Thou wilt bring down."
(Psalm 18:27.)

These are they whose hearts were riven,
Sore with woe and anguish tried,
Who in prayer full oft have striven
With the God they glorified:
Now, their painful conflict o'er,
God has bid them weep no more.

Anniversaries and Birthdays

AUGUST 1

And He that sitteth on the throne said, "Behold, I make all things new." **Rev. 21:5**

THE hurt that man suffered in the fall was great, greater than any one of us understands. Life's whole foundation went to ruin; and sin, sickness, and death became our inheritance. But in front of this closed door God opens a new way for us that leads to life, and then He shouts these great words out over the world: "Behold, I make all things new!"

That which closed the door against us was taken away by Jesus Christ, and through Him the new and living way was opened, too. He is the way Himself. Every sinner who lays hold on Christ in faith is carried over from death to life, and has come into that kingdom where all things are made new. At death every believing person is set entirely free also from sin itself; and when once the graves are opened, and the dwelling of God in fullest sense is with us on the new earth, then the promise is wholly fulfilled. The hurt is then completely healed. Spirit, soul, and body are one single harmonious life. As the drop of water becomes one with the sea into which it falls, so everything in the eternally new kingdom will unite into an unspeakable and glorified joy.

May this exalted goal become very vivid to us. Then everything here will become small in comparison with that which shall be revealed on us.

"And there shall be night no more; and they need no light of lamp, neither light of sun; for the Lord God shall give them light: and they shall reign for ever and ever" (Rev. 22:5).

O one, O only mansion!
O Paradise of joy!
Where tears are ever banished,
And smiles have no alloy;

The Lamb is all thy splendor;
The Crucified thy praise;
His laud and benediction
Thy ransomed people raise.

Anniversaries and Birthdays

AUGUST 2

Then came Peter and said to Him, "Lord, how oft shall my brother sin against me, and I forgive him? until seven times?" Jesus saith unto him, "I say not unto thee, Until seven times; but, Until seventy times seven." **Matt. 18:21-22**

THE Christian who cannot forgive those who have sinned against him, has a bad disposition; and if he is not able to overcome this, he will lose the forgiveness that he himself has received from God.

It is not always easy to forgive. It is especially difficu't when it is one of our fellow Christians, or someone who is closely associated with us, who has wronged us. But no matter who it is or how hard it is, if we are to save our souls we must conquer the bad temper. Vile as it may sound to say it, nevertheless it is true that there are Christians who seem unable to forgive. Some say that they cannot; others argue with themselves and suffer much evil, but get nowhere. That is sad. There would be much less evil in homes, family groups, and neighborhoods, and in Christian congregations if we Christians had more of the mild temper of Jesus who always forgave.

What shall we do to get power to forgive?

First, look this truth in the eye, that he who will not forgive others, loses forgiveness from God. Jesus has said that clearly. Remember also that you must receive forgiveness from God every day. Next, bring to God in your prayer the person that you dislike, mention him by name, and tell God plainly that you are unable to forgive that person. Then God will enable you to forgive.

> A broken heart, my God, my King,
> Is all the sacrifice I bring:
> The God of grace will ne'er despise
> A broken heart for sacrifice.

Anniversaries and Birthdays

AUGUST 3

Nevertheless in this rejoice not, that the spirits are subject unto you; but rejoice that your names are written in heaven.

Luke 10:20

SHOULD it not be right and Christian to rejoice because one was privileged to bring a sinner over from the power of Satan to God? Can also that joy become unclean?

He who knows the deep abyss of sin in us says Yes. It looks as though everything that our fingers touch becomes polluted. Also when God lets us run errands for Him, we stand ready to take the honor ourselves, and to rejoice over our great works. As the king of Sodom coaxed Abraham to take what was not his, so Satan and our evil nature coax us to rob God of the honor for what He lets us do. And when in one way or another we have succeeded in exalting ourselves, we have no objection to adding that all the honor belongs to God. Under this beautiful sign we rob God of His honor.

The only safe place for us is at the cross, to embrace that and have our joy in God. Then He writes our name in heaven. The joy that seizes the soul then is perfectly clean. It cannot be polluted by us, and it can never become too great. Consider for a moment this blessed miracle that God's own hand has written your name and mine in heaven! Perhaps the saved who have arrived on the other side get the opportunity of seeing our names there. Many of them know us from our being together on earth, and they surely expect us soon. A glorious thought!

I thank Thee, my God, for writing also my name in heaven.

Blessed assurance, Jesus is mine!
O what a foretaste of glory divine!
Heir of salvation, purchase of God,
Born of His Spirit, washed in His blood.
This is my story, this is my song,
Praising my Savior all the day long.

Anniversaries and Birthdays

____

____

____

____

____

AUGUST 4

For I reckon that the sufferings of this present time are not worthy to be compared with the glory which shall be revealed to us-ward. Rom. 8:18

TO think that we are going to be made more comfortable than others in this world because we are Christians, is false. No one can buy riches and good days with Christianity. Just as certain as it is that godliness is profitable for all things, just so little does it exempt us from life's heavy burdens. The Christian must endure the fruit of sin in this world together with all others. Therefore sorrow, sickness, and death knock at the door of those who fear God also.

But that is not all that a Christian must accept. Just because he is a Christian a special path of suffering is given him to walk. Only Christians have the conflict against sin, Satan, and the evil in themselves, in addition to fear and anxiety for the salvation of themselves and others. The chief reason for the sufferings of a Christian is found outside of the road on which the worldly travel. All the children of God must go to school, and learn to know themselves and God, and be trained to help others. Suffering is the head teacher in this school. We Christians must count on that.

But then God has also told us that we must count on the goal: that in a little while we will be where all suffering is exchanged for eternal glory, a glory so great that all we suffered here is not worthy to be regarded. Over yonder when we see the benefit of what we had to suffer here, we shall thank Him so much the more because He permitted us to walk in His footsteps to eternal life.

Come, Lord, when grace has made me meet
Thy blessed face to see;
For if Thy work on earth be sweet,
What will Thy glory be?

Then shall I end my sad complaints,
And weary, sinful days,
And join with the triumphant saints
That sing my Savior's praise.

Anniversaries and Birthdays

AUGUST 5

But Christ as a Son, over His house; whose house are we, if we hold fast our boldness and the glorying of our hope firm unto the end. **Heb. 3:6**

IN this Word there are among others two things that are told us that we will try to remember.

One is that all saved people are God's house. God dwells in His people. As He dwells in His heaven and in His Word, so He also dwells in a saved sinner. "Know ye not that ye are a temple of God, and that the Spirit of God dwelleth in you?" "Even as Thou, Father, art in Me, and I in Thee, that they also may be in us." He who dwelleth in light unapproachable, and who owns all heavens, He dwells with them who believe in the name Jesus.

"O what an honor,
Too great for thought to reach!"

Let us believe this, and thank God for so great an honor.

But then we must also remember that it said, "If we hold fast our boldness and the glorying of our hope firm unto the end." By this we can see that it is possible to fall away from God. If we quit believing in God and quit having confidence in Him, we are no longer His dwelling. If we depart from Him, He must also depart from us. Those who wrap themselves up in the false thought that a Christian never can fall away from God, ought to take this to heart. O yes, we can fall away! We may fall away today!

"If a wicked thought we mind,
Satan soon hath bound us."

He who is faithful unto death will receive the crown of life. He that overcometh shall inherit all things.

He that overcometh! He who is faithful!

I ask Thee for a thoughtful love,
Through constant watching wise,
To meet the glad with joyful smiles,
To wipe the weeping eyes;
A heart at leisure from itself
To soothe and sympathize.

Anniversaries and Birthdays

AUGUST 6

Even to old age I am He, and even to hoar hairs will I carry you: I have made, and I will bear; yea, I will carry, and will deliver.

Isa. 46:4

THIS is a great and comforting Word, that we should try to lay up in our hearts. If we did that we should experience more of God's help in our struggles. This Word is for him who has just planted his foot on the Lord's way and it promises him help through life; and this Word also comes to him who is old and tired of his day's work. But it may be that God thought especially of old people when He gave us this Word.

In most cases it happens that with the passing of the years we become more and more lonesome, helpless, and forgotten. Time and youth leave us, and the older generation is left to watch everything move away. Many of those that we lived together with are asleep under the sod; and those that are left we see so seldom. Our views have changed, and the friendship is ended.

But in the midst of all these things that slip away and that cause us one disappointment after another, God steps forth and promises that He will never leave us. When vitality dwindles inch by inch, when thinking tires, when sight is weakened, and knees tremble; and when friends and those nearest and dearest forget us, then the Lord is the same. He will lift, carry, and deliver even to old age and to hoar hairs. Yea, He leads us even through the valley of the shadow of death; and when we no longer are able to walk, He will carry us over.

Father, I know that all my life
Is portioned out for me;
The changes that are sure to come,
I do not fear to see:
I ask Thee for a present mind,
Intent on pleasing Thee.

Anniversaries and Birthdays

AUGUST 7

And He looked round about on them all, and said unto him, "Stretch forth thy hand!" And he did so: and his hand was restored. Luke 6:10

THE man with the withered hand prayed Jesus to make his hand well again. Jesus answered by asking him to stretch forth his hand. The man did so and his hand became well.

That is faith.

Many of us would probably have answered Jesus about this way: "You know that I cannot stretch out the hand that is withered. If I had been able to do that I would not have come to you. But if you will restore the hand, I will gladly stretch it forth." Thus many of us would have answered. But that is not faith. That is to have the experience before one believes. There are many seekers and praying people among us who do not get what they are praying for because they insist on having the answer to the prayer before they believe. They long for peace with God and pray to be saved, but they experience no peace and salvation because they want to possess peace and be assured of salvation before they believe that they are saved.

But the Word of God says that he who believes the forgiveness of sins in Jesus' name *is* saved. He who believes on the Son *has* eternal life. Believe that and you are saved.

"For God so loved the world that He gave His only begotten Son, that whosoever believeth on Him should not perish, but have eternal life."

"In Thee, O Jehovah, do I take refuge;
Let me never be put to shame:
Deliver me in Thy righteousness" (Psalm 31:1).

My hope is built on nothing less
Than Jesus' blood and righteousness;
I dare not trust the sweetest frame,
But wholly lean on Jesus' name:
On Christ, the solid rock, I stand;
All other ground is sinking sand.

Anniversaries and Birthdays

AUGUST 8

And the younger of them said to his father, "Father, give me the portion of thy substance that falleth to me." And he divided unto them his living. And not many days after, the younger son gathered all together and took his journey into a far country; and there he wasted his substance with riotous living. Luke 15:12-13

THE greater part of humanity has by degrees acquired the false faith that it is best to get as far away from God as possible. With great, proud words they boast of their freedom, and paint a bright future because they think that they are through with God. Human reason and culture are exalted as savior in place of Jesus Christ.

But while they are boasting about the paradise they are going to build on earth without God, they fear the disaster that they see drawing nearer every day. As the harlot wastes her own life and consumes the strength of man, so the godless life consumes soul-peace, morals, life-power, and a people's joy. Poverty and hunger reign there, death embraces the populace, there the way is opened to the "outer darkness" where the worm never dies and the fire never is quenched.

Just think if our generation were on the way *to* God with the same speed with which they are now going *away* from Him! Then all frontiers would be without cannon; suspicion and hatred would drown in peace; and national prosperity, godliness, and good works would bloom in joyous competition. Not a single honest person can doubt that.

You, who were in the far country but have found the way home again to God as your Father and Savior, you ought to thank and worship Him for this greatest joy of life.

Just as I am, Thou wilt receive,
Wilt welcome, pardon, cleanse, relieve;
Because Thy promise I believe,
O Lamb of God, I come, I come.

Anniversaries and Birthdays

____

____

____

____

AUGUST 9

And they bring unto Him one that was deaf, and had an impediment in his speech; and they beseech Him to lay His hand upon him. And He took him aside from the multitude privately, and put His fingers into his ears, and He spat, and touched his tongue.
Mark 7:32-33

MANY, who never saw the Lord's way and did not hear His voice, have received both hearing and sight when they were taken aside from the multitude privately. In life's mad chase they saw nothing but food, money, finery, and fun. But then there came to some of them a new time, dark and hard to bear. Riches took wings, and poverty moved in and cleared away friends and glad parties together with well-being and worldliness. Sickness came and laid these frivolous and light-hearted people on the edge of the grave. Death came and took the best that life had given. You who were so great and seemed highly loved, you are now bedfast, without friends, and apart from the multitude.

But there you met your Savior. Very slowly but gradually you received ears to hear with and eyes to see with. Now you see your sin, you hear the Word about salvation for sinners, and you praise Him who took you away from the multitude.

You who have just been taken aside and who are wondering why this should happen to you, listen! Let Him, who in grace brought you to where you are now, touch also you. Then you will find a better Friend and greater riches than you lost. And when He also takes His own aside, He does so in order that we may see our right fatherland better, and hear the melodies of the heavenly choir more clearly.

Hence with earthly treasure!
Thou art all my pleasure,
Jesus, all my choice;
Hence, thou empty glory!
Naught to me thy story,
Told with tempting voice;
Pain or loss, or shame, or cross,
Shall not from my Savior move me,
Since He deigns to love me.

Anniversaries and Birthdays

AUGUST 10

Seek ye Jehovah while He may be found; call ye upon Him while He is near! **Isa. 55:6**

THE Lord may be found as long as the time of grace lasts. The door that He opened for us in Christ stands open for all. As impossible as it is for anyone else to open the door, so impossible is it for others to close it. He has the keys of death and of hades, and only He opens and closes.

But He has also told us that the day will come when He will close the door. And so He impresses on us that he who would be saved must seek Him "while" He may be found. No one can determine the time for his own conversion. Those who desire to get to heaven must redeem the acceptable time. Not a single person would have the slightest thought of seeking God, if He did not seek us first. If the Spirit of God did not disturb us, we would surely be permitted to walk comfortably in our sins. Only when He knocks can we open the door, if we will.

You who no doubt wish to go heaven, but who yourself want to determine the time of your conversion, you forget that this is Satan's deception. Many, many who thought as you think were never saved. It is when the Lord seeks you that you can seek Him. Today is our day, God alone owns tomorrow.

You and I too who found salvation, we too have gotten our "while." We too must redeem the acceptable time. If we draw back from the grace of God, danger stands also at our door.

E'er since, by faith, I saw the stream
Thy flowing wounds supply,
Redeeming love has been my theme,
And shall be till I die.

Anniversaries and Birthdays

AUGUST 11

And after six days Jesus taketh with Him Peter, and James, and John his brother, and bringeth them up into a high mountain apart. Matt.17:1

THERE are times and happenings that make marks in our lives so deep that we never can forget them. It was such a time that John remembered when he wrote of the day he found Jesus. This impressed his soul so strongly that even in his old age he remembered the hour that he met Him. Somewhat the same was true of Matthew when he wrote: "after six days."

If we read the sixteenth chapter of Matthew's gospel we will learn a little of what happened before these six days. Jesus had spoken serious words to Peter and to the others also about taking up the cross every day, and about losing life if they wanted to save life. This gave them something to think about; but now the stripes they received on those trying days shall be healed, and darkness shall yield to the shining sun. The time is now come when Jesus is to be transfigured before their eyes. He who gives power to the faint, and increaseth strength to him that hath no might, He knows the correct time for giving comfort; and now they move upward, away from sorrow and crying.

He who would know Jesus must first learn to know himself. Knowing ourselves brings us into conflict, discouragement, and doubt; but the knowledge of Christ gives us unspeakable and glorified joy. It is in such times that a Christian receives grace to forget himself and to see "Jesus only."

Help me, for I am weak; I fight,
Yet scarce can battle longer;
I cling but to Thy grace and might,
'Tis Thou must make me stronger;
When sore temptations are my lot,
And tempests round me lower,
Break their power;
So through deliverance wrought,
I know that Thou forsak'st me not.

Anniversaries and Birthdays

AUGUST 12

And He said, "So is the kingdom of God, as if a man should cast seed upon the earth; and should sleep and rise night and day, and the seed should spring up and grow, he knoweth not how."

Mark 4:26-27

IN this Word there is great comfort for us both as Christians and as workers in the kingdom of God. We hasten to complain if we do not see fruit the day that we have sowed the seed, and we believe that only evil is growing, while the good withers and disappears. But Jesus sees it otherwise. He says that the kingdom of God grows both in us and by us. Under the rain and sunshine of His grace God's seed grows too from the blade to the ripened grain.

So let the Word from God, which God's Spirit planted in our hearts by faith, be in peace. If a Christian quits believing because he sees no growth in him of the life with God, and because he cannot taste the fruit of life, then he resembles the little boy who repeatedly dug up the pea he had planted to see whether it had sprouted or not. Much divine life loses its power in this way, and has its growth stunted.

"Go to the ant, thou sluggard;
Consider her ways and be wise,"

says the proverb. The Christian should go out to the field to get confidence in the Word of God. There let him say to himself: "So is the kingdom of God, as if a man should cast seed upon the earth." Then it is left in peace, and then it grows.

"They are planted in the house of Jehovah;
They shall flourish in the courts of our God.
They shall still bring forth fruit in old age:
They shall be full of sap and green:
To show that Jehovah is upright;
He is my rock, and there is no unrighteousness in Him"
(Psalm 92:13-15).

Oft as the precious seed is sown,
Thy quickening grace bestow,
That all whose souls the truth receive
Its saving power may know.

Anniversaries and Birthdays

AUGUST 13

Not that I already have obtained, or am already made perfect: but I press on, if so be that I may lay hold on that for which also I was laid hold on by Christ Jesus. Phil. 3:12

TO be laid hold on by Christ, and to feel oneself saved and made free in this hold, is life's greatest joy. The light that then rises in our heart shows us a great goal. And the goal is to lay hold on Him who first laid hold.

To be saved in faith is not the same as having reached the goal of faith, but it is having found the way to the goal. We are saved in order to be saved. As the skater trains that he may win the prize, so the Christian trains to win the crown of righteousness which is laid up for him in heaven. The Christian who loses this holy buoyancy is left behind. "Let us therefore, as many as are perfect, be thus minded." Not perfect in the sense that we are out of danger or entirely without evil; but perfect in Him who has laid hold on us: Christ. Then we find the right meaning in the words that we are perfect, and that we are not perfect, but that we press on. When we look at Christ, all is perfection; but when we look at ourselves, everything is imperfect.

Therefore the Christian longs, suffers, and prays so that he may win the prize of victory. As the rain drop becomes quiet only after it has reached the sea, so the Christian will not possess perfect salvation until he "enters in by the gates into the city," and sees Jesus as He is.

More holiness give me,
More strivings within;
More patience in suff'ring,
More sorrow for sin;
More faith in my Savior,
More sense of His care;
More joy in His service,
More purpose in prayer.

Anniversaries and Birthdays

AUGUST 14

And Jehovah thy God will cast out those nations before thee by little and little: thou mayest not consume them at once, lest the beasts of the field increase upon thee. Deut. 7:22

THE Israelites owned all of the land of Canaan in faith, and it was theirs as soon as they stood inside the boundary. Still they must win the land inch by inch through war.

God's people of the new covenant live under the same conditions. The day they found peace with God many Christians thought that all enemies were struck to earth, and that sin was out of their minds and thoughts for all time. But before they had finished dreaming this deceiving dream the enemy fell upon them anew. The country that we own in faith, we must fight to win.

Sure I must fight if I would reign:
Increase my courage, Lord;
I'll bear the cross, endure the pain,
Supported by Thy Word.

We have become the elect people of God not that we may lie on a sunny hillside dreaming in sweet ecstasy: we are saved to reach the goal through conflict. We win no victory except God be our strength; but neither does God win a victory for us unless we get into the fight. "Go! and I will be with thee!" That is the Lord's command and promise. So when we stand in the midst of the fight, confronted by enemies stronger than we are, and carry on according to the laws God has given in His kingdom, then the Lord gives us victory.

"Fear ye not, stand still, and see the salvation of Jehovah, which He will work for you today" (Ex. 14:13).

Thy saints, in all this glorious war,
Shall conquer, though they die;
They view the triumph from afar,
And seize it with their eye.

Anniversaries and Birthdays

___

___

___

AUGUST 15

This poor widow cast in more than they all: for all these did of their superfluity cast in unto the gifts: but she of her want did cast in all the living that she had. Luke 21:3-4

THE temple was God's house in the old covenant, and is a picture of God's people in the new covenant. The temple treasury and the gifts that were put in it are also a picture of what we ought to give to God. By this offering we shall build God's house, and be God's dwelling in the spirit. It was surely for the purpose of teaching His disciples the right generosity that He bade them stop at the temple treasury and watch those who gave of their superfluity, and her who gave all, even what she needed to support her life.

Well, how much shall a Christian give God in the offering? He shall give all he owns and all he is. But does this mean that a Christian may not own anything? Must he literally always do as this widow did? Give away too what he needs for the support of body and life? No, that is not what God teaches. But he must plan as a servant, not as an owner. He must manage and use everything that he owns as one who is responsible to God, to the advantage of himself and others, and to the glory of the Lord.

He who is manager is not owner.

A Christian is appointed to be a steward of the manifold grace of God, and he must give account of all that he receives from God. He must answer for both natural talents and gifts of grace, earthly property, and his position in society. Happy is he who gives the Lord all.

How can I, Lord, withhold life's brightest hour
From Thee; or gathered gold, or any power?
Why should I keep one precious thing from Thee,
When Thou hast given Thine own dear self for me?

Anniversaries and Birthdays

AUGUST 16

Thou hast not defrauded us, nor oppressed us, neither hast thou taken aught of any man's hand. **I Sam. 12:4**

IT made old Samuel feel bad to step down from the place of leadership, but in a patient and manly spirit he yields to the popular demand. But before he leaves the steersman's bridge he calls all Israel together and asks them whether he at any time has misused his power. Then the people answer: "Thou hast not defrauded us, nor oppressed us, neither hast thou taken aught of any man's hand." Then Samuel said: "Jehovah is witness against you, and His anointed is witness this day, that ye have not found aught in my hand. And they said, He is witness." Happy and contented, Samuel installs another man in his place, and willingly steps aside for him.

Samuel was a great man!

Many of those who have the talent to govern, misuse their power, and when they get too old to hold the rudder, they unwillingly yield to younger men better qualified to fill the place. Samuel had the courage to stand in battle, and the understanding to resign his office at the right time. He did not resist, neither did he sulk when the people demanded a different governor; he anointed his successor and prayed for God's blessing on him and the people.

May every servant of the Lord, not least those in high places, resemble Samuel both when he was in the work and when he withdrew. Then the day's work closes with peace and blessing also for coming generations, and old people teach young people wisdom.

Give me a calm, a thankful heart,
From every murmur free;
The blessings of Thy grace impart,
And let me live to Thee.

Anniversaries and Birthdays

AUGUST 17

She said, "Let me glean, I pray you, and gather after the reapers among the sheaves." So she came, and hath continued even from the morning until now. Ruth 2:7

THE story of Ruth has much to teach us, but here we shall be reminded of just two traits in this excellent woman.

One great thing about her was that she forgot herself and was faithful to her old mother-in-law. Out of love for her she left her own country and made her home among strangers. In this case she, who was a heathen, showed a larger heart and a finer disposition than many who bear the name Christian. It is so easy for youth to despise old people; yea, some even forget their own parents! Let us learn from Ruth to be true and helpful toward old people, especially toward those of our own flesh. Those who forget this, turn their backs on the promise that God has given in the Fourth Commandment.

The other great virtue that she shows is that she steadily and patiently picks up the heads of grain from what the others have let fall, and in this way supports herself and her old mother-in-law. From sunrise till late evening her back is bent and her hand is reaching out for the heads of grain, one by one, and no rest. That kind of working-life does not suit our generation. If we do not get a full hand all at once we refuse to work, and in addition demand that others shall help us. Let us all leave that devious way and together with Ruth do all we can to support ourselves. Then the words that Boaz spoke to Ruth will also become words from God to us:

"Jehovah recompense thy work."

May each child of Thine be willing,
Willing both in hand and heart,
All the law of love fulfilling,
Comfort ever to impart,
Ever bringing offerings meet,
Suppliant at Thy mercy-seat.

Anniversaries and Birthdays

____

____

____

AUGUST 18

"Fear not; for they that are with us are more than they that are with them." . . . And Jehovah opened the eyes of the young man; and he saw: and, behold, the mountain was full of horses and chariots of fire round about Elisha. II Kings 6:16-17

JUST as Satan sends out his spiritual hosts to tempt people to sin and to fall, so God has His serving spirits here below to help His children. We cannot see these friends and faithful servants, but God has told us that they are here, and the experiences of the Christian life confirm that.

How blest to be reminded that no matter how lonely we are on our way through the world, we are still never alone; and though many enemies plot against us, yet the Lord sends help that is greater than the danger.

Today, too, a disciple of Jesus can join the prophet in saying: "They that are with us are more than they that are with them." Even if we do not see these helpers, it is still God's intention that we believe that they are here, and that we in glad confidence rely on the help that He sends us. How calm and peaceful we may be in meeting dangers and difficult situations when we in child-like faith in these promises, too, put our confidence in His help. It is well that these servants of the Lord go about helping us and fighting our battles even though we forget them. But if we forget His protecting grace we neglect the thanks we owe God, and we lose the joy our hearts should feel.

People of God, remind yourselves of this again and again! It is so helpful to have this comfort, secured in the heart by a living faith.

The world is full of dangers for all of us, but heaven has an eye for a soldier of Jesus Christ. When like the servant we shout to Elisha, "How shall we do?" the answer comes, "Fear not; for they that are with us are more than they that are with them."

All little ones, awake, asleep,
And every child of Thine, they keep;
O'er all Thy kingdom, far and near,
They give their kind and loving care.

Anniversaries and Birthdays

AUGUST 19

And be not fashioned according to this world: but be ye transformed by the renewing of your mind. Rom. 12:2

THE way of the world is to live according to one's own wishes. What a person is most interested in, what one most desires, and what is to one's own advantage, that is what a person will do whether it is sinful and vulgar, or good and fine. A person who is not born of God can do no better.

But a Christian can do better because he has become a new creature. A worldly person is self-centered, but a Christian has the love of Christ as the starting-point for all that he does. We must never inquire about our own advantage, honor, or praise, but about the will of God. As New Testament priests bringing the sacrifice, we are to present ourselves as a living and holy sacrifice to God.

If we are to have strength to be steadfast in this sacrificial service, we must continually be renewed in our mind. We should not hide away from our fellow men but we should live otherwise than they. To that end we are called and saved, and for that reason we are in this world. But here it is so easy to be fashioned according to this world, and then our whole life becomes a failure.

Happy the Christian who is on his guard here, and who is victorious. He will help others onto the right way, and will live to the glory of God. Let us pray God to help us to live thus every day.

One there is for whom I'm living,
Whom I love most tenderly;
Jesus, unto whom I'm giving,
What in love He gave to me:
Jesus' blood hides all my guilt;
Lead me, Lord, then as Thou wilt.

Anniversaries and Birthdays

___

___

___

AUGUST 20

I thank God through Jesus Christ our Lord. So then I of myself with the mind, indeed, serve the law of God; but with the flesh the law of sin. Rom. 7:25

WHEN a Christian is not sinless, then what is he? He is a saved sinner who still has sin. But if that is so, then we must also reckon that the sin in us is not only a dream, or something half evil and half good, but a living power, just as vile in us as in Satan. Just as impossible as it is for God and the life we received from Him to be changed in essence, so impossible is it for sin too to be changed in essence.

We Christians struggle much more than we ourselves realize trying to make evil good. But that is something that we never can accomplish. Paul had learned this, and he had given it up entirely. He let evil be evil, and reckoned with it as being only evil. He did not try to hide from himself the evil that was in him, and he did not try to avoid the responsibility for his own sin. His deep lament, "Wretched man that I am!" tells us that he feels the responsibility for sin; but the way he sees it, he serves the law of God with the mind, but the law of sin with the flesh. In me, he says, there are two distinct lives that never can be united: each serves its own lord. "But if what I would not, that I do, it is no more I that do it, but sin which dwelleth in me." Then he thanks God for the new life he has received in Jesus Christ, and serves God in newness of the spirit.

Those are the experiences of a Christian here in the kingdom of grace. Happy the person whose citizenship is there, and who knows the way to the free city.

Now my conscience is at peace;
From the law I stand acquitted;
Christ hath purchased my release,
And my every sin remitted.
Naught remains my soul to grieve:
Jesus sinners doth receive.

Anniversaries and Birthdays

AUGUST 21

But thou, when thou prayest, enter into thine inner chamber, and having shut thy door, pray to thy Father who is in secret, and thy Father who seeth in secret shall recompense thee. Matt. 6:6

ALL true prayer is born and nurtured in the heart, and from the heart it ascends to God. If our words are the expression of a praying heart, then our mouth prays aright, too. But often the Christian does not know how to pray as he needs to: "But the Spirit Himself maketh intercession for us with groanings which cannot be uttered; and He that searcheth the hearts knoweth what is the mind of the Spirit, because He maketh intercession for the saints according to the will of God."

There are times when the Christian's burden feels so heavy that he is unable to use words, even though he sees what he needs. We have an example in the Word about Hannah in I Sam. 1:12-13: "And it came to pass, as she continued praying before Jehovah, that Eli marked her mouth. Now Hannah, she spoke in her heart; only her lips moved, but her voice was not heard." That day Hannah went home with her prayer answered.

That which characterizes a true Christian life is a praying spirit. When the heart needs nothing, and the spirit does not pray, but only the mouth moves, then a Pharisee is praying. A praying spirit protects the Christian against a worldly spirit: it is like the walls round about Jerusalem. A praying spirit carries us up toward God and helps us to stay there; it is like wings for a Christian; without it we sink toward the earth.

"Praying at all seasons in the Spirit."

God of all grace, we come to Thee
With broken, contrite hearts;
Give what Thine eye delights to see,
Truth in the inward parts.

Anniversaries and Birthdays

AUGUST 22

There is therefore now no condemnation to them that are in Christ Jesus. Rom. 8:1

THERE is no condemnation—that is the gospel that Satan preaches to people, and that he gets many to believe, live on, and die on. But if any one of these that he has deceived wakes up, then the spirit of lying turns about and tells the condemned sinner that it is quite impossible for him to be saved. So long as one continues thoughtlessly to live in sin, then everything is all right, heaven is open, and God is gracious; but if one is in dead earnest about finding God, Satan makes everything look impossible.

That is the character of the spirit who has gone forth to deceive all the nations of the earth.

But there is no condemnation to them that are in Christ. Why not walk that way? Is that not simple and clear enough? Yes, but it is Christ that the worldly person does not want to hear about. You want to live in sin, and then go to heaven when you die. In Christ we are separated from sin in this world, and that is the stumbling block for all who want to live unto themselves, and be saved when they die.

To you who wish to be freed from sin and judgment here in this life, we say, "Open your heart to Christ, and abide in Him, and then you are saved." He is like the cave in a mountain into which the defenseless person can go and make his home. Though all the biggest cannons be fired at the mountain, you who are within are safe. The simple but certain solution for us all consists in being in Christ. You are secure and there is no condemnation for you if you can truly say: No matter what happens I cannot leave Him; I must be with Him in light and in darkness, when I believe and when I doubt, yea, also when all seems lost.

Just as I am and waiting not
To rid my soul of one dark blot,
To Thee, whose blood can cleanse each spot,
O Lamb of God, I come, I come.

Anniversaries and Birthdays

___

___

___

AUGUST 23

It is a good thing to give thanks unto Jehovah,
And to sing praises unto Thy name, O Most High. Psalm 92:1

GREAT things have happened to us that we may go to God and mourn our distresses, and also know that we are always welcome. He who inclines His ear to the poor and needy that cry to Him, He will also more than gladly make alive the spirit of him who is bowed down.

Nevertheless it may be too true that it is easier to complain than to give thanks. Many look upon life as one single pitch dark night, and fill their days with despondency and complaint for both themselves and others. Many Christians have also lost their way in this dark valley, and when once a person has sunk down into this black abyss, it is not an easy matter to get out again.

How dreary it is, and how it makes one feel impotent to meet people who seem to have learned nothing in life except to complain. Unspeakably more happy is the person who sees the goodness of God through life's workday, and who in childlike trust gives thanks to God the Father for all things. Evil does not get control of the person who has learned to give thanks. His heart is open to receive the love and grace of God. He who always complains, easily becomes a victim of doubt, but the thankful person mounts up on the heights of grace, and from that vantage point he sees that the Lord does all things well. Complaining makes a Christian weak, but the thankful person becomes strong in the Lord.

And as my life is onward gliding,
With each fresh scene anew I mark
How Thou art holding me and guiding,
Where all seems troubled, strange, and dark:
When cares oppress and hopes depart,
Thy light hath never failed my heart.

Anniversaries and Birthdays

AUGUST 24

Unto me, who am less than the least of all saints, was this grace given, to preach unto the Gentiles the unsearchable riches of Christ.
Eph. 3:8

SOMETHING is wrong when our work in the kingdom of God becomes a burdensome duty. But it is still worse when we work in the kingdom of God to make our living, or to win honor and power. The sad complaint that Paul makes against some of the Christians in his time, "They all seek their own," fits, alas, on many in our day, too. When our life's work passes through the fires of judgment, it is probable that much of what we considered genuine will burn like straw.

But how these holy words impress us: "Unto me, who am less than the least of all saints, was this grace given, to preach unto the Gentiles the unsearchable riches of Christ." The man who says this about himself was the greatest and best worker God has ever had. He did not regard himself worthy of a single word, when only he could fulfill the ministry which he had received from the Lord.

To be the least of the Lord's servants in our own eyes, and to consider it grace to be privileged to bring tidings of Him to others—that is the mind we should have in all our work. And if we could see, as we ought, what we ourselves are, and what God has made us, then we would be small in our own eyes, and God's grace unspeakably great. So let us pray God for such sight and such a mind.

At Thy Word in faith I press
Onward through this vale of sadness;
By Thy grace I shall possess
Victor-palms in heavenly gladness;
To my latest hour, O Lord,
I will trust Thee at Thy Word.

Anniversaries and Birthdays

____

____

____

____

____

AUGUST 25

Stand therefore, having girded your loins with truth, and having put on the breastplate of righteousness. Eph. 6:14

THE clothes that a sinner receives by faith in Jesus must be fastened about the loins with truth. If a Christian loses that belt, he also loses the robe of righteousness that he got from Christ. Falsity in heart, life, and word toward God or men is one of the great dangers that always lurks about us. Many have fallen by the way, and have had to stand naked before God, because they lost the belt of trutn.

To sin is not the same as to live in falsehood. David sinned, Peter sinned, but they did not lose the belt. They confessed their sins before God, and saved the belt of truth. Saul sinned, Judas sinned, Ananias and Sapphira sinned, but they threw the belt away and were lost. Grace saves and cleanses from all sin, but it cannot dwell in a heart that lives in falsehood. Just as certain as it is that we may draw near with boldness unto the throne of grace, just so certain is it also that we must come with a true heart.

He who hides his iniquities does not prosper, but he who confesses them finds mercy.

He who is the father of lies walks about desiring to steal the precious belt away from us. Blessed is he who watches, fights, and makes sacrifices in order to live in the truth. He shall never lose either the belt of truth or the breastplate of righteousness.

> Let all your lamps be bright,
> And trim the golden flame;
> Gird up your loins, as in His sight,
> For awful is His name.

Anniversaries and Birthdays

AUGUST 26

And of which of you that is a father shall his son ask a loaf, and he give him a stone? or a fish, and he for a fish give him a serpent? Or if he shall ask an egg, will he give him a scorpion? If ye then, being evil, know how to give good gifts unto your children, how much more shall your heavenly Father give the Holy Spirit to them that ask Him? Luke 11:11-13

THE father who would give his hungry and praying child a stone or a serpent instead of bread and fish would resemble a devil more than a man. Nor can Jesus conceive of such a father. On the other hand, He starts from the proposition that we who are evil will give our children good gifts. Then He leads us from the evil people who give, up to Him who is good, with these comforting words: "How much more shall your heavenly Father give the Holy Spirit to them that ask Him?"

Let us take note of these words of Jesus.

The Holy Spirit is the greatest gift we can ask for. He who possesses this beautiful treasure has been given the key to everything else that he needs. God's Spirit guides us into all the truth, reveals Christ to the heart, gives us light on our way through the world, is the seal of our sonship, and the earnest of our inheritance. He is the oil that keeps us shining and living at the midnight hour when the Bridegroom comes.

Let prayer for the Holy Spirit be our first and last prayer day by day for ourselves, for all the people of God, for all men. Jesus has promised us that the Father will hear that prayer.

Come, Light serene, and still,
Our inmost bosoms fill;
Dwell in each breast;
We know no dawn but Thine:
Send forth Thy beams divine,
On our dark souls to shine,
And make us blest!

Anniversaries and Birthdays

____

____

____

____

AUGUST 27

He that overcometh, I will make him a pillar in the temple of my God, and he shall go out thence no more. Rev. 3:12

PILLARS are a supporting power. They hold a house together and make it strong. They are also used to ornament an edifice.

In our Word today Jesus says that He will make of him that overcometh a pillar in the temple of His God. This surely is not only a promise that he that overcomes shall have a place of honor in the temple at home with God: but here and now in the temple of God on earth the conquering Christian shall be permitted to be a pillar. The people of God are God's temple. "Know ye not that ye are a temple of God, and that the Spirit of God dwelleth in you?"

And if there is any place that the temple of God needs supporting power it is here on earth. If God's building among us is to stand and be intact, it must be upheld by victorious Christians.

And God be praised, we have them among us yet. From year to year, for many of them through their whole lives, they are supporters in prayer and responsibility and work, though often they get only hostile criticism and ingratitude as rewards. In some places many friends carry the load together, in other places just a few, and occasionally only one.

Let us appreciate the pillars God has given us, and let us pray that the kingdom of God in our midst may always have such Christians. Then those who follow us will also succeed.

And you who are a bearer now, hear what God says to you, and rejoice at what awaits you at home with God!

To Thee, Thou bleeding Lamb, I all things owe;
All that I have and am, and all I know.
All that I have is now no longer mine,
And I am not mine own;—Lord, I am Thine.

Anniversaries and Birthdays

AUGUST 28

Look therefore carefully how ye walk, not as unwise, but as wise; redeeming the time, because the days are evil. Eph. 5:15-16

OUR chief joy must always be the great grace that we have received the forgiveness of sins and sonship with God.

But even though all this is of God so that he that glories must glory in the Lord, we must nevertheless not forget that this glorious inheritance has also placed responsibility on us. There is no nobility and honor in the kingdom of God either, without responsibility. If we rejoice in hope of the glory of God, and acknowledge that we are heirs of eternal life, we must also walk as children of light. It is an honor to father and mother that children are good: it is an honor to God that His children live as becomes saints. Jesus said to His disciples: "Herein is My Father glorified, that ye bear much fruit."

Truly God is always glorified in Himself: in that sense no one can make Him greater than He is. But a Christian can make Him small or great here on earth by his manner of life.

What should be more important for us Christians than to walk carefully, so that we with our lives can thank and honor Him who gave us the right to be His children? "For God called us not for uncleanness, but in sanctification." The days are evil, that is true, but the grace of God is also great, and He is great enough so that we today can honor God with our life.

I need Thee every hour;
Teach me Thy will;
And Thy rich promises
In me fulfill.
I need Thee, oh! I need Thee;
Every hour I need Thee;
O bless me now, my Savior!
I come to Thee.

Anniversaries and Birthdays

____

____

____

____

AUGUST 29

Cast not away therefore your boldness, which hath great recompense of reward. **Heb. 10:35**

THERE are especially two places in life where it is easy for many Christians to lose their boldness. Those are the home and the place where one works.

Not least is it difficult for father and mother. It is not always easy to be pastor in one's own house where all know him through and through. Then comes the temptation: "Just lay the Bible and prayer book away: the others are tired of all this long ago. They see your many faults, and they expected you to be quite different from what you are. Do not speak about your Savior in your home or among neighbors. but keep up the good fight as well as you can by yourself."

Mother works hard with her flock of children. She is worn, tired, and nervous, and therefore perhaps she does not always act just as she should. Then her boldness is inclined to fail her. It is often difficult to bend the knee at her child's bed.

But, Christian, you must not lose your boldness. God has promised to reward them who do not cast their boldness away. In the first place, boldness is a protection for ourselves. It awakens us to walk carefully, and it invites us to prav God for help. In the next place we have the promise of the Word that it shall be a blessing to others too. When your child gets out into the big, cold world, if not before, it will remember what father and mother testified about God. That has been the case with many, and shall be with your children too. He who promised to recompense them that retain their boldness, He will keep His Word.

No one can expect to win and own anything good in this world without conflict.

> If in this darksome wild I stray,
> Be Thou my light, be Thou my way;
> No foes, no violence I fear
> No harm while Thou, my God, art near.

Anniversaries and Birthdays

____

____

____

AUGUST 30

And my God shall supply every need of yours according to His riches in glory in Christ Jesus. Phil. 4:19

IF there is anything that we know, it is that we have within us a deep longing for something that we have an inkling of but do not possess, something that invites and draws, and that we must get.

From our earliest years this longing filled thoughts and mind, and so we set out to find the treasure that we believed would give us what we longed for. We resemble the little boy down in the valley who thinks that he would reach heaven if he only got to the top of the mountain. Most people think they will have a joyous life if only they can get higher up and farther ahead. Well, what happens? Oh, what happened to the little boy happens to us: when one fine day he stood on the top of the mountain, heaven seemed farther away than ever. This world and all that it has to offer can never satisfy our longing. That is impossible.

But then the Word of God comes and tells us that here is a way to the goal. "God shall supply every need of yours." Every need! He is that rich. A mighty thought! Consider it! Try to believe! God shall supply all our need in Christ. "My soul waiteth in silence for God only," said he who had walked the path from being a shepherd boy to sitting on the king's throne. Only with God!

He who accepts Christ, finds the treasure that satisfies all our longing.

> In Thee my trust abideth,
> On Thee my hope relies,
> O Thou whose love provideth
> For all beneath the skies;
> O Thou whose mercy found me,
> From bondage set me free,
> And then for ever bound me
> With threefold cords to Thee.

Anniversaries and Birthdays

AUGUST 31

And if also a man contend in the games, he is not crowned, except he have contended lawfully. II Tim. 2:5

IT is one thing to be a soldier, but it is quite another matter to contend lawfully. Also on the skaters' course and in the boxers' ring there are rules that must be observed by the one who hopes to win the prize. To be the first man across the finish line, or to knock your opponent down, does not always mean that you have won. He who cheats or fouls is ruled out no matter how capable he is.

We Christians would be a great deal ahead if we always had in mind that no one is stricter in this matter than Christ. If our fight is to be good, and if we are to have any hope of winning the crown in the fight, we must be soldiers of Jesus Christ. It must be His cause, His name and glory that we are fighting for. If it is our person, our cause, and our honor that we are contending for, the General will not count on us. The Judge who sees the hearts strikes the names of all self-seeking soldiers. None of them wins the crown, no matter how spiritual and Christian the conflict appears to be.

May this truth stand before us in words of living fire in all our conflict! We will not obtain the crown unless we contend lawfully.

A characteristic of a good soldier in the kingdom of God is that he can endure evil. He who contends for himself and his own under the sign of the cross will hardly be able to endure evil; but he who contends for Christ hears a comforting voice in his soul as he receives the hardest blows: "He who sent me into this fight will heal the sores, and He will find them that struck me."

O watch, and fight, and pray!
The battle ne'er give o'er;
Renew it boldly every day,
And help divine implore.

Anniversaries and Birthdays

SEPTEMBER 1

The Jews therefore strove one with another, saying, "How can this Man give us His flesh to eat?" . . . And Jesus healed all manner of disease and all manner of sickness. John 6:52 and Matt. 9:35

WHAT intellectualists are angered at, life cries out for. The wise of this world scoff at Jesus, they hate Him, and seek to kill Him. But He has no sooner come away from these parched souls, than life's naked speech cries out to Him for help. And where the Savior helps the helpless, there arguments and imaginary wisdom drown in facts.

Although it is quite impossible to understand Jesus with our reason, He nevertheless fits perfectly where need calls for help. As tangled as everything is for us, just so easily does He solve all puzzles.

It has often happened that the Spirit of God has been able to lead to Christ someone who has been laid on a sick bed. When the child lay in the coffin, mother lay at the cross. When godlessness and sin increased in home and neighborhood, when young people scoffed at the prayers of father and mother, it has happened that a great blessing came wrapped in what we call misfortune. When father and neighbor along our extended coast found their graves in the ocean, it was not as a punishment for sin, but in order that this sad occurrence might be the voice of God to the unconverted in neighborhood and parish. In the senior class in God's school the fellowship of the sufferings and the power of the resurrection of Jesus are united into one blessed mystery for salvation for us and for others.

So, let the thorns prick us for a little while: the fragrance of the rose will endure eternally.

Why should I shrink from pain and woe,
Or feel at death dismay?
I've Canaan's goodly land in view,
And realms of endless day.

Anniversaries and Birthdays

____

____

____

____

SEPTEMBER 2

But God said unto him, "Thou foolish one, this night is thy soul required of thee; and the things which thou hast prepared, whose shall they be?" **Luke 12:20**

THE story of the rich farmer is not put into the Bible for the praise of poverty and laziness, and is not intended to make us careless about our property in this world. If we had shown less kindness to laziness, our community life and folk-happiness would now be on a higher plane. It is un-Christian to consider work an evil that must be endured. Christ Himself was a laboring man.

What sin then did the rich farmer commit?

He had nothing else to live on and to die on than buildings full of food. To eat and to drink were the only riches and joy he possessed. Jesus says that is folly.

Most people live and die in that same folly in our day, too. Their riches and happiness reach only to business, bank books, food, and pleasures. Outside of that they have nothing. As soon as death's cold hand touches their lives, everything is eternal poverty. Think of it! To be a man and to have nothing but this to live on and to die on! That *is* folly.

But He who became poor for our sakes, He who is Heir to all the riches of heaven, He can make us eternally rich. May we all be so wise that we seek first the kingdom of God. The danger of falling in love with this world and of forgetting to be rich toward God threatens all, also Christians. Be not highminded, but fear.

Thou hast no shore, fair ocean!
Thou hast no time, bright day!
Dear fountain of refreshment
To pilgrims far away!
Upon the Rock of Ages
They raise thy holy tower;
Thine is the victor's laurel,
And thine the golden dower.

Anniversaries and Birthdays

SEPTEMBER 3

Send forth thy sharp sickle, and gather the clusters of the vine of the earth; for her grapes are fully ripe. Rev. 14:18

WE know that the people of God may look forward to a complete redemption from all evil; but Satan, sin, and death, yea, everything and everybody that belong to them are also moving toward their goal. As the angels shall gather all the saints of God into eternal life, so shall also the ungodly be gathered into eternal death.

The evil and the good will not always dwell side by side as they do now. There will come a time when the evil and the good shall be separated so that no one thereafter can pass over the boundary. When the angel has gathered the clusters of the vine of the earth, all those who love sin and unbelief and live therein, shall be thrown into the wine press of the wrath of God; and the only drink in the land into which the river of life does not flow, and where death always is king, is the dregs of this fruit of sin. Heaven will have gathered in everything that is of God into the kingdom where life and light dwell: Satan and all that belongs to him will be "cast out into outer darkness."

Time is no more. No clock brings tidings of approaching day, and no sound is heard that gives the slightest shadow of hope.

The way of life and the way of death are marked out thus for us, and there are no other ways.

"Behold, He cometh with the clouds; and every eye shall see Him." Happy he who then is a branch on the true vine; for him this harvest is life's eternal spring.

The dead in Christ shall first arise,
At the last trumpet's sounding.
Caught up to meet Him in the skies,
With joy their Lord surrounding;
No gloomy fears their souls dismay;
His presence sheds eternal day
On those prepared to meet Him.

Anniversaries and Birthdays

SEPTEMBER 4

"Come now, and let us reason together," saith Jehovah: "though your sins be as scarlet, they shall be as white as snow; though they be red like crimson, they shall be as wool." Isa. 1:18

ONE might consider it a foregone conclusion that we would lose if we men should meet God in court and conduct a suit against Him. Still God promises us that we shall win. Even if we come into court with sins as red as scarlet and crimson, we shall depart as clean and white as snow and wool.

How can that be?

It happens in this way that He who knew no sin was made to be sin on our behalf, so that we in Him may be made righteous before God. Wherefore he who goes to court in Jesus' name and stands there on His account, he is already declared not guilty in the supreme court. Thus occurs the great miracle that he who has no works to show forth, but believes on Him who justifies the ungodly, becomes righteous by his faith.

It is great for a criminal to receive grace, but he that is justified appears before God as though he had never sinned. That is the way a sinner is saved for Jesus' sake. Should not this be enough to attract every single sinner to God?

"For as through the one man's disobedience the many were made sinners, even so through the obedience of the one shall the many be made righteous" (Rom. 5:19).

Jesus, Thy blood and righteousness
My beauty are, my glorious dress;
Midst flaming worlds, in these arrayed,
With joy shall I lift up my head.

Anniversaries and Birthdays

SEPTEMBER 5

For we know that if the earthly house of our tabernacle be dissolved, we have a building from God, a house not made with hands, eternal, in the heavens. II Cor. 5:1

GOD'S Word compares our body to a house, a tabernacle, a tent which some day must be torn down. Thereby God has also told us that the inner, real man is entirely independent, and can exist though he has no earthly house to dwell in.

To be sure it is sad that so beautiful an edifice must be laid in the earth. But we have no reason to be discouraged, because God has provided for building a new house for us; and we may be assured that none of us will regret the change. Paul entertained no doubts in this matter, and this deep-laid conviction is the reason that he was always of good courage, yea, that he longed to be absent from the body that he might be at home with the Lord, clothed upon with his habitation that was from heaven.

The finest and deepest wish in a Christian is to get to heaven, to be at home with God, and to meet his Savior. God has promised heaven to His own, and every single Christian should live in that comfort with full confidence every single day. That gives hope a sure anchorage, and it gives to faith courage to endure in the conflict.

The Christianity that has not the comfort that one shall get to heaven to Jesus when one dies, is poor indeed. But for him who believes this, it is good to live, and still better to die.

In heaven above, in heaven above,
What glory deep and bright!
The splendor of the noonday sun
Grows pale before its light:
The mighty sun that ne'er goes down,
Around whose gleam clouds never frown,
Is God, the Lord of hosts.

Anniversaries and Birthdays

____

____

____

____

SEPTEMBER 6

And He said to the woman, "Thy faith hath saved thee; go in peace." Luke 7:50

TO hear the great words from Jesus' own mouth, "Thy sins are forgiven thee," is perhaps the greatest joy we can experience here on earth.

And it is this joy that many long for and seek and pray for, but do not attain. What was the reason that Jesus could speak these great words of release to this poor woman? What did she do, and what was there about her faith that could release her?

She defied all "if's" and "but's" that would shut her out from Jesus. Her great sins and miserable life, Simon's anger and everything else that was in the way—to these she paid no heed, but crowded forward and threw herself poor and sinful at Jesus' feet. There she lay, bathed in tears. That is what she did. It was then that Jesus said: "Thy faith hath saved thee; go in peace."

This seems clear and easy to understand when it has to do with this woman, but not when it concerns us. And yet it is simple for us, too. To all who break through all hindrances, go to Jesus, and lay themselves and their sins there, to all these Jesus speaks the same words that He spoke to the woman. You who have come to Jesus and are lying at His feet, hear what Jesus says to you: "Your sins are forgiven. Your faith has saved you." Do not believe on what you feel in your heart, but believe God's Word; then you are saved.

Here the Redeemer's welcome voice
  Spreads heavenly peace around;
And life and everlasting joys
  Attend the blissful sound.

Anniversaries and Birthdays

SEPTEMBER 7

I have fought the good fight, I have finished the course, I have kept the faith. II Tim. 4:7

PAUL stands at the end of life's journey. He has had a fatiguing workday, and many hard conflicts. Now the end of the fight is in sight as the day wanes. It is great to be privileged to stand at the end of life with such certainty, such calm and victorious power. That is like seeing the evening sun in the sea, and the sky above covered with light, golden clouds.

What Paul seems to be gladdest about is that he has kept his faith through life's struggles. This tells us that he was one of those who not only had to battle in faith, but also for his faith. All those who have been in this struggle know that that is the most difficult thing of all. When faith in God, in Christ, in heaven and the life after death, begins to fail, then everything becomes night, then one sees no way of escape. Many of the soldiers of Jesus Christ must enter such a night. Not even a trip into "the third heaven" gives us the right to be let off.

How wonderful to have gotten through this, too, safe and sound! How unspeakably great when our feet are unable to carry us any farther, and our eyes stare ahead into darkness at midday, to have a faith that sees land, home, rest, and the eternal day! To have a faith that can make one rejoice that he soon is at his journey's end. With such a faith it is good to be allowed to quit the fight. Then autumn is more beautiful than spring, and evening is more full of life than the most beautiful morning.

That martyr first, whose eagle eye
Could pierce beyond the grave;
Who saw his Master in the sky;
And called on Him to save;
Like Him, with pardon on his tongue;
In midst of mortal pain,
He prayed for them that did the wrong:
Who follows in His train?

Anniversaries and Birthdays

SEPTEMBER 8

And one of the elders saith unto me, "Weep not; behold, the Lion that is of the tribe of Judah, the Root of David, hath overcome to open the book and the seven seals thereof." **Rev. 5:5**

OUR world is full of suffering, longing, and tears. One generation gives this dreary heritage to the next, and it looks as though everything is going to be as it was.

But in the midst of this dark night a voice shouts to us from another world that better times are soon coming. He who came to us as a poor Child, and made us rich by His poverty, and who returned home with all power in heaven and on earth, He asks us to quit weeping. What now is sealed in need and in night shall soon be released into day and life. The deep groans and painful travail of creation shall disappear for always when the children of God have reached the goal of their faith.

He on whom the star shone on Christmas night, and for whom the heavenly spirits sang their hymn of praise on the fields of Bethlehem; He who by suffering was perfected to be the Captain of our salvation, and who has the keys of death and of the kingdom of the dead, He shall soon come in power and glory, to wipe away the last tears with His own gentle Savior-hand. This comfort should be more than enough to get all the weeping children of God to smile through their tears.

With jasper glow thy bulwarks,
Thy streets with emeralds blaze;
The sardius and the topaz
Unite in thee their rays;
Thine ageless walls are bounded
With amethyst unpriced;
The saints build up thy fabric,
The corner-stone is Christ.

Anniversaries and Birthdays

____

____

____

____

____

SEPTEMBER 9

Put on the whole armor of God, that ye may be able to stand against the wiles of the devil. Eph. 6:11

GOD'S Word tells us very impressively that we must count with Satan as a real person, a fallen chieftain, who burns in anger because he lost the battle against Christ, and who stops at nothing in order to destroy the people of God. He is the father of lies, and uses all possible means to cause God's people to fall. He can meet us as a roaring lion, as an oily serpent, and as an angel of God.

All you who think that Satan is only an idea that simple-minded Christians have conceived, you just choose Christ and the cross as the only ground of your salvation, then follow in the footsteps of Jesus, and you will learn from experience that Satan exists.

No one can meet God in the robe of his own righteousness, and neither can anyone dressed in his own clothes be victorious over Satan. We must wear the armor of God. If at some point in our lives we rely on ourselves, we will be defeated. Wherefore many a time we had the distasteful experience that when we thought we were at our best, we got the worst wounds.

Satan dares not touch Christ and the cross, and therefore he tries to get us away from them. At the cross we receive the white robe of righteousness in which we can meet God, and there we also get the strong steel breastplate that no dart of Satan can penetrate.

Thy love, O God, embraces all,
And Jesus' merits cover
The guilt of all, both great and small,
The world of sinners over.
Thy Spirit doth Thy light afford
To all who will receive it,
And from Thy knowledge bars Thy Word
No soul who will believe it.

Anniversaries and Birthdays

SEPTEMBER 10

He brought him to Jesus. John 1:42

A CHARACTERISTIC of all genuine Christian life is a strong desire that others too may be saved. When a Christian succeeds in bringing others to Christ he experiences one of his highest and purest joys.

But that is also our grief when our success is small. It should be our comfort that God looks at this otherwise than we do. Therefore it may happen that he who feels the burden and the sorrows most, some day gets to see what he never could have believed. It is written, "They that sow in tears shall reap in joy." They that sow in tears shall reap!

The main point is that we have enough of the Spirit of Jesus Christ so that we draw worldly people by our life. Our words will never reach men's souls if God's love is not poured out in our hearts. First we must be what we say we are. We must prove by our life that we possess Him whom we want others to give their lives to. That always has the strongest drawing power on those who are on the outside.

Bold words without the warmth of love in the heart may wound, but cannot heal; may terrify, but do not attract. A mild, humble, and trusting presence is like the spring sun and like rain on dry ground. He who has this disposition will not forget to speak a kind word at the right time, and that will also draw others to Him whom you yourself have found.

"In due season we shall reap, if we faint not."

Shall we, whose souls are lighted
With wisdom from on high,
Shall we to men benighted
The lamp of life deny?
Salvation! O salvation!
The joyful sound proclaim,
Till earth's remotest nation
Has learned Messiah's name.

Anniversaries and Birthdays

SEPTEMBER 11

O our God, wilt Thou not judge them? for we have no might against this great company that cometh against us; neither know we what to do: but our eyes are upon Thee. II Chron. 20:12

WHEN Jehoshaphat stood before God helpless, not knowing what to do, and acknowledged that he in no way was able to overcome the enemy, God gave him victory. Also in our day the art of being victorious over evil is found in this same: to be conscious that you are entirely helpless, and then in the midst of your helplessness to attack the enemy in faith in God.

When Saul was small in his own eyes he never turned his back to an enemy; but when he thought highly of himself he suffered defeat. When David counted the people and was developing confidence in his own might, he was at the point of falling. And when Peter relied on himself, he immediately lay beaten in sin and shame.

If a Christian feels strong in his own power, he is always on the road to defeat. If we place the slightest confidence in our will, our character, our experience, or our Christianity in the battle against sin, we shall leave the conflict wounded and bleeding. But to feel your own helplessness and then throw yourself into the arms of grace, that is the way to victory. Then the Lord says to us as He did to Jehoshaphat: "The battle is not yours, but God's."

Nothing in my hand I bring;
Simply to Thy cross I cling;
Naked, come to Thee for dress:
Helpless, look to Thee for grace;
Foul, I to the fountain fly:
Wash me, Savior, or I die!

Anniversaries and Birthdays

SEPTEMBER 12

For Jehovah's portion is His people;
Jacob is the lot of His inheritance.
He found him in a desert land,
And in the waste howling wilderness;
He compassed him about, He cared for him,
He kept him as the apple of His eye. **Deut. 32:9-10**

THE Lord has a special love for His people. He purchased us with His blood, He found us on the waste plains where we were wandering without hope and without God in the world; and He carried us into the kingdom of His grace more gently than a mother carries the child that has been saved from death. As the eyelid covers the eye and guards it against danger, so God hides His own in His heart.

God's people are His children, His honor and praise. On the day of Christ He will show Himself glorious in all His saints, and wonderful in all believers. That will be a great day, not only for God but also for His people. The greatest thing possible outside of God is to be a saved man. Everything else is created by God, but a Christian is born of God. As the child is a part of the parents, so a regenerate person is a part of God.

The Lord's people are His inheritance. As the eagle circles over her young, so He spreads abroad His beam-feathers and bears us on His pinions. He who sits on these wings is carried toward heaven. They are strong enough to carry us all.

Blessed assurance, Jesus is mine!
O what a foretaste of glory divine!
Heir of salvation, purchase of God,
Born of His Spirit, washed in His blood.

Anniversaries and Birthdays

SEPTEMBER 13

I will arise and go to my father, and will say unto him, Father, I have sinned against heaven, and in thy sight. Luke 15:18

MANY of those who went away from God, see that they have done wrong, and they long to come home again. But that looks quite impossible. Sin, Satan, and the world have bound both soul and body, and the mind is drawn downward more and more.

If these words should meet you as you sit in this prison I should like to give you this advice: Do as the lost son did. He acknowledged to himself that he had sinned, and he decided to go home to his father and confess his sin. In this way he was saved. And this is the way home to God today, too. He who goes to the Savior with an honest heart and confesses his iniquities, he will be saved, how great a sinner soever he may be. But he who does not do that can never be saved.

Come home, come home, come to your Savior's bosom!
He waits so longingly, and calls by name!

"Him that cometh to me I will in no wise cast out!"

For us Christians too this is the narrow way. To see that you are a sinner, and to acknowledge that sin to God, that is to die daily. We so often try to conceal from ourselves and from Him what we at bottom are, and thus we depart from grace. To acknowledge one's sin and not depart from grace, that is the way for a Christian clear up to life's late evening.

With Thy flock I long to be,
With the flock to whom 'tis given
Safe to feed, and, praising Thee,
Roam the happy plains of heaven:
Free from fear of sinful stain,
They can never stray again.

Anniversaries and Birthdays

____

____

____

____

SEPTEMBER 14

Wherefore also He is able to save completely them that draw near unto God through Him, seeing He ever liveth to make intercession for them. Heb. 7:25

IT is through Jesus Christ that a sinner can appear before God, because in Him we are looked upon as though we had never sinned. But just as surely as we can go into the holy place and receive mercy and grace because of the atonement of Jesus, just so surely does Jesus appear before God and make intercession for us. And the Word here says that this intercession contains our complete salvation.

Not that there is anything lacking in Christ's work of atonement, but His intercession helps us to be victorious in our struggle to reach the goal of our faith. He who knows us through and through and on that account understands best what we need, He always prays the right prayer for us. And He who can show the emblem of victory that He won in the fight, He offers the prayer that is always answered. And that prayer is for us.

It is comforting to know that Jesus ever lives to make intercession for us. You who often are fearful and think that your prayer is weak and withered, listen! Take a firm grip on this comfort that the Savior prays for you, that He is praying for you today. How securely and confidingly we then can go out to our conflict and our work, in the full assurance that what happens to us today, too, is an answer from our heavenly Father to the prayers of Jesus for us.

He is faithful that promised, He will do it.

He ever lives above,
  For me to intercede;
His all redeeming love,
  His precious blood to plead;
His blood atoned for all our race,
  And sprinkles now the throne of grace.

Anniversaries and Birthdays

SEPTEMBER 15

Fear thou not, for I am with thee: be not dismayed, for I am thy God; I will strengthen thee; yea, I will help thee; yea, I will uphold thee with the right hand of My righteousness. Isa. 41:10

WHEN God sees any of His own feeling discouraged, helpless, afraid, and with a poor opinion of himself, He always comes like a mild mother to her sick child. Every tear that He sees, and every sigh that He hears from His own sets His heart aflame with a love that is stronger than anyone can understand.

"Jehovah hath comforted His people, and will have compassion upon His afflicted." "O thou afflicted, tossed with tempest, and not comforted, behold, I will set thy stones in fair colors, and lay thy foundations with sapphires." "As one whom his mother comforteth, so will I comfort you: and ye shall be comforted in Jerusalem." These are just a few words of the many from Him who loves His people. Those who have counted, tell us that the words, "Fear not!" are found 365 times in the Bible. Perhaps God also in that way wants to tell us that He will comfort His own every day.

What is important for us is to get to see this, so that we with full confidence open our hearts to God's love, and trust in Him alone. When God is for us, who can be against us? He who is kept in grace by the righteous hand of God will never be lost.

How blessed is the little flock,
Whom Jesus calls His own!
He is their Savior and their rock,
They trust in Him alone;
They walk by faith and hope and love,
But they shall dwell with Him above,
When hope and faith shall pass away,
And love shall last for aye.

Anniversaries and Birthdays

SEPTEMBER 16

If there be with thee a poor man, one of thy brethren, within any of thy gates in the land which Jehovah thy God giveth thee, thou shalt not harden thy heart, nor shut thy hand from thy poor brother. Deut. 15:7

MANY are poor because they will not work. They boast of living in poverty and laziness, and consider it quite a matter of course that others are to give them food. To such people God's Word says: "If any will not work, neither let him eat." If no help were given to laziness, our living conditions would be better than they are. They who sew pillows under the arms of the lazy, are not doing works of love, and are not walking the ways of God.

But among the poor there are also many who labor and toil hard but still are unable to earn enough for themselves and their dependents. If we close our hearts and hands against such people, we will fall under the heavy judgment of God.

Perhaps it is not right to say that it is God who lets such people dwell among us. But it says in God's Book:

"The rich and the poor meet together:
Jehovah is the maker of them all."

When the poor man knocks at our door and is helped, he is glad. And he who gives is not only glad but also blessed of God.

"He that hath pity upon the poor lendeth unto Jehovah,
And his good deed will He pay him again."

Let us try to believe this Word, too, and then we will have more success in lending to the Lord by helping the poor. He who is merciful toward us every day and gives us grace for grace, He desires that we help those who are in need.

Think of this, if you should meet a poor man today.

Praise to the Lord, who doth prosper thy work and defend thee;
Surely His goodness and mercy here daily attend thee;
Ponder anew
What the Almighty can do
If with His love He befriend thee.

Anniversaries and Birthdays

____

____

____

SEPTEMBER 17

But Jesus answereth again, and saith unto them, "Children, how hard is it for them that trust in riches to enter into the kingdom of God!" Mark 10:24

IT appears to be difficult for us men to unite Christianity and riches. Earthly goods often seem to have just as great power over us as sin. Many who are very uneasy, and who feel a burning need for eternal life, never attain to it because earthly riches have closed their hearts against the kingdom of God.

It is easy to see that the "gross" slave of sin is on the way to destruction for both time and eternity: but it is not so easy to see that a fine, worldly person is on the same way. The slave of mammon is often praised as a model, is honored and respected, not especially for what he is in himself, but because he is rich. Riches have a way of making us feel secure and proud, often without our knowing it, so that we consider ourselves better than those who have little property, if we have been so fortunate as to lay up riches. It is quite easy to understand that such a person cannot have very much room for Him who is mild and lowly in heart.

Wise was the man who prayed thus:

"Give me neither poverty nor riches;
Feed me with the food that is needful for me."

That is best for us in this world. May we all learn to have our heart free from what we own here on earth, and bound to Him who gives us the eternal riches.

As they offered gifts most rare
At that manger rude and bare,
So may we with holy joy,
Pure and free from sin's alloy,
All our costliest treasures bring,
Christ, to Thee, our heavenly King.

Anniversaries and Birthdays

SEPTEMBER 18

Whoso privily slandereth his neighbor, him will I destroy: Him that hath a high look and a proud heart will I not suffer.

Psalm 101:5

OF all the sins that have sent their roots deep down into our personality, envy, suspicion, and slander are among the worst. As Christians we can be victorious over much of our folly, but to master the desire to speak evil of others seems to be very difficult. Strong characters that are wise and firm may bridle their tongue; but their heart may be just as evil as that of those who have not sense enough to control their tongue and to conceal their passion for honor.

Some of the greatest difficulties that arise, also among Christians, have their source in suspicion and evil tongues. The heart is more deceitful than anything else, and the tongue is a fire, the world of iniquity; it defiles the whole body, and sets on fire the wheel of nature, and is set on fire by hell.

Something great has happened, also in the life of a Christian, when he no longer secretly speaks abusively of his neighbor, and when he thinks more highly of others than of himself. May we as Christians be given a deep desire for such a mind, and then in the strength of Jesus Christ be enabled to speak well of others. Then much of the evil among us would disappear.

Mightily strengthen my spirit within me,
That I may learn what Thy Spirit can do;
O take Thou captive each passion and win me,
Lead Thou and guide me my whole journey through!
All that I am and possess I surrender,
If Thou alone in my spirit mayst dwell,
Everything yield Thee, O Savior most tender,
Thou, only Thou, canst my sadness dispell.

Anniversaries and Birthdays

SEPTEMBER 19

Blessed are they that have been persecuted for righteousness' sake: for theirs is the kingdom of heaven. Matt. 5:10

WHEN a Christian is scoffed at and persecuted he must always ask himself whether the reason for this is that he is unfaithful and slovenly, or if this is visited on him because he lives godly and righteously. Alas, it often becomes evident that Christians think they are suffering for Christ's sake, while the truth is that they are suffering because of their own slovenly life.

It is humiliating to receive righteous blows from unrighteous hands, but it is glorious when lying, gossip, ridicule, and persecution are heaped on us because we live as true Christians. In such times the angels of God come down to us with such happiness as only heaven owns and can give. If we had less regard for men, if we flattered people less, if truth and righteousness in word and deed had more free course in our lives, we should surely get more both of persecution and of blessedness, of ridicule and of comfort. Because the spirit of our time so quickly grinds off the sharp point and the keen edge of our righteousness, it is also given us to pass through the world easily, without blows, but also without experiencing God's help.

It is a great thing to escape blows because of our poor Christianity, but it is greater to be scoffed at because we resemble our Savior. That Christian is indeed fortunate who has the will and the power to live so holily that he eggs on worldly people to opposition and scoffing. It is God's will that we live thus. Then the kingdom of heaven is ours.

Perfect truth will never waver,
Wars with evil day and night,
Changes not for fear or favor,
Only cares to win the fight.

Anniversaries and Birthdays

SEPTEMBER 20

And this is life eternal, that they should know Thee the only true God, and Him whom Thou didst send, even Jesus Christ.

John 17:3

THE word about eternal life is the morning star that sheds its light on the graves of earth. If this star should be extinguished, and if we were assured that death was the end of everything, human life would become a big, wild absurdity. That would not only extinguish our hope, but all suffering would increase, and strength to bear the burdens that life lays on us would dwindle away.

But now matters do not stand thus. We have hope of eternal life. That gives a person strength to bear all that life lays on him, even the heaviest burdens, and it makes of death an entrance to life.

You discouraged person, busy walking in circles around yourself, lift your eye to the land that Jesus has told us about, the land where the sun never sets, where graves are never found, and where all the suffering that earth gave you is exchanged for eternal peace! Try with your heart to grasp the thought that such a future awaits you, too, if you believe in Jesus. Then you have found the key to life's puzzle.

Use this key! Then it will be great to be a man. The fight that used to take the heart out of you, will then teach you the melody and the song about Him who is the way, the truth, and the life. He who stood on His grave on Easter morning gives life eternal to all who believe on His name.

My Jesus, as Thou wilt!
All shall be well for me:
Each changing future scene
I gladly trust with Thee.
Thus to my home above
I travel calmly on,
And sing, in life or death,
My Lord, Thy will be done!

Anniversaries and Birthdays

SEPTEMBER 21

For they all seek their own, not the things of Jesus Christ.

Phil. 2:21

THIS word contains a severe judgment on Christian people. The powers of temptation are always active to trap Christians in this snare, perhaps more now than ever before.

In the first place, this danger lurks around the people of God just as it always has done more or less: that one works in the kingdom of God only for his living, or to win honor and power. There would surely be many vacant pulpits both in churches and chapels, and many empty seats on boards and in societies, if all those were removed who now are there to make a living, or to win honor and power.

In addition to these, there are the special dangers that originate in the fact that Christians now are divided into so many parties and societies for the work. That makes the danger so much greater that I will be working for "me" and "mine."

When I want to do something to the advantage of myself and my group I can so easily harm what others are doing for God. No one who wants to be honest can close his eyes to the fact that the vile results of this evil have worked their way into our midst.

The Christian who is to be victorious here will find that there are many things to watch over, fight against, and give up. If the love of God does not become the ruling power in our hearts, we will go wrong. But happy is the Christian that wins, and who has the will of God as the goal for all that he is and does.

Give me a true regard,
A single, steady aim,
Unmoved by threatening or reward,
To Thee and Thy great name;
A jealous, just concern
For Thine immortal praise;
A pure desire that all may learn
And glorify Thy grace.

Anniversaries and Birthdays

SEPTEMBER 22

For we must all be made manifest before the judgment-seat of Christ; that each one may receive the things done in the body, according to what he hath done, whether it be good or bad.

II Cor. 5:10

A CHRISTIAN must not appear before the judgment-seat of Christ to be judged in the matter of his salvation. He has settled that at the throne of grace, and what is done there is valid in the court that is to judge the living and the dead. The same God that invited us to the throne of grace, and who received us when we came, sits on the judgment-seat: and the charter of liberty that He gave us at the throne of grace, is good also in the judgment.

But what then has a Christian to do at the judgment-seat? It is our life-work, our work in the kingdom of God, that is going into the fires of judgment. There is so much in many of us that is not done in God, so much hay and stubble that the fire will consume.

A worldly person, too, can do much good, but none of the deeds he does stands God's test. They all originated in human nature, and therefore their root is not genuine. The Christian's works may also start from that same root, and in that case the same judgment will be pronounced on them as on others. Only that which is of God, which is done in God, and which has its root in the love of Christ will stand in the judgment. On that day much will be different from what we thought.

Our comfort is that what Jesus has done will stand the test. If all else is consumed by fire, that will stand, and that is the ground of our salvation.

On my heart imprint Thine image,
Blessed Jesus, King of grace,
That life's riches, cares, and pleasures,
Have no power Thee to efface;
This the superscription be:
Jesus, crucified for me,
Is my life, my hope's foundation,
And my glory and salvation.

Anniversaries and Birthdays

SEPTEMBER 23

Then shall the kingdom of heaven be likened unto ten virgins, who took their lamps, and went forth to meet the bridegroom. And five of them were foolish, and five were wise. Matt. 25:1-2

THAT is the way things will look in the kingdom of God on earth at the end of our age. All will go to sleep, both the true Christians and those who have lost the life in God, and those who never had it. They go forth together to meet the bridegroom. And they all fall asleep. In that respect they were all so much alike that no one could tell the one from the other. Not until the light from the bridegroom shines toward them in the darkness of night do the five see that they are deceived.

What intense earnestness there is in these words of Jesus!

To walk together with true Christians, to consider yourself a Christian, and then at the last moment when any change is impossible, to hear that the Lord does not know you—that is awful to think about. Gradually as the day of Christ's return draws near, we are carried on toward such a time. The people of God will more and more mingle with the religious world, and they will tear down the boundary stones that God has set up between the converted and the unconverted. This mixing together will rob the people of God of power, and will bind them in impotence and sleep.

A Christian who is awake ought easily to be able to see how everything is working to carry us into this time.

In this dark night there is comfort and light in the fact that sleep need not be the same as death. If the Holy Spirit has not departed from us, we still have the earnest of our inheritance, and the Lord knows us as His own. God be praised for this comfort!

Be on your guard,
Keep watch and ward,
Beware of Satan's cunning!
Watch and pray and trust your Lord
Till ye see Him coming!

Anniversaries and Birthdays

SEPTEMBER 24

And bear ye also witness, because ye have been with Me from the beginning. John 15:27

TO witness is not the same as making a speech. Neither is it the same as saying some good words about Christ, or preaching the Word about the kingdom of God. When we are to bear witness we must not repeat talk we have heard from others. Nor must we say what we think and consider to be true. To witness is to tell what we have seen and experienced. "I have seen it and I bear witness of it," says John. Yes, that is the way to be a witness. See, and then bear witness.

If you are to be sure that you are an entirely credible witness you must above all things not say more than you have seen. That demand is made in an earthly court, and we ought always to remember that when we appear as witnesses of Jesus Christ. A Christian should also remember that his life must never contradict what he says about Christ. A holy life is the clearest and strongest witness that a Christian can offer about his Savior. To live, work, serve, direct, and be such wherever we are that people have reason to say, "There is a Christian," that is bearing witness about Christ.

May it be truly said of us that we live as Christians! Good children are an honor to father and mother. Bad children are their sorrow and dishonor.

God's honor on earth is good Christians.

'Tis all in vain that you profess
The doctrines of the Church, unless
You live according to your creed,
And show your faith by word and deed.
Observe the rule: To others do
As you would have them do to you.

Anniversaries and Birthdays

____

____

____

____

____

SEPTEMBER 25

Ye did not choose Me, but I chose you, and appointed you, that ye should go and bear fruit, and that your fruit should abide: that whatsoever ye shall ask of the Father in My name, He may give it you. **John 15:16**

THE deepest content in the Word about being chosen by God no man will understand until the consummation of all things.

But some of the words about being chosen are clear, and they contain great comfort for all the people of God. First and foremost one must mention the Word in Ephesians 1:4, that God chose us in Christ before the foundation of the world. Before there was life on earth our salvation was ordained by God in Christ. Think about this a little.

Before the world created was by Him who loves,
God had in Christ elected me to be His child.

It was to accomplish this election of salvation that Christ became man, and had to take the way to Calvary and through the grave. For the same reason we received the Holy Spirit to guide us into this salvation. We did not pray God for this: He gave us all of His free will. Neither did we first seek this salvation: it was Jesus who sought us first. And of all who permit themselves to be saved, God says: "Ye are an elect race.... Ye did not choose me, but I chose you." He who accepts this election of salvation in Christ, is elected to be God's child and a worker together with Jesus Christ in the kingdom of God.

May all God's people find some of the comfort which is contained in all this.

He sent His Son with power to save
From guilt and darkness, and the grave:
Wonders of grace to God belong;
Repeat His mercies in your song.

Anniversaries and Birthdays

____

____

____

____

SEPTEMBER 26

But Martha was cumbered about much serving. . . . Mary sat at the Lord's feet and heard His Word. Luke 10:39-40

MARTHA'S strength lay in working for Jesus, and Mary's in listening to His Word. Martha is absorbed in her work for Jesus: Mary is absorbed in Jesus Himself. Mary is laid hold on by Jesus and what He says: Martha is gripped by the work for Him. She had no thought for anything else.

If Jesus had not told us what He did about these two sisters, we should certainly have considered Martha the more God-fearing of the two. How wonderful! She thought of nothing except serving Jesus! Could you imagine a better Christian? But Jesus does not look at it that way. To come to rest in Him and His Word, to devote everything to Jesus Himself, that, He says, is greatest.

Many of us Christians of the present time resemble Martha more than Mary. Our time tends strongly in that direction because there is so much to do in the kingdom of God. As a consequence we get so busy working for Jesus, that we forget to live with Him. Then the result in our case is as in Martha's: we are worn, dissatisfied, and begin to complain. Little by little as we suffer inward defeats we become more and more exacting and critical toward other Christians, and consider that they accomplish altogether too little. It is wrong of a Christian to demand more from others than he demands of himself.

May none of us ever get so busy working for Jesus that we forget to live with Him.

> Nearer, O Jesus Christ, to Thee!
> Nearer whate'er the cost may be!
> Nearer tomorrow than today;
> Nearer, O Lord, through years that come.

Anniversaries and Birthdays

SEPTEMBER 27

Therefore let us also, seeing we are compassed about with so great a cloud of witnesses, lay aside every weight, and the sin which doth so easily beset us, and let us run with patience the race that is set before us. Heb.12:1

IT is always an advantage when one sets out on a difficult and dangerous road, to know that someone has traveled it before us, and has arrived at his destination. Every wise traveler makes inquiries of those who have traveled the road he is to take, but is not acquainted with. One of the secrets of Roal Amundsen's successful expeditions over ice and ocean, was that he always studied carefully the reports of those who had tried to get through before him. A Christian will always benefit by listening to those who before him have traveled the road that leads home to God.

The first big lesson we must learn from those who already have won the prize of victory, is to lay aside every weight. He who fills his mind with love for this world, with money, finery, honor, and power—he will be left behind. The Israelite, who wishes himself back in Egypt, will never reach Canaan.

The cloud of witnesses that we read about in Hebrews XI saw the heavenly fatherland before them, and longed for the city that God had prepared for them, and they arrived. Let us try to have the same mind and we too shall win the prize. If we believe in Jesus and long for and desire the heavenly city we shall not come short of it.

Ye saints, who here in patience
Your cross and sufferings bore,
Shall live and reign for ever,
When sorrow is no more.
Around the throne of glory
The Lamb ye shall behold,
In triumph cast before Him
Your diadems of gold!

Anniversaries and Birthdays

SEPTEMBER 28

Who sinned, this man, or his parents, that he should be born blind? John 9:2

IF a special misfortune overtakes one, people consider that that is punishment for a special sin. This manner of reasoning is so deep-rooted in our nature that it seems almost impossible to think otherwise. Call at a few homes, see how people are getting along, and hear what they say! In one place you will find that the child that father and mother had pinned their hopes on has become helpless for life. In another place you will find that the father, who was relied on to provide food for many mouths, is no more, and mother has lost her health. Many who laid their child up to the heart of Jesus before it was born, now that the child is grown up, spend their days and nights waiting for this child to come home. They know that their child is lost in sin and shame, and they know the child will not come home, but nevertheless they wait. This and much more you will see and hear.

Then comes the question: "Am I worse than others, since God must strike so hard?" The heart says Yes, and neighbors and acquaintances say Yes. But Jesus says No. Wonderful Man! Does He not know the laws of Moses and the laws of heredity? O yes, but He also knows God's love and grace. There have been many, very many who in thoughtless pride said No to Christ in the good days, who came when God chastised them. When the child lay in the coffin father and mother lay at the cross. What God was unable to give us His children in good times, we accepted when He punished us. So when the Lord sees that He can give us eternal happiness through a misfortune that lasts but a moment, He lets the misfortune overtake us.

On this ground thy anchor cast;
Safe thou art, in Christ confiding;
All the griefs which here thou hast
Are but shadows unabiding.
Soon thy cross shall pass away,
Joy shall come that lasts for aye.

Anniversaries and Birthdays

SEPTEMBER 29

For in hope were we saved. **Rom. 8:24**

NEVER does a Christian experience joy more holy than when he looks up and into the place where the sun never sets, where tears never flow, and where Death never knocks at Life's door. With that land before him, in full assurance that it soon is won, no adverse fortune will get a Christian to complain, and no storm can drag the anchor that was thrown "within the veil."

The wonderful and comforting part of it is that hope is most alive and strong in those Christians who are having the hardest time in this world. Comfort and prosperity are like lead on the wings of hope, but the chastening grace of God lifts us anew. As a rule you never will find Christians that are more holy and happy than those who have the heaviest loads in this life. Living hope also has the miraculous power of making time here below seem short. Gradually, as hope carries us upward toward our homeland, we forget time and strife.

One day you met a Christian whose hands were full of all the things of this world: he complained and was dissatisfied with everything. On another day you meet him again, this time at a grave where he has laid away the dearest one that God gave him. There at the grave he says: "Soon I shall be at home, too. Soon I shall go home, too."

Hope is revived again, and to his inner vision time has become short.

"Blessed be the God and Father of our Lord Jesus Christ, who according to His great mercy begat us again unto a living hope by the resurrection of Jesus Christ from the dead" (I Peter 1:3).

In a land where all are strangers,
And our sojourning so short,
In the midst of common dangers,
Concord is our best support;
Heart with heart divides the smart,
Lightens grief of every sort.

Anniversaries and Birthdays

SEPTEMBER 30

And it came to pass, when He went into the house of one of the rulers of the Pharisees on a sabbath to eat bread, that they were watching Him. Luke 14:1

THE enemies of Jesus were always on the lookout to find something that could be used against Him. Today many worldly people are watching and hunting for faults in Christians. In much greater degree than we ourselves think, we are pursued by those who rejoice in our faults. They are seeking to justify their own sins, and say to themselves: "We are just as good as these people who claim to be better than all others." They are not conscious that it is contemptible to comfort themselves with the folly of others.

But even if this is so, one cannot deny that we Christians often are the cause of both criticism and scoffing. We easily forget our responsibilities and that we "walk in danger all the way." And then we also forget to watch and pray. That is when we stumble and fall.

Therefore the Word warns the people of God against both hidden and manifest enemies. We must expect, wherever we move among people, that there is always someone watching us. For besides the need of walking carefully, not as unwise but as wise, we are also to be a sweet savor of Christ unto God, in them that are saved, and in them that perish.

"Herein is my Father glorified, that ye bear much fruit; and so shall ye be My disciples," says Jesus.

Jesus, perfect my trust;
Strengthen my spirit's faith;
Nor let me stand, at last, alone
Upon the shore of death.

Anniversaries and Birthdays

OCTOBER 1

For thus said the Lord Jehovah, the Holy One of Israel, "In returning and rest shall ye be saved; in quietness and in confidence shall be your strength." **Isa. 30:15**

TO be converted is to have a change of heart and a change in the direction of one's life. He who formerly turned away from God and walked his own ways in unbelief, sin, and worldliness, turns to God with his life as it is, and acknowledges his folly. To be converted is not to conquer evil and then go to God as those who have helped themselves; but it is to be saved by Another, when one sees that he cannot save himself. To be converted is to cease opposing God, it is to quit running away from Him, and to say: "Here I am. You may now save me if You will." He who then hears the words of the Savior, "I will!" and throws himself trustingly in His arms, he is saved.

The great art for a Christian later in life too is to possess a childlike confidence in God. No power can overcome him who builds his life in small matters and great on what Jesus has done, and on what God has promised in His Word. He may be wounded in the fight, but if he does not let go of his Savior, he is unconquerable. The helpless person can be safe with Jesus. In Him hell is closed and heaven is open. But outside of Jesus hell is open and heaven is closed.

All of you who wish to be victorious and reach heaven, you must come to Jesus and remain with Him in life and in death. Then He will lead us through conflict and death to the land of the living.

With my burden I begin:
Lord, remove this load of sin!
Let Thy blood, for sinners spilt,
Set my conscience free from guilt.

Anniversaries and Birthdays

OCTOBER 2

Beware of the dogs, beware of the evil workers, beware of the concision. Phil. 3:2

EVIL workers have this characteristic that they show no particular anxiety for bringing worldly people to Christ. Their one and great goal is to "convert" those who already are converted.

They believe that they have discovered the only correct teaching about God, the Word of God, and the life to come. They tell us that all others are on the wrong track. So if we—we who have found Christ—want to save our souls, we must go to them. If we do not, we must at any rate remain here below when Christ comes for His bride. Only when we are with them can we have assurance of a full salvation. With them there is the right light and the right faith. With them is the Spirit, and the earnest of entry into the wedding feast. These are some of the claims of "evil workers."

And many are led astray. But when this loud-voiced, spiritual boasting no longer can support them, they are left lying on the ruins torn and broken. Where formerly Christianity bloomed, beautiful in human lives, there are now only dry branches.

That Christian is wise who turns away from all those who want to disturb the souls that have found peace and salvation in Jesus alone. Those who call sinners away from the salvation in Jesus with their cries of, "Here is the right way! Here is Christ!" they are not from God, and Jesus has said that we shall not believe them.

Ponder all God's truth can teach you,
Let His Word your footsteps guide;
Satan's wiles shall never reach you,
Though he draw the world aside:
Lo! God's truth is thy defense,
Light, and hope, and confidence;
Trust in God, He'll not deceive you,
Pray, and all your foes will leave you.

Anniversaries and Birthdays

OCTOBER 3

By which will we have been sanctified through the offering of the body of Jesus Christ once for all. . . . For by one offering He hath perfected for ever them that are sanctified. Heb. 10:10, 14

WHAT Christ has done for us has been done perfectly. By His will and in His body we are sanctified. When He died for our sins and rose for our justification, He sanctified us in Himself for God. He who grasps Christ in faith stands in Him holy and without blemish before God's face. Ye are holy in Christ, and ye are called saints, says the Word of God.

But when He has perfected forever them who are in Christ, how then can it be that they also shall be sanctified? Because that which is prepared for us in Him, and that we possess in faith, must be made a part of our person, not only so that we believe it, but also so that it abides in us. We are to grow in the grace and knowledge of Christ. And we shall be sanctified in soul, spirit, and body, and shall perfect our holiness in the fear of God.

"Sanctify in your hearts Christ as Lord." "Present your members as servants to righteousness unto sanctification" . . . "for without sanctification no man shall see the Lord."

If faith in Jesus does not lead us to growth and sanctification we will soon be blind again and lose our vision of the Lord. He who is holy shall be sanctified.

More love to Thee, O Christ,
More love to Thee!
Hear Thou the pray'r I make
On bended knee;
This is my earnest plea,
More love, O Christ, to Thee,
More love, O Christ, to Thee,
More love to Thee!

Anniversaries and Birthdays

____

____

____

____

____

OCTOBER 4

Why sayest thou, O Jacob, and speakest, O Israel, My way is hid from Jehovah, and the justice due to me is passed away from my God? Isa. 40:27

MANY people believe that when God established the laws of nature, He Himself stepped aside and bestowed His omnipotence on lifeless, blind forces in nature. Everything that happens in nature and in the lives of men, is a command from this hard, cold king, the laws of nature. Not even God can do anything contrary to this will of nature. That is what many believe!

If this were true it would be grievous indeed to be a man. Think it over! Do you not have a sensation of something strangling your very heartstrings, when you imagine your fate resting in the hands of a blind, lifeless, adamant, unyielding power that has neither a will nor a heart?

How different to open your Bible and to see there that God stands above all the laws that He has established in nature. He directs and rules, He does as He wills. As the Ruler of all, as the Law above all laws He walks among us, as a father and mother walk among their children.

This view of God and existence opens to us a world of responsibility, of the right to decide our own fate, and an ocean of grace. Then no one need think that our way is hid from the Lord. No, He takes us by the hand, and leads us on the narrow way, and guides us "in the paths of righteousness for His name's sake." And if we do not find the way, He is a lamp unto our feet, and light unto our path.

"Thou wilt guide me with Thy counsel,
And afterward receive me to glory."

Be not dismayed, thou little flock,
Although the foe's fierce battle-shock
Loud on all sides assail thee;
Though o'er thy fall they laugh secure,
Their triumph cannot long endure:
Let not thy courage fail thee.

Anniversaries and Birthdays

OCTOBER 5

And Jesus rebuked him, saying, "Hold thy peace, and come out of him." And the unclean spirit, tearing him and crying with a loud voice, came out of him. Mark 1:25-26

EVIL spirits have more power over many people than we believe and understand. The worst and most Satanic things that people think of, are brought forth by evil spirits. Even though we are evil by nature, there is reason to believe that most of the evil that is done would not be done if Satan and his host were not on earth. The Word of God foretells a time when evil shall lose its power over man. That is the time when Satan shall be bound.

Evil spirits are governing the souls of men when enmity, jealousy, vulgarity, and hatred rule over people. When homes are filled with strife, and happiness between husband and wife, parents and children is destroyed, when relatives hate each other, and one neighbor is at war with the next, then one can at times be conscious that evil spirits are abroad in the countryside, and that they dwell in the homes.

And what shall we say about all the young people, middle aged, and old who are awakened, who long for peace with God, but who get no further? What else but evil spirits is binding them?

Why are not you a Christian? Do you not know that that is best? Do you not want peace? Yes, you do, but—well, what is it? You are bound by the power of an evil spirit. Be wise enough to admit this to yourself, and go to Him who can liberate you from the power of Satan, and make you a free and happy person. He can do it if you will let Him.

Awake, thou that sleepest, arise from death's slumber!
Christ on thee shall shine;
The daylight, now glowing in rays without number,
Shows mercy divine;
Repose now no longer,
Lest night's dark and danger
Soon come o'er thy soul.
Awake now, arise, and be whole!

Anniversaries and Birthdays

OCTOBER 6

I have set watchmen upon thy walls, O Jerusalem; they shall never hold their peace day nor night: ye that are Jehovah's remembrancers, take ye no rest. Isa. 62:6

THE watchmen that we now hear about have been given the great task of bearing the people to God in prayer. They are to stand before the Lord's face day and night and never let either Him or themselves have any rest.

God has given us such watchmen, too. Round about in our country we have men and women who stand as watchmen without growing weary. They intercede for people in township and city, for neighbors, relatives, friends, people known and unknown, for converted people and for the worldly, they cry for grace for the missionary, for the heathen, and for those who are being won for God. They intercede day and night for preachers in the home land, and they often sense that one or another is in some special danger.

Occasionally I have succeeded in finding some who through many years have performed such a guard duty for me, too. After I had had an opportunity to look somewhat into their watch tower I understood more clearly many of the things that had happened to me in my life. What grace is ours that there are women and men who give God no rest night or day—for us.

Let us, too, be counted among those who serve the Lord in intercession. The disquiet that then settles on our heart shall also seize the Lord, a disquiet that He likes. And some day we too shall find the answer to our prayers.

These, like priests, have watched and waited,
Offering up to Christ their will,
Soul and body consecrated,
Day and night they serve Him still.
Now in God's most holy place,
Blest they stand before His face.

Anniversaries and Birthdays

____

____

____

____

____

OCTOBER 7

And why beholdest thou the mote that is in thy brother's eye, but considerest not the beam that is in thine own eye? Matt. 7:3

IT is just as easy to see the faults of others as it is difficult to get your eye on your own faults. From our earliest childhood and on to the late evening of life this evil power pursues us and creates discord in land and kingdom, in house and home. I have often wondered why it is so easy to see the faults of others but not our own. Although we try to be upright it seems almost impossible to place ourselves in the right light. We may have great talents for studying the soul-life of others, but we are very incapable at learning to know ourselves. This, too, one can see best when one looks at others!

It is a settled fact that the Christian who can get his own person and the faults of his own character up before his vision for examination has attained to something great and has won high wisdom in life. The person who has learned to know his own folly, has taken a long forward step on wisdom's way.

How shall we learn to take this step? We shall say to ourselves: "Remember that you see the faults of others much better than your own! Remember that one of the most difficult things a person has to do is to find the beam in his own eye!" If one tries to awaken himself in this way, it will be helpful for him who desires to know the truth. And then, if we can be humble enough to accept the light and the correction that come to us from God's Word and God's Spirit, we will be kept so busy with ourselves and our own faults, that we will think more mildly of others. But then we have gotten onto the road that a Christian should travel.

May we be more successful in this endeavor after this.

Wherever in the world I am,
In whatsoe'er estate,
I have a fellowship with hearts
To keep and cultivate;
A work of lowly love to do
For Him on whom I wait.

Anniversaries and Birthdays

OCTOBER 8

If ye abide in My Word, then are ye truly My disciples; and ye shall know the truth, and the truth shall make you free.

John 8:31-32

OUR life with God cannot be preserved except we abide in God's Word. He who lays his Bible away and still believes that he is a Christian, he is living on a lie.

But to abide in the Word of God does not mean only to read the Bible. It is first and last to give the Word room in your heart and to live according to it. Next, it is to be in all of God's Word. Some of the disciples of Jesus prefer to study and ponder and apply to themselves only the words that make demands, and pronounce judgment, and show the way, but the word about grace and forgiveness they leave untouched. Others wish to know only the words that comfort and lift up, and make happy.

Both of these practices are one-sided and contain a danger. If the truth is to make us free, then demands and judgment and comfort must all find a place in our hearts. If the truth about ourselves is shoved aside, then the heart will also be closed against liberating truth. The fundamental law, that always must rule in a Christian life, is the word about sin and grace. Where all acknowledgement of sin is absent, grace can no longer work; but when the sinner knocks at the door of grace, God gives "grace for grace." Thus the truth sets us free.

If we are disciples of Jesus in this matter, then the truth will both make us free and be our power to live a holy and happy Christian life.

Deep and glorious, Word victorious,
  Word divine that ever lives!
Call Thou sinners to be winners
  Of the life that Jesus gives;
Tell abroad what God hath given;
  Jesus is our way to heaven.

Anniversaries and Birthdays

OCTOBER 9

Blessed are they that mourn: for they shall be comforted. Matt. 5:4

WORRY and complaint about food and clothes and all else that belongs to "daily bread" is as common as it is un-Christian and unprofitable. All the disquiet and agony that anxiety for daily bread has in its train is enough to rob us of our courage for the problems of life and our strength to work. God has therefore been so good to us that we are spared the need of worrying about such matters.

Jesus said to His disciples: "Be not therefore anxious, saying, 'What shall we eat?' or, 'What shall we drink?' or, 'Wherewithal shall we be clothed?' For after all these things do the Gentiles seek; for your heavenly Father knoweth that ye have need of all these things."

For what kind of mourning does Jesus call the Christians blessed? It is sorrow for sin, sorrow because of our weak Christianity, and because we do so little for Him who did everything for us. It is the feeling that we need more of God's Spirit and power in our lives, so we can be living letters for our fellow men to read about Christ. It is mourning for all those who are living without God and without hope in the world. This is the right Christian mourning.

The tears that we shed for such reasons our Savior gladly wipes away; and He comforts the heart that feels oppressed by sorrow for sin and sympathy for others.

> Cleanse us, Lord, from sinful stain,
> O'er the parched heart, O rain!
> Heal the wounded of its pain.
>
> Bend the stubborn will to Thine,
> Melt the cold with fire divine,
> Erring hearts to right incline.

Anniversaries and Birthdays

____

____

____

____

____

____

OCTOBER 10

In My Father's house are many mansions; if it were not so, I would have told you; for I go to prepare a place for you.

John 14:2

WHAT will become of me when I die? A Christian, too, can ask that question in the dark hours of life.

Jesus has told us what becomes of a Christian when he dies. He goes to the Father of Jesus Christ, to heaven, to God. When "the earthly house of our tabernacle is dissolved, we have a building from God, a house not made with hands, eternal in the heavens." "We are of good courage, I say, and are willing rather to be absent from the body, and to be at home with the Lord."

It looks as though it is very difficult for us Christians of today to keep a firm hold on the Word about the heaven that awaits us, and to grasp it with a living faith. We surely believe it after a fashion, but it is so loose, gray, and unreal. If we accept it as a truth that cannot be shaken, that when we leave this world we are going to a real home, a place where we shall live a fully conscious life, without sin, sorrow, and death, then we shall surely be less earthbound and we shall long more for heaven. Then we shall also understand more of what these words contain: "We are willing rather to be absent from the body, and to be at home with the Lord."

God grant us Christians a more living faith in heaven!

"The sun shall be no more thy light by day; neither for brightness shall the moon give light unto thee: but Jehovah will be unto thee an everlasting light, and thy God thy glory."

Blessed are the heirs of heaven,
The dead, who die in Christ forgiven,
They from their labors have release;
Saith the Spirit: they are resting,
No sting of death is them molesting,
For they have found the home of peace;
In peace they sweetly rest,
Forever they are blest,
Hallelujah!
Before God's throne to His dear Son
Do follow them their works well done.

Anniversaries and Birthdays

OCTOBER 11

For narrow is the gate, and straitened the way, that leadeth unto life, and few are they that find it. Matt. 7:14

IN Christ the door is opened for us that leads to eternal life. In Him there is no narrow gate and no straitened way. On the contrary there is such a plenty of room that the worst and greatest sinner can be saved by faith in His name; and the way is so direct and well marked that not even fools need err therein.

It is not what Jesus has done for us that is narrow and straitened: the narrow and straitened part is found in us and in the world that we must pass through. If we desire to go through the door into life, and walk the way that leads home to God, we will meet no hindrances in Christ, but in our sinful nature, in the spiritual hosts of wickedness in the heavenly places, and in the spirit that is the world-ruler.

To be a Christian is to row against the stream. There are many swift rapids to get by, but upstream we go toward life. He who floats downstream is on the way to death. To save your life is to lose it, Jesus says; but he who loses his life saves it. The soul wills to ascend, our evil nature wants to let things slide: wherefore all who would save their life must lose it. There the gate is narrow and the way straitened, but all those who press into the kingdom of heaven with violence, take it by force.

"To him that overcometh, to him will I give of the hidden manna, and I will give him a white stone, and upon the stone a new name written, which no one knoweth but he that receiveth it" (Rev. 2:17).

Glory, honor, and thanksgiving,
Be unto God the ever-living,
And to the Lamb for sinners slain!
Ransomed host that now victorious
Have won the crown of life all glorious,
Extol the Lamb, enthroned to reign!
For us Himself He gave,
He sank into the grave,
He is risen!
He went before, death's pathway o'er,
We follow to the heavenly shore.

Anniversaries and Birthdays

OCTOBER 12

Happy is he that hath the God of Jacob for his help,
Whose hope is in Jehovah his God. Psalm 146:5

"HAPPY" does not always mean to feel that one is lifted above this world and up toward heaven. Neither does "happy" always mean to feel released and certain of salvation. Happy—this word has an ascending scale in the Bible, from the lower deeps to the heights above, from the soul's first heavy sigh for release and peace till we finally stand saved in eternal life.

Happy—that is to weep over yourself, and to long for release from sin, and for peace with God. It is to be prostrate at the throne of grace, and to receive mercy, and sonship, and peace.

Happy—that is also to live under God's discipline. When in life's hard conflict we are wounded and smitten by sin, Satan, and the world, by Christians, and by ourselves—and when in the midst of all this we may nestle close to God as our Savior and our Father, and hide ourselves in His pavilion in the day of trouble—then we are happy.

Happy—that is to get your wounds healed, to be able to give thanks for everything in Jesus' name, and then to go out into the conflict again with a freshly washed face, with a calm mind, with courage to live, with power to love and serve, and with a smile for death.

But we shall be happy first, last, and greatest when we have crossed the river of death, and enter the heavenly city, when angels stand on the heavenly shore and sing their songs of welcome, when all tribulation is ended, and sorrow and sighing are no more.

"Happy art thou, O Israel:
Who is like unto thee, a people saved by Jehovah,
The shield of thy help,
And the sword of thy excellency!
And thine enemies shall submit themselves unto thee;
And thou shalt tread upon their high places" (Deut. 33:29).

So now, until we die,
Sound we Thy praises high,
And joyful sing.

Anniversaries and Birthdays

____

____

____

OCTOBER 13

He said therefore, "Unto what is the kingdom of God like? and whereunto shall I liken it?" Luke 13:18

THE kingdom of God is the net that is cast into the sea of humanity, so that it can draw people in, onto the beach of grace. It is the seed that is planted in the soil of humanity, and it grows and becomes a large tree. It is the yeast that eats its way into the life of humanity; it is a wedding in the palace of the king; it is the treasure that makes us eternally rich; it is the pearl that adorns us in life and in death and in all eternity. It is grace for grace, it is righteousness, peace, and joy in the Holy Spirit.

Most wondrous is of all on earth
The kingdom Jesus founded.
Its glory, peace, and precious worth
No tongue has fully sounded.

But the kingdom of God is not only a gift: it is also a task.

We are called not only to sonship and eternal riches, but also to work and responsibility. What God has given us He wants us to use to help others, for our own happiness, and to His glory. We must make an accounting for all that God has given us, and if we lay it away, or dig it down in the earth, we will fare ill, for the kingdom of God is also the King who makes a reckoning with us.

A true Christian must live both in the gift and in the service, in full freedom as a child in the Father's house, and in complete responsibility as a worker together with God. And the responsibility and the task reach from the home and place of work and out to the ends of the earth.

God desires that His children serve Him, and when evening comes He pays the wages, and invites us into His glorious kingdom, to eternal rest.

Let foes against the kingdom rage
With hatred and derision,
God crowns its reign from age to age,
And brings it to fruition.

Anniversaries and Birthdays

____

____

____

____

OCTOBER 14

And I heard the voice of the Lord, saying, "Whom shall I send, and who will go for us?" Then I said, "Here am I; send me."

Isa. 6:8

IT was because his sin had been taken away that Isaiah hearkened to God's call and stated his willingness to go. When we get an eye on our own sins, we see that also others are in danger; and if we find salvation we also want others to be saved.

This is according to the will of God: He wants His children to serve Him. "And ye also bear witness," said Jesus to His disciples, "because ye have been with Me from the beginning." The Christians who never feel any strong desire "to proclaim the acceptable year of the Lord," and to ask men to repent, ought again pray that the live coal from the Lord's altar might touch their mouth.

How wonderful that there continually are young people who accept calls to tell the message from God not only in the home land, but also out in the missionary fields. They bid farewell to parents, home, and fatherland, and with a blessed and quiet joy they answer the Lord: "Here am I; send me." He, who gave His life for all men, loves that answer.

May we, each in our own place, be found among those who gladly run errands for the Lord to those who are walking away from Him. We will surely meet people who not only need a helping hand in order to get to God, but who also are waiting and longing for help. There are more of these than we think.

When Jesus enters land and nation,
  And moves the people with His love,
When yielding to His kind persuasion,
  Our hearts His truth and blessings prove,
Then shall our life on earth be blest
The peace of God on us shall rest.

Anniversaries and Birthdays

OCTOBER 15

Blessed is the man that . . .
But his delight is in the law of Jehovah;
And on His law doth he meditate day and night.
And he shall be like a tree planted by the streams of water,
That bringeth forth its fruit in its season,
Whose leaf also doth not wither;
And whatsoever he doeth shall prosper. Psalm 1:1-3

THAT which characterizes a regenerate man, just as soon as he has received the life with God, is a profound desire to do the will of God in all things. When we, who now are old Christians, think back to that time, we are reminded that the slightest thing that we feared might have offended God, was enough to drive us to our Savior to get everything straightened out again. If we were in doubt about anything we sought light in the Word and in prayer: we could not endure the thought of getting into something that God hated.

There are surely many Christians who have great reason to ask themselves if this inner sanctuary is in order now, too. Life among erring men, and the evil in us and about us may easily harm just this side of our life with God. And if we are not on our guard, we will soon become careless with both the inner and the outward life. That is when the Christian life is weakened and withers. We become like a tree planted on a rocky knoll.

But he who protects this holy need—always to obey God's will—he makes great demands not only on himself but also on God and on His grace. In such a Christian the roots of life will find their way to the rivers of water that keep life healthful also in dry times. That is the kind of Christians God wanted to us to be.

Give me a calm, a thankful heart,
From every murmur free;
The blessings of Thy grace impart,
And let me live to Thee.

Anniversaries and Birthdays

OCTOBER 16

Where sin abounded, grace did abound more exceedingly.

Rom. 5:20

JUST as certain as it is that Christ was victorious over sin and Satan at Golgotha, and just as certain as it is that His grave is empty and that He now sits at God's right hand with all power in heaven and in earth, just so certain is it that grace is greater than sin.

But what seems to go beyond all bounds is this that as sin gradually becomes great, grace becomes still greater. It is almost as though Paul here is alarmed at what he himself has said, and therefore immediately asks this question: "Shall we continue in sin, that grace may abound?"

It is likely that worldly people will often draw such a conclusion from these words about grace, because they do not know what it is to be a lost sinner saved by grace alone. But the Christian knows that as his life gradually grows into the fellowship of God, and as he is privileged more and more to look into God's being, he also more and more sees the evil in himself, and becomes in his own eyes a greater and greater sinner. If then grace does not also abound more exceedingly for him, he will lose courage and will despair.

But he need not do that. The fact is that grace is as great as God is great; and as the cataract increases in power with the length of the fall, so grace increases in proportion as sin becomes great to us. In that way it is fortunate to be a great sinner

And when, redeemed from sin and hell,
With all the ransomed throng I dwell,
My raptured song shall ever be,
God has been merciful to me.

Anniversaries and Birthdays

____

____

____

____

____

____

OCTOBER 17

Be strong and of good courage, fear not, nor be affrighted at them: for Jehovah thy God, He it is that doth go with thee; He will not fail thee, nor forsake thee. Deut. 31:6

MOSES told the children of Israel to be of good courage when they in a short time should attack the enemy and take possession of the land that the Lord had promised them. God was going with them, and therefore they should be bold and strong in the fight.

It is right for a Christian not to trust in his own strength. Nevertheless there is a despondency and a distrust of one's own powers which are not good. When we hide away from the conflict and the work in the kingdom of God because discouragement tells us that God cannot use us for anything, then we are giving away the self-respect that God had thought to make use of.

A Christian who withdraws into himself and considers everything impossible is not only hindering the power of God in his own life, but he may also steal away the courage from those who are in the fight.

The right Christian mind must hold fast to the comfort that God both will and can use us, and in that faith we are to go into the fight gladly and boldly. Let us grant that in this courage there may be mixed too much self-respect and even some arrogance. The experience we get in the fight will little by little lead us away from self, and unto the power of God.

In that way the Lord will train His own to become capable soldiers.

"Jehovah is my rock, and my fortress, and my deliverer;
My God, my Rock, in whom I will take refuge;
My shield, and the horn of my salvation, my high tower"
(Psalm 18:2).

Fight on, my soul, till death
Shall bring thee to thy God!
He'll take thee at thy parting breath
Up to His blest abode.

Anniversaries and Birthdays

OCTOBER 18

But it is good for me to draw near unto God:
I have made the Lord Jehovah my refuge,
That I may tell of all Thy works. Psalm 73:28

THAT which characterizes a worldly person is fear of drawing near to God. Everything that brings one face to face with God creates disquiet and leaden thoughts. If a worldly person is to feel free and happy, it is best that God seem far away. Not until need and great misfortunes knock at the door does such a one wish for God's help: but then He must also leave at once as soon as the danger is past. The strange thing is that these people live in the delusion that after death they will get along nicely with God. On this big lie many live and die—and are lost.

But what characterizes a Christian is a deep longing to draw nearer and nearer unto God in this life. A child of God has no greater joy than when he through God's Word, in prayer, in the fellowship of other Christians, or in some other manner, is privileged to sense that God is near. Then the deepest sorrow can be changed into joy, and the heaviest burden to wings. But if God seems far away, a Christian always becomes troubled and anxious.

This is something that we experience. How wonderful that God has performed the great miracle that we sinful men become happier the nearer we get to a holy God! How great the happiness will be when we shall see Him as He is.

"Nevertheless I am continually with Thee:
Thou hast holden my right hand.
Thou wilt guide me with Thy counsel,
And afterward receive me to glory" (Psalm 73:23-24).

Though like the wanderer,
The sun gone down,
Darkness be over me,
My rest a stone;
Yet in my dreams I'd be
Nearer, my God, to Thee,
Nearer to Thee!

Anniversaries and Birthdays

OCTOBER 19

Let us draw near with a true heart in full assurance of faith.

Heb. 10:22

TO draw near to God with a true heart must be to come exactly as one is without making oneself either better or worse. It is to lay bare before God disposition, heart, thoughts, the outer and the inner life just as one sees it himself. If we try to conceal or excuse a part of what we see, and that we know we have done, then we have not a true heart, then we are false and untruthful. Then the salvation road is closed, not to Christ but to us.

"Jehovah, who shall sojourn in Thy tabernacle?
Who shall dwell in Thy holy hill?
He that walketh uprightly, and worketh righteousness,
And speaketh truth in his heart."

Let us note this: He that speaketh truth in his heart. The honest man shall be successful, but the Lord will let go him that turns to crooked ways.

"Stand therefore, having girded your loins with truth."

That robe of righteousness with which a sinner is clothed by faith in Jesus will fall off if it is not girded on with the belt of truth.

He, who thinks that it is altogether too easy to be allowed to go to God just as you are, he has not learned to know himself.

Let us pray God for help to draw near unto Him with a true heart.

May the dear blood, once shed for me,
My blest atonement prove,
That I from first to last may be
The purchase of Thy love.

Anniversaries and Birthdays

OCTOBER 20

My soul waiteth in silence for God only:
From Him cometh my salvation. Psalm 62:1

DAVID had come to life's evening, and he stands looking back over times that were past. He sees the days when as a carefree herdboy he played among the animals on hills and flowering plains. He also sees his course on hard and narrow roads to the kingly throne. He sees himself far down and high up, and when he is to weigh everything on life's true scales and determine where happiness lay, he concludes that in all his long course it was not to be found except in God.

We are slow at learning the lesson that our happiness is found neither in riches nor in poverty, in honor or dishonor, in sickness or in health, but only in God. Most people use their entire lives in hunting for happiness in this world. The soul hears this song day and night: "If I could only get so far and own so much, then I would be happy!" But the truth is that no one becomes happy before he finds God. David wept more as king than as herder. The rich man has as a rule more sorrow and anxiety than the poor man. He that increaseth riches, increaseth sorrow, but he who cheerfully lays his life into God's Savior-hand and Father-hand, he drinks from the river of life and finds the treasure that gives peace.

Everyone who desires to possess the true peace and joy in life must first find God.

Perverse and foolish, oft I strayed,
But yet in love He sought me,
And on His shoulder gently laid,
And home, rejoicing, brought me.

Anniversaries and Birthdays

OCTOBER 21

And the Word became flesh, and dwelt among us (and we beheld His glory, glory as of the only begotten from the Father), full of grace and truth. John 1:14

OF all those that learned to know Jesus it is likely that no one else looked so deeply into His being as John. And when he wants to show us Christ and His glory in a few words, he says: "glory as of the only begotten from the Father, full of grace and truth."

Others also have at various times beheld a little of God's glory before John saw it in Christ, but all these saw only a consuming fire that the sinner could not approach without dying. But when God's glory meets us in Jesus Christ the situation is quite the opposite. Then it is grace and truth.

Apart from Christ, the glory of God is like lightning: it kills and destroys everything that draws near to it. Moses said to God: "Show me, I pray Thee, Thy glory." But the Lord said: "Thou canst not see My face; for man shall not see Me and live." But the destroying power of lightning can be transformed to light, heat, and motive power to the unspeakable benefit of a whole generation. That is true of the glory of God, too. In Christ it is grace and truth.

But remember that grace and truth never can be separated, if one is to win and possess the life with God. "Everyone that is of the truth heareth my voice," says Jesus. Through Jesus the voice of God becomes to us a voice of grace. In Him we are saved by grace, so that we can live in the truth by grace.

As Thou dost will,
Lead Thou me still,
That I may truly serve Thee.
My God, I pray,
Teach me Thy way,
To my last day
In Thy true faith preserve me.

Anniversaries and Birthdays

OCTOBER 22

First of all beware ye of the leaven of the Pharisees. Luke 12:1

THERE must be something especially dangerous to the Christian in the Pharisee's view of life when Jesus can say to His disciples, "First of all beware ye of the leaven of the Pharisees." There are surely great reasons why we too should listen to this warning, not the least of which is that we have so little fear of this danger. We are most inclined to believe that it is the dead Christianity of habit that is leavened by this dough, and we forget that it may easily enter into the life of a living Christian, too.

What is it then that is so dangerous to us in Pharisaism?

A Pharisee passes himself off for what he is not. What he boasts about with his mouth, he does not own in his heart. This is the most essential trait in a Pharisee, and that is surely also what we are most tempted to resemble him in. To be entirely true in one's Christianity, and to possess in the heart what one testifies to with his mouth, that is more difficult than one thinks before he has tried it.

We are tempted in many ways to appear better than we are. So many a time do we try to conceal the emptiness of our inner life by using strong words and long prayers. I think you can consider it the general rule, that when the inner life is enfeebled we try to patch it up by polishing the outward life. Many, many large Christian words would never have been spoken if we had been entirely true.

O yes, Jesus is quite right: "First of all beware ye of the leaven of the Pharisees!" To identify oneself with an inner untruth through false spirituality and religious talk, that is the surest way to the "outer darkness." Let us therefore beware!

Use thou the Word
Of God, thy Lord;
All else is unavailing;
Every thought and passion guard
With this shield unfailing.

Anniversaries and Birthdays

OCTOBER 23

And Jesus came and touched them and said, "Arise, and be not afraid." And lifting up their eyes, they saw no one, save Jesus only. Matt. 17:7-8

IT is easy to understand that the disciples were frightened when the waves beat over the boat, and when Jesus was taken in Gethsemane. But that they should be afraid on Mount Tabor, where it was so unspeakably good to be, that sounds unreasonable.

Nevertheless a deep Christian truth is found in all this.

If a Christian is long in the dark and in a hard struggle he becomes afraid. Then he asks himself: "Can I be a Christian, I who experience so little of victory and joy in God?" But if he becomes happy again, and this happiness lasts a while and seems so great that he thinks that conflict, temptation, and doubt are far away, then also is he afraid. "Can I be in the right spiritual state now when I have no struggle or temptation? Is it not the people of God that Satan tempts, and is it not Satan that a Christian shall fight against?" And so he becomes afraid in the midst of his joy.

How can this be? It is this way, that a Christian cannot have a peace that is whole and full in anything else, save in Jesus only. There is no salvation in either conflict or joy: if we build on anything of that sort, evil will befall us. In wonderful, divine wisdom the Christian life is arranged so that nothing apart from Jesus, no matter how good it is, can make a Christian secure.

It was not only in Gethsemane that the disciples went to sleep: they went to sleep on Tabor, too.

It is Jesus, only Jesus, who can save us. With Him we are always safe.

For I shall see my Jesus,
He is my hope and stay;
The cross that me oppresses
Anon He takes away.
Then nothing more shall grieve me,
And no adversity
Shall of my joy bereave me;
Soon I shall Jesus see.

Anniversaries and Birthdays

OCTOBER 24

And ye have forgotten the exhortation which reasoneth with you as with sons,

"My son, regard not lightly the chastening of the Lord,
Nor faint when thou art reproved of Him." **Heb. 12:5**

MANY a Christian often asks himself and God: "How shall I get more true godliness and desire for heavenly things?" No matter how badly off we are, we are eager to be different from what we are. So we go to the Bible to get light, and then we pray to get power, but nothing seems to help. Sin clings to us, and our heart cannot be set free from this world, and so we get nowhere.

But while we are sighing and struggling in this way the Lord is sending help. We sense the fact that the answer will be found in the black clouds that are overcasting the sky of our life. We shall be set free and lifted through chastening. The liberating power is found in the rod, in blows, in night, in storm, and in tears. The rose will blossom among the thorns, the air will be cleansed by the storm, and the silver is separated from the slag by fire.

You who just now are under God's chastening hand and feel the smart of the rod, you perhaps ask quite often why you must endure all this suffering. But you should try to lay your wounded soul up to the heart of Him who says: "Whom I love I chasten."

Try to believe that this is true, even if you do not understand it! Then you will find the Lord's grace in every blow, and then the day will come when you will glory in your tribulations, and kiss the hand that struck you.

God calling yet!—shall I not hear?
Earth's pleasures shall I still hold dear?
Shall life's swift passing years all fly,
And still my soul in slumbers lie.

Anniversaries and Birthdays

OCTOBER 25

If we confess our sins, He is faithful and righteous to forgive us our sins, and to cleanse us from all unrighteousness. I John 1:9

IT is sin to commit sin, but there is something that is still worse, and that is to turn away from God and hide the sin from Him. Our deepest hurt is not that evil dwells in us, nor that sin rules over us: the deepest hurt is that we refuse to confess our sin to God. We try in every way to wriggle away from admitting sin itself; or we try to find a cause for it here or there—only not in ourselves.

Right there is our deepest hurt.

Pride carried man away from God, and pride is the chief obstacle when man is to find his way back to God. We can indeed admit that we are sinners, and that we commit sin too, but we are often real masters at getting around sin itself, also when we appear before God. Of all the things that humble us, there is hardly anything that is so difficult for us to agree to do as to confess sin itself. If we can surrender to God also this stronghold in our life, then victory is won by Him who gives grace to the humble. Then joy and peace come forth in the soul anew, because He who forgives the sin that we have confessed, He cleanses us from all unrighteousness.

Nothing ought to be too dear to sacrifice in order to possess life's greatest joy.

> Thy light to every thought impart,
> And shed Thy love in every heart;
> The weakness of our mortal state
> With deathless might invigorate.

Anniversaries and Birthdays

____

____

____

____

____

____

OCTOBER 26

Abstract from every form of evil. **I Thess. 5:22**

WHEN we have given our life to Christ, we have crossed the boundary into the kingdom where all sin must be our enemy. We must abstain from all that is evil, beginning with the most hidden thought in the heart, and on to the life that is open to the gaze of all. We have not the right to let sin rule in one single instance. If this truth always stood clearly before us, many things would be different in our daily life.

Another domain where we Christians must be careful is the realm of what are called "middle things," or adiaphora, or things indifferent: acts that some people consider sin, and others not. Perhaps you can take part in many of these things without damage to your soul: you do not consider them sinful. But by taking part you may cause some other Christian to fall. Paul was so careful on this point that if he knew that anyone was caused to stumble by his eating meat, then he would eat no flesh "for evermore." Among us Christians of today there are many who never taste alcohol, not because they themselves are tempted to drunkenness, but because they do not want to cause others to fall. That is a healthy, Christian view. That is obeying the Bible Word about being a good example for others.

A Christian must also be on his guard lest he be deceived by that which in itself is good. When home, business, money, buildings, and land become dearer than God, then there is grave danger. Surely more people have fallen away from God through love for the world, than by a sinful act.

My soul, be on thy guard,
Ten thousand foes arise;
And hosts of sin are pressing hard
To draw thee from the skies.

Anniversaries and Birthdays

OCTOBER 27

And Aaron shall bear the names of the children of Israel in the breastplate of judgment upon his heart, when he goeth in unto the holy place, for a memorial before Jehovah continually. Ex. 28:29

IN the breastplate that the high priest in Israel wore there were set twelve precious stones. The names of the twelve tribes of Israel were engraved on these stones. The high priest must always wear this breastplate when he appeared before the face of God, so that the Lord always would remember His people.

As God's people in the old covenant rested on the heart of the high priest in these stones, so the people of God of the new covenant rest in the heart of Jesus Christ. He has not entered into a holy place made with hands, but into heaven itself to appear before God for our sake. From there God looks upon His people as if they had never sinned, and from there He always remembers them. From there He also sees His people as one people. God does not see His people from the sign on a church door, but from the heart of Jesus Christ. We are all one in Christ.

May our eyes be opened more to see the glory in the face of Jesus Christ. Then we will experience in greater degree that the Gospel is the power of God unto salvation to everyone that believeth.

"If then ye were raised together with Christ, seek the things that are above, where Christ is, seated on the right hand of God. Set your mind on the things that are above, not on the things that are upon the earth" (Col. 3:1-2).

One in the Spirit's union,
We onward march, a pilgrim throng,
And sing in sweet communion
The ransomed Zion's victor-song;
Through night and tribulation,
Through death our way we wend,
With hope and expectation
To see our journey's end—
The cross, the grave, death's prison,
We leave behind, and rise
To meet our Savior risen,
And enter Paradise.

Anniversaries and Birthdays

____

____

____

OCTOBER 28

Wherefore, putting away falsehood, speak ye truth each one with his neighbor: for we are members one of another. Eph. 4:25

ONE would think it a matter of course for a Christian to speak the truth, but it is not. A Christian also is tempted to all kinds of sin, and the temptation to tell falsehoods is surely one of those that lurks most around many Christians. If we try to weigh our words on the scales of truth, we will find how easily untruth and falsehood lay hold of us.

But the worst of it is that it seems so difficult for us to see that falsehood is sin. We make promises but do not keep them; we buy on credit but do not pay; we borrow and promise that on a certain date we will repay the loan, but nothing is done. Evangelists permit it to be advertised that they will be the speakers both here and there, although they know that they will not be able to come. That is the way things look among us Christians.

After a statement has been reported, it often happens that someone remarks, "O, you must not pay any attention to what he or she says, for they are so loose-mouthed." It is surely time that we wake up and see this sin both in ourselves and in others. Not till then can we have any hope of victory.

"Blessed is he that watcheth, and keepeth his garments, lest he walk naked, and they see his shame."

Our evil mind,
To sin inclined,
Is drawn by sin around us;
If a wicked thought we mind,
Satan soon hath bound us.

One word from hell
Cast its foul spell
On Adam with temptation;
So by one man all men fell
Under condemnation.

Anniversaries and Birthdays

____

____

____

____

OCTOBER 29

And in like manner the Spirit also helpeth our infirmity: for we know not how to pray as we ought; but the Spirit Himself maketh intercession for us with groanings which cannot be uttered. **Rom. 8:26**

OUR thought, our knowledge of Christian truth, what we have grasped of the truth does not really extend very far. Our consciousness can grasp only a small particle of what is deposited in our soul and mind. We often notice that this is so. Not only when we look out toward created things and up toward that world that faith alone can lay hold of, but also when we look into our own bosom and try to plumb bottom there. Then we have an inkling that we are face to face with something that thought cannot attain to.

A Christian comes to know this most clearly when he goes to God in prayer. Then we understand very well that we are unable to look into our great need and to present what lies deepest in our soul. And then we are stuck. But He who knows us through and through, He has arranged matters so wisely that He does what we are unable to do. God's Spirit understands the soul's groanings and so He makes intercession for us with God. What we ought to pray for, but which thought and tongue are unable to express, this the Spirit presents.

A Christian would gain much if he laid hold on this comfort. Then we should also rejoice more in the faith that He who looks into our hearts, where all true prayer has its origin, He hears the praying Spirit and inclines His ear to our groans.

I know of a peaceful eventide;
And when I am faint and weary,
At times with the journey sorely tried,
Through hours that are long and dreary;
Then often I yearn to lay me down,
And sink into blissful slumber.

Anniversaries and Birthdays

OCTOBER 30

Who shall lay anything to the charge of God's elect? It is God that justifieth. Rom. 8:33

PREVIOUSLY in this chapter Paul has said that there is no condemnation to them that are in Christ Jesus, and that what the law could not do, God did when He sent His Son. He has also said, "If God is for us, who is against us?" And "to them that love God all things work together for good."

After having shown us this great miracle of salvation, it is as though he in thought is made free from himself, places himself in the midst of all creation, and then shouts, "Who shall lay anything to the charge of God's elect?" One gets the impression that Paul directs his question to everything and all people without limit. He asks heaven, he asks hell, he asks the earth, but no one stands forth and says, "I can."

When with few words he is to tell us the reason that no one stands forth he says, "It is God that justifieth." God! He who shall render an accounting to no one, and who has the key to death and hell, He justifies us!

He who has seen the content of these words, he has seen the greatest thing a man can see on this earth. You who have grasped Christ in faith: go on to your grave cheerfully. On the judgment day you will meet no other judge than your Savior.

The just is he—and he alone—
Who by this faith is living,
The faith that by good works is shown,
To God the glory giving;
Faith gives thee peace with God above,
But thou thy neighbor, too, must love,
If thou art new created.

Anniversaries and Birthdays

OCTOBER 31

And let the peace of Christ rule in your hearts, to the which also ye were called in one body; and be ye thankful. Col. 3:15

PRIDE and suspicion make us selfish, always demanding something, and complaining; but he who has a humble and trusting spirit has found the road that leads to thankfulness.

He who complains loses his courage, his strength for work, and his joy. He makes life a burden to himself and to those that he lives with, and he dishonors God. It is easy to learn to be dissatisfied with everything and everybody, except yourself. But to be kindly disposed and thankful toward one's fellow men, and to give "thanks always for all things in the name of our Lord Jesus Christ to God, even the Father"—that is the way that leads to the power of God and to a happy life.

It is no trick to say "Thank you" to people that we meet when on the go, but it is difficult to be thankful to those that we live with daily. It is a great art to be able to thank those of your own household. But just where it costs the most, the greatest happiness awaits those who are victors in the test.

We would have been spared much evil in our lives, if we had learned to give thanks instead of complaining and making demands. The man who is regularly greeted with complaints when he gets home tired and worn, often finds a a haven beside a pack of cards and a bottle. And the housewife who is on the point of giving up, would greet a new day of hard work strong and glad, if the grumbling and complaining of husband and children were changed to gratitude.

One of the greatest accusations to reproach us when our dear ones have left us, is that we were not thankful enough toward them while they lived and toiled for us.

Let us try to correct that today!

Jesus, Thou our footsteps guiding
May we never stray from Thee;
Jesus, near us still abiding,
Thou our constant guardian be:
Jesus, Thou our thoughts inspire,
Jesus, be our hearts' desire.

Anniversaries and Birthdays

____

____

____

NOVEMBER 1

Jesus therefore, being wearied with His journey, sat thus by the well. John 4:6

IT is a great blessing to know and believe that He who today sits at the right hand of God and has all power in heaven and on earth, has walked here on earth as one of us. He appreciated friendship highly, and felt wounded and disappointed when friends went away and left Him to fight alone. He lay down in the boat and slept while the storm raged and the billows beat against it, and He sat down by the well of Sychar, tired and hungry after a wearisome journey.

We human beings well know what it means to get tired and hungry. Let us only think of mother. While others sleep, she must often stay awake, and when others have had their rest, she must go to work together with them. But in general there is more than enough of that which makes us weary. Boat and plow, factory and motor, store and office, all wear on mind and nerves: a struggle on land and sea regularly every day to get food for self and family—those are the working conditions for most of us until we lie down to sleep the last sleep. But He who has tried life here below both on land and on sea, He extends His hands to bless all this toil and struggle. He who has innumerable hosts of angels at His disposal, He sends them to guard us in the strife, and to help us in the work.

Let us today also go to our toil cheerfully. Jesus is going to be with us. It is in this work-church that He wants to serve us. We are to conduct worship in working clothes.

Work, for the night is coming,
Work through the morning hours;
Work while the dew is sparkling,
Work 'mid springing flowers;
Work when the day grows brighter,
Work in the glowing sun;
Work, for the night is coming,
When man's work is done.

Anniversaries and Birthdays

NOVEMBER 2

We are not able to go up against the people; for they are stronger than we. Numbers 13:31

Jehovah is with us: fear them not. Numbers 14:9

DESPONDENCY and doubt are a misfortune not only to the person who is seized by these powers of darkness, but they are also a spiritual disease which is contagious. This epidemic spreads with special rapidity when it comes from people that the common crowd looks up to.

When the spies spoke to the people about how impossible it looked to get into Canaan, because the inhabitants there were so much larger and stronger than the Israelites, then they collapsed in black despair. Although Joshua and Caleb tried to imbue them with courage, they could not be moved, and Israel did not cross the border.

This word ought to awaken all Christians, and especially leaders, so they will be on their guard not to put unbelief and discouragement into God's people. How often we can hear that done! Everything is becoming more and more impossible, they tell us; sin and Satan are ravaging and laying everything waste; true Christianity is dying out, and we are on our way to destruction. And then we forget that the only thing such talk accomplishes is to sow discouragement, impotency, and doubt in the minds of God's people. But have we not enough of those already? Should we not rather resemble Joshua and Caleb who looked with hope on the future course of God's people, and then say today as they said in their day: "Jehovah is with us. Fear not!" We can be certain that that is God's will.

If you and I do that we shall enter our right fatherland together with Joshua and Caleb, and we shall also be privileged to help others to enter in.

What our Father does is well:
Though He sadden hill and dell,
Upward yet our praises rise
For the strength His Word supplies,
He has called us sons of God;
Can we murmur at His rod?

Anniversaries and Birthdays

NOVEMBER 3

For we are God's fellow-workers. I Cor. 3:9

PERHAPS we may say that when the gate to paradise was closed, that was the end of the rest that God entered on when He had created all things. After that time a new work-day began for God, and this has not come to an end yet.

A watchful Christian eye can see how all that God is and all that He rules over, works for us. On a Sunday morning on an island John saw what was to happen hereafter. He saw the last part of God's work-day clear to its end. He also saw the great, new sabbath rest.

But what we wish to be reminded of here is that God has called us to be His fellow-workers. Have we considered what this means in honor, confidence in us, and grace for us? You and I shall be privileged to work together with God, and He Himself invites us to this. As a father rejoices to get help from his children in his work, so God is glad to get the cooperation of His people in what He has to do.

It is pathetic that mere habit shall be able to make one forget life's nobility and honor. Should not this get us to give thanks in glorified joy, and to run to meet Him for a happy work-day? Paul did not forget it, but said jubilantly, "But I hold not my life of any account as dear unto myself, so that I may accomplish my course, and the ministry which I received from the Lord Jesus, to testify the gospel of the grace of God."

We too have received this ministry.

We bless Thy Son, who bore
The cross, for sinners dying;
Thy Spirit we adore,
The precious blood applying.
Let work and worship send
Their incense unto Thee,
Till song and service blend,
Beside the crystal sea.

Anniversaries and Birthdays

NOVEMBER 4

And there is no creature that is not manifest in His sight: but all things are naked and laid open before the eyes of Him with whom we have to do. Heb. 4:13

IT is painful for people who thrive in worldliness and sin to be reminded that God sees them. If they are to be in good humor and keep their courage up they must do all they can to put away thoughts about God. Worldly people can feel free and happy only when they are at some distance from the Lord.

That is not the way with a Christian. He rejoices that God sees everything: all sin, all wounds, all longing, and the reason for all tears. Then one can safely go to Him who sees everything, who can do everything, and who has enough love and grace to forgive sin, to heal sores, and to free us from all dangers.

With full confidence and in childlike faith a Christian can open his heart to the eternal, almighty God, and then be permitted to experience that He has a heart full of love for us. That is riches in life, that is light in death, and glory through all eternity.

You young people who must leave father and mother and go out into a cold and dangerous world, listen! Open your heart to Him, and give Him your hand; then you will walk safely through all dangers. Since He sees all, you are to open every room of your heart to Him. Let Him have your sin, and you shall receive His grace! Then come what may, if God is for us, who can be against us?

The eye that sees all is a Savior-eye and a Father-eye for all those who give their hearts to the Lord.

> For God observes our thoughts and deeds,
> The secrets of our heart He reads;
> The wicked cannot be concealed,
> Their evil ways shall be revealed,
> He every true believer knows,
> And love and grace on him bestows.

Anniversaries and Birthdays

____

____

____

____

NOVEMBER 5

I know thy works (Behold, I have set before thee a door opened, which none can shut), that thou hast a little power, and didst keep My Word, and didst not deny My name. Rev. 3:8

WHEN God opens a door for us, no one can shut it. But if He shuts the door, all is lost. No matter how much we then knock and shout, "Lord, open to us!" the door will never be opened. God Himself has said that.

If you who still are outside of the kingdom of God would think this over, I wonder if you then would not redeem the time. The door still stands wide open, we are still living in the time of grace. "Yet there is room." So when you still are standing outside the door that God has opened, the reason is that the door of your heart is shut. It is at this closed door that God knocks. If you open the door, He enters; but if you do not open, you will one day find God's door closed. He who does not seek the Lord while He may be found, will never find Him.

But this word about the open door is spoken primarily to Christians who in the midst of their weakness and poverty cling to the Word of God, the Word that in the name of Jesus increases strength to him that has no might, and promises to fill the poor with good things.

You who know your wretchedness, and who think that everything that is yours looks incredibly small—remember the door that God has opened. He never closes the door against the afflicted. He who knows nothing unto salvation save Jesus Christ and His cross, he will find God's door open both in life and in death.

That gate ajar stands free for all
Who seek through it salvation;
The rich and poor, the great and small,
Of every tribe and nation.

Anniversaries and Birthdays

NOVEMBER 6

Who saved us, and called us with a holy calling, not according to our works, but according to His own purpose and grace, which was given to us in Christ Jesus before times eternal. II Tim. 1:9

GOD did not let the call to salvation go out to a lost race without having salvation ready.

That one is awakened to see that he needs salvation, and to turn and believe, that has nothing to do with salvation itself. Faith without a prepared salvation would be like an empty spoon and like a pocketbook without money. The Savior-will and the salvation-work sprang out of the heart of God before the world was, and they were put into the first promise to the first men. Everything is according to the counsel and purpose of God and the grace which was in Christ before times eternal.

Jesus saved us and called us. Nothing of what we are or are not has anything to do with the essence of salvation. We received it from eternity in Christ. It is this great, prepared gift that God asks us to come and accept without money and without price. No virtue can save us, neither can any sin condemn us. But to reject what God gave us in Christ, that is the condemnation. What most people consider unimportant, namely, to turn away from Christ, that is the way to the fire that is never quenched and to "The outer darkness."

"By grace have ye been saved through faith; not of works, that no man should glory." Come, all, and accept Christ, and you are saved!

That salvation is sufficient for all of us. All else is not enough, no matter how good it is. Only the salvation in Christ is enough.

Praise the Rock of our salvation,
Laud His name from zone to zone;
On that rock the church is builded,
Christ Himself the corner-stone;
Vain against our rock-built Zion
Winds and waters, fire and hail;
Christ is in her midst; against her
Sin and hell shall not prevail.

Anniversaries and Birthdays

NOVEMBER 7

The sower went forth to sow his seed: and as he sowed, some fell by the way side; and it was trodden under foot, and the birds of the heaven devoured it. Luke 8:5

HE who knows us to the very depth of our being, He says that we are either like the wayside where people plod along, and where birds snap up every seed; or like a rock with a little soil on it where all plants wither away; or like a field overgrown with thorns; or like good ground where the seed sprouts, grows, and bears fruit. Jesus says that that is the way it looks among us who hear the Word of God.

Many hear the Word without hearing. As the water runs off the sea fowl when it has dived and again sails on the surface of the ocean, such is their heart when they have heard God's Word. The soul is like a polished stone on the beach, and like the road that human feet have made hard by tramping on it. You can go from church to a dance hall, from a prayer meeting to a liquor party, from the singing of hymns to the songs of the harlot, and from the altar to the seat of scoffers. Everything suits you about equally well. God's awakening voice may indeed reach your ear, but not your heart. The waters of grace flow over you like the deep river over the stones that are hard and slippery —and you never tremble in the presence of a holy God. If you are not better than others, you are at any rate not worse, you think, and the God that is not satisfied with you as you are, you do not care for.

Thus you have thought to live and to die and to meet God. And if a serious word should fall very near to your heart some time, the birds from the kingdom of darkness will see that it is plucked away.

You unhappy person! If God's holy plow could cut a furrow through your heart, you, too, could be saved.

May we, in unfeigned repentance,
  Seek forgiveness in Thy name,
Nor the law's condemning sentence
  Fill our hearts with fear and shame;
Thou alone canst pardon give,
Dearest Lord, our sins forgive.

Anniversaries and Birthdays

____________ ________________________________

____

____

NOVEMBER 8

And those on the rock are they who, when they have heard, receive the Word with joy; and these have no root, who for a while believe, and in time of temptation fall away. Luke 8:13

THE Word about the human heart, that resembles a rock with a little earth on it, is easy for us to understand. It means these people who quickly are gripped by things either bad or good. When the message from God is delivered with both power and fervor, these are the first to be persuaded to repent.

With great boldness they express their thanks that they now are saved. But when spring, warmth, and light gave way to coldness and tribulation, when the way became narrow and the hill steep, when rising prices made building too expensive, and war broke out, everything became only loss and bankruptcy.

Life wilted just as rapidly as it had appeared.

When Jesus once met a man of the sort that easily becomes enthusiastic and who cried out, "I will follow Thee whithersoever Thou goest!" He answered him: "The foxes have holes, and the birds of the heaven have nests; but the Son of man hath not where to lay His head."

If many of the preachers of the Word had had a little more of the same knowledge of souls, and then with a gentle hand had restrained such people, the kingdom of God would have been much better off. But it is so tempting and so easy to win a name as an evangelist at the expense of such superficial souls. And if one can manage it, he also tries to scrape away some of the earth, of which there already is altogether too little, so that the seed shall sprout still sooner.

But you who are older and more mature as a Christian, you must help these people with love, poise, and persevering courage. Then the rock may crumble into earth, and the root from this life seed may go down deeper, and thus the life of faith may be preserved. This has happened before: it may happen also now.

Divine Instructor, gracious Lord!
Be Thou for ever near;
Teach me to love Thy sacred Word,
And view my Savior there!

Anniversaries and Birthdays

NOVEMBER 9

And that which fell among the thorns, these are they that have heard, and as they go on their way they are choked with cares and riches and pleasures of this life, and bring no fruit to perfection.

Luke 8:14

THE saddest part of the Word about the sower is that which is said of the seed that fell among the thorns. There was enough earth, and good earth, and the seed had a chance to take root. So far all was in good order. But then the weeds grew up and choked everything.

What kind of people are these? There is nothing wrong about their awakening, conversion, and faith. They have not allowed themselves to be carried away in an unthinking transport of feelings. They are people of sound mind, quiet courage, good understanding, and practical judgment. The kingdom of God got a capable worker when it got you; one with courage, with an aggressive will, and with ability to accomplish something. But the danger of weeds came exactly to you with your natural aptitudes and your practical sense for the common good of humanity. It was such fun to have a part in money making, to get on and up in the world, and all these things were good. No one could say that you were doing anything wrong. But the care for the many things, the seducing power of riches, might, and honor —these got a larger place in your heart than fellowship with God, and thus the life with God was choked to death.

How much life, healthy and beautiful life with God, has lost its strength and has faded away in riches and worldly lusts! While the living grain billowed in the wind, the thorns were piercing, and the soul got bleeding sores.

Thou thorn-filled earth, how much beautiful life with God thou hast pierced to death!

O Father, may Thy Word prevail
Against the gates of hell!
Behold the vineyard Thou hast tilled
With thorns and thistles filled.
'Tis true, Thy plants are there;
But, ah, how weak and rare!
How slight the power and evidence
Of Word and Sacraments!

Anniversaries and Birthdays

____

____

____

NOVEMBER 10

And that in the good ground, these are such as in an honest and good heart, having heard the Word, hold it fast, and bring forth fruit with patience. Luke 8:15

WHAT a happy life! It begins in sunny spring, grows till radiant autumn, and matures ripe fruit. How blessed to be able to stand among these when fall comes!

But who are these that have such honest and good hearts? How do they live, and what kind of people are they?

It must be the people who have as their one great object in life to be in the blessed fellowship of God. It must be those who, with an honest heart, live their entire lives in the light of God's Word and Spirit and will, and who do not inquire about loss or gain, poverty or riches, honor or dishonor. It must be those who can lose everything in life: name, honor, position, future, earthly well-being, money, and friends, but not their good conscience, their God, their Savior, their peace, and their hope.

Everything that is offered by the will, faculties, natural aptitudes, and open doors, must first be weighed on God's scales and show their worth in the light that comes from God and eternal life. What one cannot be, do, or own with the entire assent of God—that is laid aside.

But it must be more than that. It must also be: to be able to receive the hardest blows with faith and thanksgiving and confident poise; it must be to kiss the rod and to glory in tribulations. In that soil steadfastness grows, and approvedness, and hope. There that fair flower opens that bears still fairer fruit: love, joy, peace, longsuffering, kindness, goodness, faithfulness, meekness, self-control.

That must be the good ground. That is fruit.

Word of the ever-living God,
  Will of His glorious Son;
Without Thee how could earth be trod,
  Or heaven itself be won?

Lord, grant us all aright to learn
  The wisdom it imparts;
And to its heavenly teaching turn,
  With simple, childlike hearts.

Anniversaries and Birthdays

NOVEMBER 11

But I have this against thee, that thou didst leave thy first love. Remember therefore whence thou art fallen, and repent and do the first works. Rev. 2:4-5

TO fall away from the inner fellowship with God and at the same time to be a zealous worker for God—that seems to be a form of backsliding which is just as dangerous for the people of God as it is easy to get into. Outwardly all may seem proper. We can have an open eye for evils found among Christians, we may love the truth, be patient, teach correctly, and work with great zeal in the kingdom of God, and yet, in the midst of all this we may have lost the kernel and the spark, yea, life itself.

We may hide from ourselves our entire inner defeat with great concern for everything that is right and true and good; yea, also by working for Jesus' name's sake without growing weary. We may hide our internal wound with external works. Life in Christ's love can drown in reasonable and Christian correctness. There is the danger, and the danger is great.

But what then is the first love?

That which characterizes all true life with God from its beginning is a tender conscience, an honest spirit, and an entirely open attitude toward God. The slightest thing that we feared might be wrong in heart or deed, was enough to drive us into the presence of God, so that we might tell Him all. We could hide nothing from God. That is the way he lives who has not lost his first love.

It is this fellowship with God that we can so easily lose.

There is a blessed home
  Beyond this land of woe,
Where trials never come,
  Nor tears of sorrow flow;
Where faith is lost in sight,
  And patient hope is crowned,
And everlasting light
  Its glory throws around.

Anniversaries and Birthdays

___

___

___

NOVEMBER 12

And the peace of God, which passeth all understanding, shall guard your hearts and your thoughts in Christ Jesus. Phil. 4:7

MAN can steer the largest ships on sea and in the air, he can tame the strongest of wild animals, and can chain the forces of nature, but he cannot tame his own heart or control his thoughts, not even the least.

The more we apply our will and energy to conquer ourselves, the more certainly and the sooner are we defeated. It is like the case of the big river: it grows in strength according as the opposition grows, and at last breaks down all hindrances. That is the way our evil heart and our unruly thoughts play with us, when we try to resist. Many an upright person wears himself out in a hopeless struggle, and wonders that God does not help.

There is one place where heart and mind can be guarded against evil, and that place is the peace of God. The peace of God—that must presumably be the peace that is in God. If we get heart and thoughts into His peace, then we are saved. The problem then is to find the way, so that we can arrive there. I think the secret lies in the words just preceding our text: "Rejoice in the Lord always!" The fact of the matter is that we are taken captive by that in which we find our joy. Consequently, if our joy is in the Lord, our thoughts and heart are in Him also. They do not provoke each other there, there is no mind for opposition; there heart and thoughts drown in peace—in the peace of God in Christ Jesus.

Peace, to soothe our bitter woes,
God in Christ on us bestows;
Jesus bought our peace with God
With His holy, precious blood;
Peace in Him for sinners found,
Is the gospel's joyful sound.

Anniversaries and Birthdays

NOVEMBER 13

Lay not up for yourselves treasures upon the earth, where moth and rust consume, and where thieves break through and steal.

Matt. 6:19

TO lay up treasures upon the earth cannot be the same as to have something to spare.

Just as little as being poor is the same as being rich toward God and having treasure in heaven, just so little is owning something the same as being separated from the riches in God. It would surely be more to the honor of God if every farmer owned his farm, every fisher his boat, and if every town man had a bank book, than it is when they have assumed bigger debts than they can pay. Jesus had money left, and when the people had had enough to eat in the desert, He asked the disciples to gather up the fragments, so that nothing should be lost.

One of the greatest misfortunes in our time is that people want to use up at once everything they can get their hands on, and then when they have nothing left, society is to feed them. I suppose that no one will dare to say that that is a Christian way.

But what then does Jesus mean by saying that one shall not lay up treasures on earth? If we are to understand Jesus aright, we must emphasize the words "lay up" and "treasures." A treasure is something that one loves very specially, it is something that has laid hold on us and owns us. Treasure and heart cannot be separated, but earthly property and the heart can exist separately. Many, who own much in this world, have their treasure in heaven; and many poor fellows are the most arrant of earth-bound slaves.

The chief thing for us is not owning much or little of earthly goods, but to be rich toward God, and to have a heart detached from everything in this world. That is what Jesus reminds us of. And we sorely need this reminder.

Our hope is sure in Jesus' might;
Against themselves the godless fight,
Themselves, not us, distressing;
Shame and contempt their lot shall be:
God is with us, with Him are we,
To us belongs His blessing.

Anniversaries and Birthdays

NOVEMBER 14

Let not your heart be troubled: believe in God, believe also in Me.
John 14:1

IT was in the quiet hour in the upper room that last night that Jesus spoke these words to His own. Now He has Himself gone through the world, and He knows what it has to give. He knows, too, that what it gave Him, it will also give His people.

Jesus not only knows about all the difficulties and dangers that are going to meet us; but He also reckons with them! He who so clearly sees the restless heart in His people, He has Himself said with His own mouth, "My soul is exceeding sorrowful even unto death." We ought to try to remember that. He remembers it when He sees His own on the point of losing courage.

But we forget it, and the sad part is that we forget it most easily when we need it most. Yes, we not only forget it, but we think that He can no longer care for me, poor wretch that I am. And so He looks cold and hard to us when we most need to see Him meek and mild.

Though a mother may forget the child at her breast, yet I cannot forget thee, says the Lord. Least of all can He forget when His people are in danger. When life's sombre struggle makes the heart uneasy, then His love awakens, and as a mother comforts her child, so the Lord comforts His people. So lay your troubled heart close to the Father-heart and Savior-heart of God. Then it will be full of peace.

Ye who with guilty terror
Are trembling, fear no more;
With love and grace the Savior
Shall you to hope restore:
He comes, who contrite sinners
Will with the children place,
The children of His Father,
The heirs of life and grace.

Anniversaries and Birthdays

NOVEMBER 15

So then as through one trespass the judgment came unto all men to condemnation; even so through one act of righteousness the free gift came unto all men to justification of life. Rom. 5:18

ADAM'S sin is the inheritance that he gave his race. As we received his body and blood, we also received his sin. Through his trespass the judgment came unto all men to condemnation, because his trespass made sinners of us all.

No one can slip by this hard fate nor remove it from his nature. Life's naked truth lays it at our feet night and day from generation to generation.

But what no one understands, what many do not know, and only a little flock believes, is that Christ is the father of a new race, and that He has thereby won us a new inheritance. As Adam by his fall gave us sin and judgment, so Christ gave us redemption and life by His acts of righteousness. "For as in Adam all die, so also in Christ shall all be made alive." This sets our brain in a whirl, but the crushed heart becomes alive in those who believe it, and without our understanding it, our lost life cries out: "This is what we must have! This is our salvation!"

We shall receive the merit of Christ as our heritage and inheritance just as surely as we received Adam's sin. The new father of our race is Christ. As we have inherited what was contained in Adam's flesh and blood, spirit and nature, so we do also inherit what is contained in Christ's flesh and blood, spirit and nature, and by the latter we are redeemed from the former.

Once on the dreary mountain
We wandered far and wide,
Far from the cleansing fountain,
Far from the pierced side;
But Jesus sought and found us,
And washed our guilt away;
With cords of love He bound us
To be His own for aye.

Anniversaries and Birthdays

NOVEMBER 16

"Never man so spake." "Is not this He whom they seek to kill?" So there arose a division in the multitude because of Him.

John 7:46, 25, 43

JESUS stood forth in the midst of the people and spoke. Then when some believed in Him, He turned to them and said, that if they wanted to be His true disciples, they must abide in His Word: only then could the truth make them free. But they would not agree to this, and their faith changed to anger and hatred.

So Jesus leaves these brain-worshipping slaves of the letter, and goes out among the people, to the helpless. When He meets people who are in trouble, no one says that He has a devil or is possessed, but even the evil spirits who must flee before His Savior-might cry out that He is the Son of the living God.

Just as impossible as it is for the conceited person to submit to Him, just so loud do those who are in trouble call upon Him. As warmly as He is loved by the latter, so ardently is He hated by the former.

No one has been so loved and so hated as Jesus. Some see in Him their greatest antagonist, others their only salvation and eternal welfare. Some give property and life in order to get Him, His Word, and Spirit, and power out of the world. Others sacrifice everything: life and property, father and mother, home and fatherland, in order to make Him known among the peoples. I pray you to ask yourself: What is Jesus to me?

O Bringer of salvation,
  Who wondrously hast wrought,
Thyself the revelation
  Of love beyond our thought:
We worship Thee, we bless Thee,
  To Thee, O Christ, we sing;
We praise Thee, and confess Thee
  Our gracious Lord and King.

Anniversaries and Birthdays

NOVEMBER 17

He Himself knew what He would do. None that wait for Thee shall be put to shame. My people shall never be put to shame.
John 6:6; Psalm 25:3; Joel 2:27

THERE were too many people and too little food, and no matter how Philip figured, there was too little for all. Is it not strange that not one of the disciples thought to count on Jesus? They had surely seen His miracles many times, each greater than the previous one. But no, they did not think of that; they had forgotten that.

How humanity at all times is true to form! While our life is interwoven with benefits which are built on one miracle after another, we nevertheless continue to calculate. And when we fail to make things come out as we desire, or as we think they must be, then we see no way out.

But He who has staked out the way for His own, He who knows what He wants to do, and who has the ability to accomplish what He desires, He does not come to counsel with us before He sets His will to work. As the potter takes a lump of clay and makes whatever he will out of it, so Jesus does with His own, those that He has bargained to help home to God. He who knows our nature, and the tricks of Satan, He sees best on what way He must conduct us, and He also knows what He will do. So, Christian, lay aside all your arithmetic, quit your road building, and all your heavy thoughts. Try to count on Him who does not need to count, on Him who has enough for all, also for you and me. You will find out that His will and His way are the best. Those who looked up to Him radiated joy, and their faces never blushed with shame. The Word of God says that. Believe it.

Only be still, and wait His leisure
In cheerful hope, with heart content
To take whate'er thy Father's pleasure
And all-discerning love have sent;
Nor doubt our inmost wants are known
To Him who chose us for His own.

Anniversaries and Birthdays

___

___

___

NOVEMBER 18

Now when Jesus was in Bethany, in the house of Simon the leper, there came unto Him a woman having an alabaster cruse of exceeding precious ointment, and she poured it upon His head, as He sat at meat. Matt. 26:6-7

JESUS will permit Himself to be anointed King before He seats Himself on the foal of the donkey and rides into Salem city. But He does not go into Israel's national sanctuary, there to receive the homage of the most reverend priests, of the chosen and the learned men of the country, and to be anointed by them. No, He enters a poor home where saved sinners dwell, and there He permits Himself to be anointed by a thankful and believing woman.

The fact that this ointment brings a message about a grave must not cause us anxiety: the kingly crown lies on the edge of the grave. On Easter morning it was placed on His head by almighty God, and it shall never be removed.

It was a woman who brought sin into the world, but it was also the same woman who received the promise that her Seed should bruise the serpent's head. It was a woman who poured the ointment on the head of the Savior of the world, and it was a woman who first brought the message that He was risen from the grave. Thus God rewards the sinner! In everything that He does He is different from us. When we expect judgment and punishment, He comes to meet us with eternal life in Jesus Christ our Lord; and He redeems us from sin and judgment with grace for grace.

Come, let us, too, anoint Him and do homage to Him as our King! He who opens the door of his heart to Him and permits himself to be ruled by this King, he will find the way home again to the land where there is no unhappiness. There the redeemed will sing to the honor of Him who from the throne of grace helped us and brought us out of darkness into His marvelous light.

Ah, dearest Jesus, Holy Child,
Make Thee a bed soft, undefiled
Within my heart, that it may be
A quiet chamber kept for Thee.

Anniversaries and Birthdays

NOVEMBER 19

For many walk, of whom I told you often, and now tell you even weeping, that they are the enemies of the cross of Christ. Phil. 3:18

THE holiest war that a man feels, and the purest tears that a Christian sheds, are sorrow and tears that others may be saved. Much of what also the children of God weep for has, alas, its cause in a heart that is selfish and bent on earthly things. But those who have an unceasing sorrow for the many who are moving on toward the grave without hope, and who are struggling to win them for God, they have gotten some of the mind of Jesus.

Such sympathy is more than human. No one can enter into the fellowship of the sufferings of Jesus, and feel holy sorrow for others without being laid hold on by God.

When the servant intercedes with prayers and tears for his master and mistress, when the refined lady cries out to God for her servants, when a believing man brings his worldly and contrary neighbor to God in prayer year after year, then the love from Christ has found a place in the heart. And when talented young people, who might have had a bright future among their own countrymen, bid farewell to everything, and go out to a strange people that try to kill them, and wear themselves out there just to win others for Christ, then heaven has come down to earth.

We will praise God who gave us this desire, and we will confidently hold fast to the Word, that he who sows in tears shall reap in joy.

Lord, Thou needest not, I know,
Service such as I can bring;
Yet I long to prove and show
Full allegiance to my King.
Thou an honor art to me;
Let me be a praise to Thee.

Anniversaries and Birthdays

NOVEMBER 20

Not of works, that no man should glory. Eph. 2:9

WHEN we feel very seriously the need of fellowship with God, and the question of salvation becomes life's greatest question, then the thought takes root in us, that if we are ever to be saved, we must first become different and better than we are now. Then we must conquer sin; and thoughts, heart, and disposition must be changed.

So we exert ourselves with all our will and all our might, and try to break the power of sin and evil in the heart. This manner of going at it is so deep-rooted in our nature that no one will escape it except by a God's miracle.

Just as impossible as it seems to us to believe that we are saved just as we are, just so little are we able to improve ourselves in any domain. Then we forget, or more correctly, we do not see that it is just those who cannot become good by their own power, who need salvation. Those who are able to do nothing, those who in their own eyes become worse and worse, they who like a drowning man have not as much as a straw to cling to, it is they who must be saved by Another.

You who are living in this impossible toil and who think that you must become different and better before you dare believe that you are saved, you must get out of this false way. If you should be unfortunate enough to make your plan work as you wish, then you would again be pleased with yourself, and you would stand forth as a Pharisee instead of as a saved sinner. All those who desire to enter God's heaven must travel by way of Jesus as helpless and lost sinners.

"For by grace have ye been saved through faith; and that not of yourselves, it is the gift of God."

Nor alms, nor deeds that I have done,
Can for a single sin atone;
To Calvary alone I flee:
O God, be merciful to me!

Anniversaries and Birthdays

NOVEMBER 21

And He beheld a publican, named Levi, sitting at the place of toll, and said unto him, "Follow Me!" Luke 5:27

WHEN I think back over those years of my life that I have been permitted to follow Jesus, I can truthfully say that they have been good years. If I said anything different, I should be denying the best things in my life. That I have many times been a poor companion for Him, that is my sorrow and my shame; but He has never left me. He has in spite of everything filled my life with grace for grace.

Now I see better than ever before that He has never done anything except good to me. In changing times, in prosperity and in adversity, in sorrows and in sins, His love and sympathy have been with me from day to day. When I did wrong, He forgave all; He healed the wounds that I got in the conflict, He wiped my tears away, and when I felt most lonely and deserted by men, He was nearest to me. He always punished me in love, and made the tribulations of life into the fairest treasures. In cases where I did not understand myself He understood all; in times of greatest weakness He gave most strength, and in the midst of darkness He threw light toward the goal. My soul longs to thank Him with a spirit made free and a liberated tongue for all His benefits in a long life.

Come all, and follow Jesus! Come, young and old, come, high and low, come, poor and rich, you who knock around in the human multitude, come! and also you who are walking through life lonely. He is the only One of those you meet who graciously will follow you through both life and death.

I walk with Jesus all the way,
His guidance never fails me,
Within His wounds I find a stay,
When Satan's power assails me;
And by His footsteps led,
My path I safely tread,
In spite of ills that threaten may,
I walk with Jesus all the way.

Anniversaries and Birthdays

NOVEMBER 22

For I say unto you, that except your righteousness shall exceed the righteousness of the scribes and Pharisees, ye shall in no wise enter into the kingdom of heaven. Matt. 5:20

MANY of the people who say that they believe in God, and who also want to go to heaven when they die, live in the faith that they will get there if they do their best morally. It is sad to find how many there are who get angry when they meet someone who doubts this faith of theirs. They ask: Do you believe that God can condemn those who live as morally as they can? Is the God that you believe in as cold and unmerciful as that? And then they may also add, "I don't want anything to do with that kind of God."

This sounds quite right to short thought, but if we will go over this matter seriously, we will find that that position is both meaningless and un-Christian. To be saved by living as morally as one can is altogether impossible. We must understand that if there were a heaven for such people there would be no Savior there, and no saved sinner. All who might be there, would be there because they had lived as morally as they could, and therefore they would have no one else to thank for being there than themselves. They cannot thank God, and much less Jesus. But all the people who want to have anything to do with Christianity should be able to understand that this is as far from salvation as the east is from the west.

Those that get inside the door in the kingdom of God dressed in their own clothes are thrown out. Jesus has said that. It is only the righteousness of Christ that gives us the right to enter the kingdom of God. All others will be left standing outside.

I have naught, my God, to offer,
  Save the blood of Thy dear Son;
Graciously accept the proffer:
  Make His righteousness mine own.
His holy life gave He, was crucified for me;
His righteousness perfect He now pleads before Thee;
His own robe of righteousness, my highest good,
Shall clothe me in glory, through faith in His blood.

Anniversaries and Birthdays

NOVEMBER 23

But when thou shalt be old, thou shalt stretch forth thy hands, and another shall gird thee, and carry thee whither thou wouldest not.
John 21:18

HE, who in faith has accepted Jesus as His Savior, has at the same time given God the right to rule him as He wills. To say, "Thy will be done," and also to demand the right to get what one wants for himself in this world—this is not possible in the kingdom where Christ is King. Although this should be self-evident, it is here that we have our hardest struggles.

What often causes us to consider God cold and unmerciful toward us is that our way of looking at life is different from God's way. We look at the advantages to be gained in this world: He looks at life's goal. We plan for the short time we are to be here: He sees what import there is for us in the alternative, eternally lost, or eternally saved. And if He sees that an earthly advantage can rob us of eternal life, then He carries us whither we would not. He has marked out the road that we are to travel, and He has made ready the school that we are to attend, and He will not alter His plans, no matter how much we complain and weep. So long as we are in His fellowship, He treats us as He pleases. Together with Peter many of God's best people must pass through the most distressing kinds of adversity; and the strange part of it is, that for many the uphill climbing becomes steepest as they draw near the end of life.

But if we walk in faith and patience, if not always willingly, then everything that we meet will be a hand that looses the earthly ties, that sanctifies our souls, and that helps us to honor God.

> But if thou ne'er forsake Him,
> Thou shalt deliverance find;
> Behold all unexpected,
> He will thy soul unbind.
> He from thy heavy burden
> Will soon thy heart set free:
> Yea, from that weight no evil
> Hath yet befallen thee.

Anniversaries and Birthdays

____

____

____

NOVEMBER 24

I thank Thee, O Father, Lord of heaven and earth, that Thou didst hide these things from the wise and understanding, and didst reveal them unto babes. Matt. 11:25

JESUS does not mean to say that being learned and wise is the same as being unable to find and to possess God's wisdom. Neither does He mean that all ignorant people are as a matter of course on the way to heaven, but He does mean that wisdom and knowledge cannot help anyone to find God. It is this that He thanks our heavenly Father for.

Just think what it would mean, if it were necessary to be wise and learned in order to be saved! How would we fare then? Then the prospect would be gloomy indeed. In the first place, relatively few people are wise and learned; and in the next place, the majority of us have neither the ability nor the means to get us knowledge. But when God has arranged matters in a way so divinely great and good that we can find Him through a childlike mind, then all who will, can be saved.

Then the learned person can step down to the person who is uneducated and childlike, and trustingly accept Him who casts no one out. The way to God lies down in the valley where we helpless ones look up to Him whom the learned find as impossible to search out as the ignorant. Both Nicodemus and the thief found the way to paradise at the cross of Jesus: there was no difference. There God has given us the opportunity to lay aside wisdom and folly, nobility and poverty, sin and imagined virtues.

You who are wise and learned, come and bow down to the God of wisdom, and acknowledge that you know nothing of what you especially ought to know. Then you, too, will find light and life in a childlike faith.

Cheer up, faint heart, rejoice and sing,
All anxious fear resign;
For God, the sovereign Lord and King,
Is thy God, even thine:
He is thy portion, He thy joy,
Thy life, and light, and Lord;
Thy counsellor when doubts annoy,
Thy shield and great reward.

Anniversaries and Birthdays

NOVEMBER 25

All forsook me: may it not be laid to their account. II Tim. 4:16

ONE would think that so truth-loving a man and so holy a Christian as Paul would have been spared being forsaken by his friends; but he, too, had to see them go when he most needed them. A heavy and dark philosophy of life lies in the words, that we must not rely on men. So we, too. must count on losing our best friends. Life tells us, too, that gradually as the years pass, many must put up with being more and more lonely and friendless.

Think only of all the fathers and mothers who wore themselves out to help their children get on in the world, and who in their old age were left alone, to sit forgotten by all! Brother forgets sister, and sister brother, and in a pinch the person that you expected most help from can add the heaviest stone to your burden. Many who worked together in the kingdom of God as Christian brothers and good friends for many and long years, pulled apart as evening came on. That is the way we men are. We are no more reliable than that. "All forsook me," says Paul. All!

But the big thing that we must learn of Paul is that he faces all this with a loving and forgiving heart. "May it not be laid to their account," he says. He who can say that is unspeakably happy. It is the will of God that we forgive everybody, and in the midst of adversity glorify Him who has said: "I will not fail thee, nor forsake thee." When you have the Friend who never fails you, then you are surely not lonely either in life or in death.

Let the world despise and leave me;
They have left my Savior, too;
Human hearts and looks deceive me,
Thou art not, like them, untrue;
And while Thou shalt smile upon me,
God of wisdom, love, and might,
Foes may hate, and friends may shun me;
Show Thy face and all is bright.

Anniversaries and Birthdays

NOVEMBER 26

But Jesus said unto him, "Judas, betrayest thou the Son of man with a kiss?" Luke 22:48

COULD not Jesus have refrained from taking Judas as treasurer? Perhaps he then would have been saved? Many think thus. But such a thought is false.

A man must have the position that harmonizes best with the faculties that he possesses. He, who is not capable as a business man or politician, should be neither. He who does not have language at his command and who has not a voice strong enough so that people can hear what he says, must not be a preacher.

The will of God and the law of life are that every man shall have a position and responsibility in accordance with his ability and aptitude. That is the way it is in the kingdom of God, too. Christ does not give us new natural attributes when we become Christians, but He puts a gift of grace into the natural characteristic, and then He gives us a task that is in keeping with both. That is where the battle must be fought. Victory or defeat for us all.

It is the keen business man who will be most tempted to make money in a dishonest way, and it is the ablest business manager who most clearly sees how he can take money from the till. Likewise it is the most talented preacher of the Word of God who is most tempted to pride; and he who is gifted as a leader is in greatest danger of misusing his power. Where ability, call, and task are present, danger also lies in waiting. It cannot be otherwise. If we suffer defeat, if the steel cracks in the fire, then what happened to Judas will happen to us. But if we are victorious we will be "men in Christ." As gold is purified in the fire, so by the grace of God the Christian is steeled through tasks, responsibility, struggle, and victory.

> O watch and pray,
> My soul, the way
> Of safety lies before thee;
> Lest thou shouldst be led astray,
> And the foe come o'er thee.

Anniversaries and Birthdays

____

____

____

NOVEMBER 27

Blessed are the eyes that see the things that ye see. Luke 10:23

THE one great art in life consists in this: to see Jesus. All that we try to see and possess apart from Him, also in the matter of our salvation, is without worth if we do not see Him. But if our gaze is directed toward Him who bore our sins in His body, who nailed to the cross the bond written in ordinances that was against us, and reconciled us to God, then we see that in Him we are saved.

In Him everything is taken care of for us with God. There is the covenant of peace signed with the blood of God and of the Son of man, there death is conquered, and eternal life given to all who believe.

When Satan tempts us, when sin allures and the world would ensnare us, then the look at Jesus can save us from all these, because we in Him see grace and redemption. If sickness, sorrow, and poverty come knocking at our door, we can by seeing Him, look up to God as our Father, and thank Him in the midst of storm and darkness, because He lets everything work for our good. And in our last struggle, when everything in us and about us fails, when we are too weak to pray, yea even to draw one prayerful breath, then it is enough to see Him who casts no one out, and who will fill all heavens with saved sinners.

When the last shadow of this world vanishes in the light of the new Jerusalem, and our eyes behold the King in His beauty, then life's highest happiness shall be attained. As the ocean fills the fjord with water up to its own level, so shall saved man become one with God without being God. "If He shall be manifested, we shall be like Him; for we shall see Him even as He is" (I John 3:2).

My Father's house on high,
Home of my soul, how near,
At times, to faith's foreseeing eye,
Thy golden gates appear!

Anniversaries and Birthdays

NOVEMBER 28

Beloved, believe not every spirit, but prove the spirits, whether they are of God. I John 4:1

A SAD experience that we often have in life is that many of those that we considered the best Christians can be ensnared by false, destructive spiritual doctrines and movements. If men stand forth who consider themselves spiritual-minded to a high degree, and who at the same time believe that they alone have found the whole truth, then many of those that one least expected it of, are entrapped.

The reason for this seems as a rule to be that these refined, soft souls are so fearful of making a mistake and thereby offending God that they do not dare to prove the spirits. In the next place, they have the wrong view that when a preacher uses the Word of God, and with much mental energy bolsters his opinions with Bible passages, then he must be from God.

It would be no trick for a Christian to know that the spirit did not come from God, if the false preacher would have nothing to do with the Word of God, with prayer, and with Jesus. It is just there the deception lies: the false spirit appears in Christian garb. But that is also the reason the apostle asks us to prove the spirits whether they are of God.

How then shall one find it out?

God's Spirit always makes a man small in his own eyes and poor in spirit. The Word about sin and grace, about salvation and atonement, is the highest note where the Spirit of God rules. But he who makes his mind a judge of God's Word, and who believes that he is better than other Christians, he is ruled by a false spirit. God's Spirit makes us think humbly of ourselves, so that we always need help, and again and again seek Jesus as our only salvation.

Grant my mind and my affections
  Wisdom, counsel, purity,
That I may be ever seeking
  Naught but that which pleases Thee,
Let Thy knowledge spread and grow,
  And all error overthrow.

Anniversaries and Birthdays

NOVEMBER 29

"But, according to His promise, we look for new heavens and a new earth, wherein dwelleth righteousness." **II Peter 3:13**

SOME time there will come a different age from the one we are now living in. It is impossible to think and believe that everything will continue through all eternity as it now is. Life is pregnant with the idea that a decisive break must come, when good and evil shall be separated forever. It is certain that God's people and the whole creation look forward to that time: it is clear that God has told us that that time shall come.

If then it appears to us that all things continue as they were, we must remember that God counts in a manner different from ours. When one day is with the Lord as a thousand years, we have indeed not waited long. That He delays doing what He has promised is caused by His Savior-love. He wants to save that which can be saved, and a few years of waiting are nothing to Him when only He can save more of those that He bought so dearly and loves so highly.

But it is glorious to remember that the day of liberty will soon appear for the world that is subjected to the bondage of corruption, and for the creation that longs and waits. Soon the new Jerusalem will come down out of heaven from God, adorned as a bride for her bridegroom, and—all things are new!

"Yesterday is past, the morrow we have not seen, and today the Lord helps." Israel! wait for the Lord; the day is not far distant!

I know a home of joy eternal,
Where all the pilgrim hosts shall meet
In radiancy and bliss complete
Around the Christ in realms supernal.
From east and west, from ev'ry zone,
They gather there before the throne,
At home in joy eternal.

Anniversaries and Birthdays

NOVEMBER 30

Fear not, daughter of Zion: behold, thy King cometh, sitting on an ass's colt. John 12:15

WHEN Christ had conquered sin, Satan, and death He sat down at the right hand of God. He took the book out of the hand of Him who sat on the throne, and since then He has gone forward from one victory to another. Even though it may not look that way to us, it is nevertheless He who has all power not only in heaven, but also on earth. He has tamed the world's wild steed, and is strong enough to hold him in check.

We Christians have a right to appropriate for ourselves the comfort that is found in this, both for what meets us in our own lives, and in regard to what happens out in the world. To us it may appear as if only sin and Satan are ruling, but in the midst of all, Christ goes forward as King, and opens one seal after another in the book that He holds in His hand.

Christ is King in the whole creation. But first and last He desires to be King for and over His people. When we accepted Him as Savior, we accepted Him as King also. He desires to direct our thoughts, heart, and the whole course of our life, so that "all our life may be devoted to His honor, who has redeemed us dearly."

Our great misfortune is that we desire to begin again to govern ourselves. Then there is an end to both struggle and victory. If we had more courage to give Christ leave to govern us, we should the more find Him our victorious King.

"Lift up your heads, O ye gates;
And be ye lifted up, ye everlasting doors:
And the King of glory will come in" (Psalm 24:7).

All hail the power of Jesus' name!
Let angels prostrate fall;
Bring forth the royal diadem,
And crown Him Lord of all!

Anniversaries and Birthdays

____

____

____

DECEMBER 3

"For the grace of God hath appeared, bringing salvation to all men, instructing us, to the intent that, denying ungodliness and worldly lusts, we should live soberly and righteously and godly in this present world." Titus 2:11-12

GRACE, which has appeared bringing salvation to all men, is given us in Christ. Grace is not to be found in one place or another out in the universe, in thoughts, and human opinions. Grace is in Christ. It is hidden there, and there it is revealed for all men.

In Christ we meet God as the God of all grace, with grace enough for all men, and for all kinds of sinners. Grace is the justice that the criminal receives. But as it is the sinner who receives grace, it is grace too that increases strength to him that has no might. Grace makes the dishonest person honest, the hard-hearted mild, the godless God-fearing, the evil good, the thoughtless wise, and the hot-tempered quiet.

By the grace of God we may become the first to forgive, the last to make trouble. Grace makes the stingy person generous, the weakest character strong, and of the greatest slave of sin it makes the most God-fearing and victorious Christian. Grace sets us free from sin itself, it gives us the desire and the power to hate evil and to love the good, it creates new life in the children of death, it cleanses and makes holy, gives peace in the soul, peace in the home, and peace in life and in death.

Be made strong by the grace which is in Christ! There is grace for grace, there is grace enough. Enough for you, for me, enough in life, and enough in death. Enough also to conquer the evil that will meet us today.

Thy grace alone, O God,
  To me can pardon speak;
Thy power alone, O Son of God,
  Can this sore bondage break.
No other work save Thine,
  No meaner blood will do;
No strength, save that which is divine,
  Can bear me safely through.

Anniversaries and Birthdays

____

____

____

DECEMBER 4

"Be ye angry, and sin not: let not the sun go down upon your wrath: neither give place to the devil." Eph. 4:26-27

TO get angry is not always the same as committing sin. There is a deep, holy wrath that springs out of zeal for the good. When godlessness and immorality are permitted to spread themselves freely, perhaps even defended and praised by leaders in society, then the Christian has both the right and the duty to feel angry.

When one thinks of the thousands of homes and lives that are destroyed for time and eternity by drink, and then sees that this agency of Satan is highly esteemed by those who are reputed to be the greatest and best people in society—this is not the least of the causes that make anger burn in one's heart. Can a Christian fail under those circumstances to feel both anger and resentment?

There is also much else in daily life both outdoors and indoors that tempts to anger. Happy he who then does not sin! Just at such times the heart is so inclined to give place to the devil. May we then find strength in Him who has promised to govern our tongue. Then we shall safely get through this narrow pass: to be angry without sinning.

But if we are defeated, we must go to the fountain in the house of David and cleanse our souls, so that the sun does not go down upon our wrath. He that rules his tongue is stronger than he that takes a city.

"Cease from anger, and forsake wrath:
Fret not thyself, it tendeth only to evil-doing" (Psalm 37:8).

Come down, Thou Holy Spirit,
And fill our souls with light;
Clothe us in spotless raiment,
In linen clean and white;
Within Thy sacred temple
Be with us, where we stand,
And sanctify Thy people
Throughout this happy land.

Anniversaries and Birthdays

DECEMBER 5

Passing through the valley of Weeping they make it a place of springs:
Yea, the early rain covereth it with blessings.
They go from strength to strength:
Every one of them appeareth before God in Zion. **Psalm 84:6-7**

MOST people have to struggle and suffer much through life. Poverty, heavy work, sickness, and sorrow are faithful companions of most people. Our way through life is indeed a valley of weeping. Occasionally one must marvel that people really have the courage to live; at any rate it is strange when one thinks of those who believe that life ends with death. To step into a world just to enter on a laborious conflict that ends in a grave—that must be the most meaningless idea of all.

But those who believe what the Bible says about God, about salvation, about grace, about eternal life in the land beyond death—for them life in this world with all its burdens and tears, nevertheless is filled with hope of glory with God. When such a future awaits one, not only does life itself get a meaning and a purpose, but there is also a reason for everything that we must go through on the way to the goal. In the valley of Weeping the river of life flows for those who believe in God, and where others are found lying mortally wounded, there the Christian gathers strength. Through tears the sun of grace shows its wonderful play of colors, and it is the storms of life that bring us up toward God.

"He hath swallowed up death for ever; and the Lord Jehovah will wipe away tears from off all faces; and the reproach of His people will He take away from off all the earth: for Jehovah hath spoken it" (Isa. 25:8).

Though thousand times ten thousands stand
White-robed in glory there,
There is a place at God's right hand
||:For thee in heaven so fair.:||

In Jesus' heart there still is room,
In heaven is room also,
The Gospel message bids thee come,
||:Praise God who loves thee, too.:||

Anniversaries and Birthdays

DECEMBER 6

Forget not to show love unto strangers: for thereby some have entertained angels unawares. Heb. 13:2

THE Word of God strongly emphasizes the fact that Christians should be given to hospitality. He who opens heart and home to his fellow men, at the same time opens the door to God's blessings. God has ordained the law of life that he who gives also receives. But he who is stingy and inhospitable loses God's blessing, and gets a gnawing worm at the root of all his toil.

Those were great men at Abraham's table at the oaks of Mamre the day that he opened the door for the three unknown wanderers. And today too it may be our lot to have both angels and the Lord Himself as our guests, if we have the same mind as Abraham. But it is probably the hospitable disposition that is lacking. Everything is swallowed up in business and money; and the number of those who give people lodging and meals without pay seems to be growing smaller and smaller. But as hospitality decreases, money decreases, too. Angels and God's blessings pass by our door together with those that we refuse to give lodgings, and then we are left alone complaining about hard times and too little income. But in God's book it is written: "For with what measure ye mete, it shall be measured to you again."

Just think, if we believed this and lived according to it!

Open the door for the Lord's friends, and be hospitable! He who asked us to do this, is rich enough for all. He never forgets what He has promised.

How happily the working days
In this dear service fly!
How rapidly the closing hour,
The time of rest, draws nigh!
When all the faithful gather home,
A joyous company,
And ever where the Master is,
Shall His blest servants be.

Anniversaries and Birthdays

DECEMBER 7

In nothing be anxious; but in everything by prayer and supplication with thanksgiving let your requests be made known unto God.
Phil. 4:6

GREAT things have happened to us when we have gotten peace with God, and in Jesus Christ have believed the forgiveness of our sins.

But what we many times must see both in ourselves and in others is that it often is easier to believe in God as our Savior than as our Father. We can boldly testify that we are saved but at the same time be weighed down and restless about many of the things that meet us in daily life. Father may lay both his soul and his sin confidingly on the Savior-heart of Jesus, but is bowed down by anxiety for food and clothes for himself and the family. Mother sings joyfully about freedom in Christ, but is full of uneasiness when she thinks about the future of her children. Young people are happy about having found peace with God, but cry themselves to sleep out of fear for the future.

You can lay your sins on God but not your anxiety. You can believe that God is able to bring you through life and death into heaven, but you cannot believe that He is able to keep you in food and clothes. You can believe that He defends your soul against the power of Satan, but you cannot trustingly give Him your children.

But it is just this that God wants us to do. He wants us to lay every last thing on Him in prayer, in faith, and in thanksgiving. Let us make use of the right that He has given us.

Thy truth and grace, O Father,
  Behold and surely know,
Both what is good and evil,
  For mortal man below:
And whatsoe'er Thou choosest
  Thou dost, great God, fulfill,
And into being bringest
  Whate'er is in Thy will.

Anniversaries and Birthdays

____

____

____

____

DECEMBER 8

"For to me to live is Christ, and to die is gain." Phil. 1:21

SOMETHING unusually exalted and holy envelops these words. And they become especially gripping when one remembers that it is a saved sinner who testifies thus about himself.

Everything that is found in this widely traveled spirit, everything that rests in that hard-as-steel will, all faculties and all learning are given to this One: Jesus Christ. What life, time, and eternity have to offer is nothing to him any more, when it is not in harmony with Christ. There he has found all that he wishes to possess and to be. He does not see, he does not know, and he does not want to know or be anything outside of what he possesses in Him who walked by way of Golgotha. Even the best that life on earth can give is for him like moths and mold, when one compares it with Jesus Christ.

What things were gain to him he counted but refuse so that he might gain Christ. Everything was laid aside for this One; he lives in Christ and for Christ. Outside of Him there is nothing that is worth either love or fear. Death, that makes so many tremble, is for Paul only a welcome driver, who takes him across to the One that he loves.

This is the touchstone for us who confess faith in Christ now. Is He the One who is entirely sufficient for us, and whom we joyfully give our life and our strength for work? This way is unspeakably plain and exalted: "For to me to live is Christ, and to die is gain." How happy that person is who has found Christ, and who has surrendered himself fully into His will!

Take my humble adoration
While on earth below I dwell.
Let my songs in exultation
Of Thy boundless goodness tell,
Till in heav'n above, my King,
Endless hymns of praise I sing.

Anniversaries and Birthdays

DECEMBER 9

For we who have believed do enter into that rest; even as He hath said. . . . There remaineth therefore a sabbath rest for the people of God.
Heb. 4:3, 9

WHEN a person, tired of sin and a restless conscience, finds the way to Christ and trustingly accepts Him as his Savior, then that person finds rest for his soul. It is like having arrived in a quiet harbor after lying on a wreck between rocks and reefs in a stormy sea.

I now can rest, supremely happy,
The soul enjoy pure heaven's food.
The heart is cleansed, the debt is paid,
So I am nothing, Jesus all.

And yet—even if a Christian can experience this, we have still not come to the perfect rest. Here we rest in faith, here there is rest for the soul in the midst of the battle, a rest that by the grace of God brings into our life the happiness that only a Christian can own. But in the midst of this happiness we still long for something more. We long for the adoption of sons, for the redemption of our body, to be where no danger threatens, where no conflict awaits us, and where no earthly need calls us to a new day of fatiguing work. About this rest the Word of God says: "Blessed are the dead who die in the Lord from henceforth: yea, saith the Spirit, that they may rest from their labors; for their works follow with them" (Rev. 14:13).

Thus the long day of the future beckons to God's people to come into the eternal sabbath rest.

Blessed is he who attains thereto.

Who are these like stars appearing,
These, before God's throne who stand?
Each a golden crown is wearing;
Who are all this glorious band?
Hallelujah! hark, they sing,
Praising loud their heavenly King.

Anniversaries and Birthdays

DECEMBER 10

But what are these among so many? **John 6:9**

GOD has placed in man two wonderful forces that He has called blessing and curse. As a hidden but strong current they glide through every single human life, through house and cabin, and out to people and country. When we have God's blessing there is always enough. Then crops grow in the fields, then the food in the kneading-trough, in the kettle, and in the platters, increases. But if the curse comes upon us, hidden worms crawl into everything. They consume and cause everything to vanish away right out of our hands.

Where there has been enough, there is much too little for just a few.

That is the way life speaks to us, and all who wonder about this would do well to read Deuteronomy XXVIII. There they will find the answer to the question.

Where Philip gets altogether too little, no matter how he calculates, there is more than enough under the blessing of Jesus' hands.

Well, what shall we do that we may own God's blessing?

To me a part of the answer falls thus: Be an honest and diligent worker in the position that you now have. Be content with what you have, and do not envy others. Take care of what you own, save what you can, and help others as far as possible, where you consider it right to give help.

Let nothing be wasted. He who owns all says that.

Then fold your hands and pray God to bless your work, your food, and all that you own. That is where the way leads in under the hands of God outstretched to bless.

O feed the hungry, God of love,
Who sigh for bread to heaven above;
Give to our land prosperity,
And bless the earth, the sky, the sea!

Anniversaries and Birthdays

DECEMBER 11

Good Teacher, what shall I do that I may inherit eternal life?
Mark 10:17

THE desire to win eternal life brought the young rich man to his knees before Jesus. But even though he had gotten that far, he had to go away without receiving what he sought because this world was dearer to him than the winning of eternal life.

This man has many spiritual kinsmen. There are multitudes of people, not least among the young, who are torn in the struggle with themselves in the question of peace of soul and love for the world.

From the depth of the soul, forces come forth that cry for light and life. One feels like an imprisoned man, shut up in a room where there never yet has been light. But the door to that room cannot be opened by human hands, and so we are left standing there. It is then that people feel drawn to Jesus. As the little child turns to mother for food and drink, so the soul feels drawn to Jesus to get this closed door opened, to attain to release and life.

But then one meets the great hindrance: That which must be gotten out of the way in order to gain life becomes too costly to give up—and the road is closed. Love for this world is of greater importance than gaining life eternal, and shadows from the land of death have shut out life's sun.

You who are walking that road, ask yourself this question: "What doth it profit a man, to gain the whole world, and forfeit his life?" Perhaps that might help you to pay the price.

Only a step to Jesus!
Believe, and thou shalt live;
Lovingly now He's waiting,
And ready to forgive.

Only a step to Jesus!
A step from sin to grace;
What has thy heart decided?
The moments fly apace.

Anniversaries and Birthdays

____

____

____

DECEMBER 12

Let us fear therefore, lest haply, a promise being left of entering into His rest, any of you should seem to have come short of it. Heb. 4:1

IN God's Word there is wonderful harmony that to us seems to be built on two great contrasts.

On one side are the many words about a complete salvation and the open door, and all the solid promises that God will keep us. No one shall be able to snatch us out of the hand of our Savior, and nothing shall be able to separate us from God's love in Christ Jesus our Lord.

But then there are other Bible passages that tell us that our danger is great. If we want to have any hope of reaching the goal we must watch, pray, struggle, purify our souls, work out our salvation with fear and trembling, and perfect our holiness in the fear of God. How can two series of statements so unlike, be true? Because the first refers to God, the second to us. That which is unshakable, rock-ribbed, that never fails, *that* rests in God who is our Savior and Father. With Him we are always safe, but we must always be fearful of ourselves. In our own bosom danger always lurks. "Not a sparrow shall fall on the ground without your Father";—and, "Ye are of more value than many sparrows." Thus we can be safe in God. "But I will warn you whom ye shall fear: Fear Him, who after He hath killed hath power to cast into hell."

Those are the conditions for the Christians in this world. Afraid of himself, secure in God.

Let us fear therefore!

O when, thou city of my God,
Shall I thy courts ascend,
Where evermore the angels sing,
Where sabbaths have no end?

There happier bowers than Eden's bloom,
Nor sin nor sorrow know;
Blest seats! through rude and stormy scenes
I onward press to you.

Anniversaries and Birthdays

DECEMBER 13

Be ye merciful, even as your Father is merciful. And judge not, and ye shall not be judged. Luke 6:36-37

EVERY person has both the right and the duty to have an opinion about himself and others. He who believes that he must go through life with eyes closed and without the right to see life truly, he will not get very far before he is trampled under foot by his fellow men. We have received an understanding in order to use it. And the Word of God also cries: "Woe unto them that call evil good!"

When life's naked speech tells us that this one or that one lives in a worldly, godless, and sinful manner, then it surely is not the will of God that we shall call such people Christians. We are not only told not to judge, but also to judge righteous judgment.

But what does Jesus mean by telling us that we shall not judge?

I believe that He means especially this, that what we think, say, and judge about our fellow men which has its root in an evil and selfish mind, that is wrong even if what we say is true. If our words about other people come from that kind of disposition, if we enjoy advertising the folly of others, we are on the wrong road with our judgment. Be ye merciful, and judge not! The judgment lies in the unmerciful disposition that permeates the words: it is this that always is wrong. There our beam lies. It is this beam that Jesus asks us to draw out of our own eye.

If our thoughts and words about others are characterized by good will and love, then we do not judge, in an evil sense, even though we say the heaviest words, keen-edged with truth. Then we have a right to say to the guilty person: "Thou art the man!"

Judge not hastily of others,
But thine own salvation mind;
Nor be captious to thy brother's,
To thine own offenses blind;
God alone discerns thine own,
And the hearts of all mankind.

Anniversaries and Birthdays

DECEMBER 14

Finally, brethren, whatsoever things are true, whatsoever things are honorable, whatsoever things are just, whatsoever things are pure, whatsoever things are lovely, whatsoever things are of good report; if there be any virtue, and if there be any praise, think on these things. **Phil. 4:8**

A CHRISTIAN is not only to be spiritual, he shall also move as a good man among other men.

First of all we are to see that we are on a right footing with God. Nothing, neither bad nor good, must deflect us from this. But if we are standing on life's solid Rock, we ought from this vantage point help promote everything that can create more happiness among people and better living conditions. There is nothing that belongs to human life of which the Christian may say that it does not concern him. The Christian who in this way, too, joins in, serves, and helps as far as he can, does God's work.

In a place which the preacher of God's Word never reached, a servant, a fisher, a farmer, a carpenter, a deaconess has opened men's hearts to God's grace. Where a Christian helped to improve living conditions among people, he walked in the footsteps of Jesus, who died for our sins. To assist in promoting what is beneficial, righteous, and clean, and to do it in the Spirit of Christ, that is the worship of God that heaven loves most.

Jesus, Master! at Thy Word
I will work whate'er betide me,
And I know Thou wilt, O Lord,
By Thy Word and Spirit guide me;
At Thy Word my faith shall see
All things work for good to me.

Anniversaries and Birthdays

DECEMBER 15

Then opened He their mind, that they might understand the Scriptures. Luke 24:45

THE Word of Scripture is different from all other words, not only because it is God's Word, but also because no one can find the real content of God's Word in the Bible unless God Himself opens the door to the Word in the Word, and gives a new light in our understanding.

Those who read the Bible with unbelieving and worldly eyes find only absurdities, and are offended. But where the Bible by the grace of God opens itself so that we find the law of the Spirit of life in the Word, there it gives life to the dead. The condemned person is set free and transformed to a man of God. The heaviest burden becomes light, the broken heart is healed, and where everything before was puzzling and dark, there we now see the way of the Lord.

But if God closes against us the door that opens to the law of the Spirit of life in the Scriptures, we may read the Bible as long as we wish and no light will shine, we find no solution, no grace, and no comfort. Together with the disciples who went to Emmaus we can only walk heavy of heart and ponder on that which was, but is no more. Only when He, who has the key also to His own Word, opens it to us, do we find light and see the glory in the face of Jesus Christ.

We cannot often enough remind each other that we must ask God to open the Scriptures to us by His Spirit. Not till then do we find the way through life and death.

All our knowledge, sense, and sight
  Lie in deepest darkness shrouded,
Till Thy Spirit breaks our night
  With the beams of truth unclouded.
Thou alone to God canst win us,
  Thou must work all good within us.

Anniversaries and Birthdays

DECEMBER 16

Let no corrupt speech proceed out of your mouth, but such as is good for edifying as the need may be, that it may give grace to them that hear. Eph. 4:29

THE ability to speak is one of God's greatest gifts to us. By our words we can understand each other, express our thoughts, and tell what is on our hearts. By our words we can dry each other's tears, remove burdens, let light shine in darkness, and help each other to find the way through both life and death. No music brings us such beautiful melody and gives us so much riches and happiness as good words. Where the love of Christ rules, our words are interpreters of heaven.

But who can describe the damage that our words do when they are evil? God's Word says that then the tongue is a fire, a world of iniquity, it defiles the whole body, and sets on fire the wheel of nature. It is this tongue that we are exhorted to use right, so that it may work to the upbuilding and benefit of those that hear us, instead of doing damage.

If we listen to much of the conversation that can be heard among Christians, we must admit that there is not little of empty words, thoughtless talk, evil words, and gossip. God shouts to us that we must watch our tongue, and that is a shout that we sorely need to hear. Empty and evil talk is the cause of much of the spiritless and half dead Christianity in our time. Whoso keepeth his tongue, keepeth his soul from troubles, and is stronger than he that taketh a city.

We shall one day give account of every idle word.

So let your tongue, your heart, and mind,
Agree to banish every kind
Of malice, falsehood, and disguise,
And here on earth a paradise
Of peace and harmony maintain,
Where concord and good will shall reign.

Anniversaries and Birthdays

____

____

____

____

____

DECEMBER 17

If we say that we have no sin, we deceive ourselves, and the truth is not in us. I John 1:8

AGAIN and again, with more or less power, the doctrine pops up that to be a Christian is the same as being sinless. Sensible people can stand up, and in the strongest language testify that they are sinless. Apparently the only thing that can make such people speak in a somewhat lower voice is what life itself says.

This delusion is one of the most dangerous and meaningless ideas that a Christian can get entangled in. Even if one would not pay any attention to what the Bible says, not much Christian sense would be required to see that Christians, too, have sins and faults. If "sinless" is not to be anything more than what one can experience in himself and in other Christians in this world, well, then the heaven that God has promised His people is on a low plane.

One of the reasons that this doctrine is taught and believed, is that we know that no one who has sin can enter heaven. And so they say: "Death cannot remove sin!" No, but God can remove sin in death. He who cannot believe that must have a poor opinion of Him who has promised to transform us in a moment, so that we become like Him when we see Him even as He is.

Until the moment when we are transformed a Christian is a sinner who is saved by faith, and who must be cleansed from his sins in the blood of Jesus Christ. He who ceases from this cleansing becomes a branch that withers and is taken away.

God deliver us from that fate!

> We wait for Thee 'mid toil and pain,
> In weariness and sighing;
> But glad that Thou our guilt hast borne,
> And cancelled it by dying.
> Hence, cheerfully may we with Thee
> Take up our cross and bear it,
> Till we relief inherit.

Anniversaries and Birthdays

DECEMBER 18

And behold, they brought to Him a man sick of the palsy, lying on a bed: and Jesus seeing their faith said unto the sick of the palsy, "Son, be of good cheer: thy sins are forgiven." Matt. 9:2

THESE words contain a comfort that many of us have good use for. There is so much that goes to pieces and is robbed of power by sickness and sin. Then when one sees this, and is moved by sympathy, and tries in a small way to help, one realizes how helpless and incapable he is.

But in the midst of all this impotence in us and around us, there is nevertheless something that a Christian can do. He can help carry others to Jesus. To Him we can safely go, not only because He is able to help, but also because He asks us to bring everything to Him.

One day a father brought his child to the disciples of Jesus, but they could not help him. When Jesus heard that, He said, "Bring him hither to Me!" Then the father brought the child and Jesus healed it. This is the Word of Jesus also to us today. Hearken to it, not least you fathers and mothers who have children living in sin and shame, ravaged by impotence and evil spirits. "Bring them to Me!" says Jesus. Shall we not take our children to Him when He invites us to do so? If the load proves too heavy for us to carry alone, others will help in our day, too. When Jesus sees a united group of believers bringing someone to Him, He will help and He will say now as before: "Thy sins are forgiven!"

Let us grasp this comfort when we bring our fellow men to Him! He has given us the right to believe it.

I sing to Thee with voice and heart,
Of all my joys the well;
I sing, that, what I know Thou art
My lips to all may tell:
That Thou a fountain art of grace,
With blessings richly stored
For all, in every time and place,
This well I know, O Lord.

Anniversaries and Birthdays

DECEMBER 19

And let us consider one another to provoke unto love and good works; not forsaking our own assembling together, as the custom of some is, but exhorting one another; and so much the more, as ye see the day drawing nigh." Heb. 10:24-25

IT is impossible to deny that there are many Christians who are almost unbearable. The more fully we get to know each other, the more ready are we to acknowledge that being a saved sinner is not the same as being perfect.

But just because this is true we must help and forgive each other as God helps and forgives us. If it is true that you or I are better than certain others, we must remember that precisely to us comes the charge to help those who are weaker. To love, that is also to serve, forgive, endure, and help our fellow Christians. Insofar as we are capable of these assignments, insofar do we love. If we begin to judge and to criticise instead of provoking one another to love and good works, there is great danger that we will depart from the company of God's people. We think the most peaceful way is to go into hiding. But many of those who hid themselves away from God's people, also got away from God.

One of the greatest tasks God has given His people in this world is to help each other to be victorious. Let us not forget that. If we always have an eye for that, that, too, will create in us a greater desire to forgive and serve.

Good and pleasant 'tis to see
Brethren dwell in unity,
When the law which Jesus taught,
Rules each word, and deed, and thought.

Anniversaries and Birthdays

DECEMBER 20

Looking carefully lest there be any man that falleth short of the grace of God; lest any root of bitterness springing up trouble you, and thereby the many be defiled. Heb. 12:15

THAT grace is the door by which we have access to salvation and peace with God, a Christian can become more and more sure of, but that we have nothing else later on for comfort and help in our Christian life except grace—that is more difficult for us to believe. One is so inclined to think—and it looks so godly, too—that what we have received and experienced by grace, is to comfort and strengthen us in the days to come. Accordingly, when darkness, doubt, and impotence overwhelm us, we look to ourselves for the help that is found only in the grace in Christ.

We are saved by grace alone. We must also live by grace alone. Nothing else can give us strength, and keep the evil root down. If we get away from grace, evil will again overpower us. The sins that we thought we were entirely through with, were only fettered by grace. Then, when grace left us, the old root sprang up again, often stronger than before.

No—"not of works, that no man should glory." Grace can never store up power in a Christian. It is like the manna that the Israelites kept till the next day: there were worms in it. For every new day there must be new grace. Therefore, say the Scriptures, rivers of living water shall flow from within believers. It is running water that makes power, not still water.

"By the grace of God I am what I am: and His grace which was bestowed upon me was not found vain."

O may that grace be ours,
In Thee for aye to live,
And drink of those refreshing streams
Which Thou alone canst give.

Anniversaries and Birthdays

____

____

____

____

____

DECEMBER 21

Behold, I stand at the door and knock: if any man hear My voice and open the door, I will come in to him, and will sup with him, and he with Me. Rev. 3:20

IN this life no one will ever be able to find the dividing line between God's omnipotence and our free will. But even though we cannot do that, we must still hold fast to the truth that we ourselves are responsible in determining whether we shall be saved or lost. The key to the heart is in our own hand in this matter.

The Savior stands outside and knocks, but He does not break in, and He takes no one by force. He knocks, He asks permission to save, He invites, yea, He weeps when people do not know the time of their visitation: but He never uses force.

What a miracle of love that God seeks us, that it is the almighty, the eternally rich God who knocks at our door and asks permission to save us. Should not we have knocked at His door, to ask whether He in grace would receive the lost sinner. But, No, no one seeks Him, if He does not seek us first.

If all of you who have not opened the door to Him, would remember this, then must you soon understand that the greatest sin you can commit is to keep the door closed against Him. Beware of that great sin, and open the door!

A word to you who earnestly desire to be saved, but who dare not believe that you are saved. Cannot you, too, understand that He who now knocks at your door has a much greater desire to save you, than you have to be saved?

> Behold, He at the door is knocking!
> Hark, how He pleads our souls to win!
> Who hears His voice—the door unlocking—
> To sup with Him He enters in!
> How blest the day, my soul, how blest!
> When Jesus comes to be thy guest!

Anniversaries and Birthdays

____

____

____

____

____

DECEMBER 22

For God sent not the Son into the world to judge the world; but that the world should be saved through Him. John 3:17

WE need no judge from God. The whole creation groans in aching pain under the judgment, and every man carries the judgment in his own bosom. All fear of meeting God tells us that we are guilty and condemned. But He who saw the burden that we bore, He surely did not desire to make it heavier. So He sent His own Son to us, and laid the sin, guilt, and condemnation on Him.

The Judge Himself for death's grim captives died;
Our God's atoned, He took the sacrifice.

Though we so well know this, it seems to be so difficult for us to see and grasp this great, redeeming grace. Terror of the Holy One and fear of judgment are so deep-seated in us, that also those who have found Christ often tremble at thought of the day when they shall appear before His holy face. There are so many things in the daily life that cause one to fear to meet God. If we lose sight of Jesus as our Savior, we are down again fearing the judgment.

All of you who are struggling to be victorious, but who think it appears hopeless: Try to grasp this great word of comfort! Grasp it now and take it with you into life's conflict today, that God sent not His Son to condemn he world, but that the world should be saved by Him! Live in this Word, believe it, and turn your face toward Him who became a curse for us! Then you will be set free from the judgment, and be made strong in God.

Now mark, O man, and ponder well
Sin's awful condemnation.
For whom were all those wounds endured?
To purchase thy salvation.
Had Jesus never bled and died,
Then what could thee and all betide
But fiery reprobation?

Anniversaries and Birthdays

DECEMBER 23

He shall be great, and shall be called the Son of the Most High: and the Lord God shall give unto Him the throne of His father David. **Luke 1:32**

IT is a strange greatness that begins in a manger and ends on a cross, and that during the whole time between these two poles, knows nothing but poverty, contempt, and persecution. And still it is on this road that our Savior not only was great, but also becomes great. The way of suffering is the king's highway. That He came down to a helpless and lost race, and at last gave His life to save that race, that makes Him great to us, too. That which finally more than anything else coaxes a proud sinner to give himself to Jesus voluntarily, is that He gave all for us.

In one sense it is easily learned that for us, too, it is necessary to step down to get on the road that goes upward. But to do this, which we know is right, is not learned so easily, because it means passing through death to life. For us the first step upward is to give ourselves wholly to Him who gave Himself wholly for us; and from this point the road goes upward, away from sin, death, and the kingdom of Satan. It is also from this point that we must step down to helpless men, if we are to bring them to Him who can help all into the presence of God. Every new day opens a way for us to this serving love. *With* Jesus and *for* Jesus, there the road goes upward, there we become truly great.

God, give us the will and the power to go through life together with Him!

O ye who sorrow, sinking
Beneath your grief and pain,
Rejoice in His appearing,
Who shall your souls sustain:
He comes, He comes with gladness!
How great is His good will!
He comes, all grief and anguish
Shall at His Word be still.

Anniversaries and Birthdays

____

____

____

____

DECEMBER 24

There was no room for them in the inn. **Luke 2:7**

THERE has always been a scarcity of room for Jesus in this world, and no change for the better is in sight either: quite the contrary. All men know indeed that He is good, but He is too good: He does not suit the self-sufficient generation that chooses to live according to its own lusts. We can build churches and altars for Him, and on festival days and at a grave we can sing, too, about Him and His heaven, but then that will also have to be enough. The aim of our life is to live as we please, without having anything to do with Jesus. But when we die He is expected politely to have a door open for us right into heaven. We are about ready to dare Him to fail us there.

That is the way most people think and live. During life they want nothing to do with Jesus, but when they die they must at all costs go to Him. He who must stand outside the door of your heart, home, business, parties, and the whole course of your life, He must have a place for you in His heaven, because you want to get in there. What are you going to do there? You will not get a new mind in death: you must get that here. No; the Jesus that you have no room for, He has no heaven for you. If you wish to find room with Jesus when you die, then you must have room for Him while you are living.

But you and I who once gave Him room, let us be on our guard, and keep away from everything that would make the place of Jesus smaller in our lives. It is hard to find room for Jesus with many of us Christians, too. This world deceives and draws so many of the Lord's little ones, also.

Come, Jesus, glorious heavenly Guest,
Keep Thine own Christmas in our breast;
Then David's harp-string, hushed so long,
Shall swell our jubilee of song.

Anniversaries and Birthdays

____

____

____

____

____

DECEMBER 25

There is born to you this day in the city of David a Savior, who is Christ the Lord. Luke 2:11

AS the strokes of the Christmas bells are heard over vale and beach every Christmas day, so the Word about the Savior who was born sounds forth from generation to generation. We need a Savior: we are in trouble. Satan, sin, and death have found us and struck us to earth. No one can any more get up by his own strength. "Our need is great, in the night of death we dwell."

But He who had to lock the gate against us to the land of life, He promised to find a way to open it again. It is impossible for us to understand it, but the Bible tells that even before the foundation of the world God had arranged for help. And when the time came, He Himself came to earth and became our Savior. He by whom all things are created, He lies in the stable on straw to make us rich by His poverty. Now God no longer deals with us: now He deals with Him who said, "Demand of Me!" He has entered into our race, as a man among men, as the second Adam, so that He can take away the evil that the first Adam gave us as an inheritance.

In joy over what now happens to us men, angels and heavenly hosts sing songs of praise up to God, and the message of salvation down to earth. So come, and sing with us, all you who have a heart, mouth, and voice, and let us worship Him who came and desired to save us who were lost!

To David's city let us fly,
Where angels sing beneath the sky;
Through plain and village pressing near,
And news from God with shepherds hear.

O let us go with quiet mind,
The gentle Babe with shepherds find,
To gaze on Him who gladdens them,
The loveliest flower on Jesse's stem.

Anniversaries and Birthdays

DECEMBER 26

And this is the sign unto you: Ye shall find a Babe wrapped in swaddling clothes, and lying in a manger. And suddenly there was with the angel a multitude of the heavenly host praising God, and saying,

"Glory to God in the highest,
And on earth peace among men in whom He is well pleased."

Luke 2:12-14

IT was an angel that sang the first Christmas song on our earth, together with a heavenly host. Heaven opens and sings its joy down to us lost men, because God will save us and be well pleased with men.

If we see this aright we will find rich comfort in the fact that those who dwell on high rejoice that "there is born to us a Savior." We who dwell in such lowly conditions with sin and shame over us, are so inclined to think that perfect and holy spirits must depart from us. But that is not the case. Everything that is in and around God in His glory rejoices that we are to be saved. If this truth were given room in our thinking and faith, we, too, would jubilantly sing out our joy. Yea, who indeed should sing louder and more joyously than we? We are the ones who are to be served by all this. So when the heavenly hosts rejoice at our good fortune, we know that we are welcome in their company.

It is true indeed that we have reason to complain, when we look at ourselves and all the evil round about us. But if we look upward to Him who became poor for our sakes so that we might become rich, then

We sing of peace, the peace profound,
That hell shall tremble at the sound,
Our Christmas anthem hearing.

We gather round Thee, Jesus dear,
So happy in Thy presence here;
Grant us, our Savior, every one,
To stand in heaven before Thy throne.

Anniversaries and Birthdays

____

____

____

____

DECEMBER 27

Are they not all ministering spirits, sent forth to do service for the sake of them that shall inherit salvation? Heb. 1:14

GOD cares wonderfully for all His people. He gave us His Son to be our Savior, He Himself wishes to be our Father, and we received the Spirit to be our Guide, Light, Teacher, Chastener, Comforter, for a seal and an earnest of our inheritance.

And then He has that great host of angels that He sends forth to serve us. They accompany us as a holy guard day and night, just as faithful and sure as the beating of a heart. Occasionally we afterward have an inkling that invisible hands held us fast, and that protective beckonings turned us back from roads that would have led to disaster. They follow every Christian family in the daily toil, and take children by the hand when they thoughtlessly plunge into danger. When the fisherman steps into his boat, the angel of the Lord goes along and stills the storm that would otherwise send everything to the bottom. Angels stand on the captain's bridge in the dark, stormy night, and occasionally ask the mate to change course and steer toward a wreck where the crew is calling to God for help.

Abraham met angels at the oaks of Mamre, Paul met one on the sea, and on Christmas night they filled the heavens with song about the Savior of the world.

They will serve us today, too, and guard us against dangers.

"The angel of Jehovah encampeth round about them that fear Him, And delivereth them."

I walk 'mongst angels all the way
  They shield me and befriend me;
All Satan's power is held at bay
  When heavenly hosts attend me;
They are my sure defense,
All fear and sorrow hence!
Unharmed by foes, do what they may,
I walk 'mongst angels all the way.

Anniversaries and Birthdays

DECEMBER 28

And Simeon blessed them, and said unto Mary His mother, "Behold, this Child is set for the falling and the rising of many in Israel; and for a sign which is spoken against." Luke 2:34

AS the rock in the midst of the falls, so Christ stands in the midst of the race for falling or for salvation. We cannot meet Him and pass Him in the same way that we meet and pass other persons. As the sun either burns and destroys, or gives life, so the meeting with Jesus brings about either falling or rising. No one gets by Him and escapes this choice. "And he that falleth on this stone shall be broken to pieces: but on whomsoever it shall fall, it will scatter him as dust."

Meeting Jesus entails responsibility. To learn to know Him through the Word of God, to know that He died for our sins and was raised for our justification, to be called into the kingdom of His grace, and then not accept Him, that is adding sin to sin, and judgment to judgment. "And this is the judgment, that the light is come into the world, and men loved the darkness rather than the light."

But as many as received Him, them He raised up and made to be free, saved people. "If therefore the Son shall make you free, ye shall be free indeed." You who do not give yourself to Him who who gave Himself wholly for you, you are lost. When the bottomless abyss forever has shut you out from the last hope, then your fall is great. Then you will know what it is to be lost. But happy are you who accept Him. When you have entered within the gates of the city, you will know what it is to be eternally blessed.

Ne'er think the victory won,
Nor lay thine armor down;
Thine arduous work will not be done,
Till thou obtain thy crown.

Anniversaries and Birthdays

DECEMBER 29

And Joseph said unto his father, "They are my sons, whom God hath given me here." And he said, "Bring them, I pray thee, unto me, and I will bless them." Gen. 48:9

JACOB is come to the end of his life. He is old and blind, but his mind is clear, and his heart warm. Times that have gone, pass in review before his mind; and he looks into the future. During a long life he has learned to esteem highly his ancestors, their God, and the blessings they gave him through faith and godliness. He now desires to portion out this inheritance to children and grandchildren before death knocks at his door. Joseph's sons shall also have their part. So he lays his old, worn hands on their heads, and blesses them with these words: "The angel who hath redeemed me from all evil, bless the lads."

Of all that we can give coming generations, nothing is so valuable as God's blessing. When we take our children to grandfather or grandmother, that they may lay their hands on them and bless them, then we give them an inheritance that no one can take away from them, and that always brings happiness with it. Money and good times have brought poverty and misfortune to so many; but those whose young lives are blessed by the hands of Christian fathers, will have light and happiness on their work, struggles, and tears. When evening comes for them, too, they can give the same heritage to the race after them, which God has promised to maintain through a thousand generations.

Take my heart, O Lord, and ordain it
To proclaim Thy love unto man;
Let me lose my life to regain it
In devotion to Thee and Thy plan.

Anniversaries and Birthdays

______

______

______

______

______

______

DECEMBER 30

Now lettest Thou Thy servant depart, Lord,
According to Thy Word, in peace;
For mine eyes have seen Thy salvation. Luke 2:29-30

CAN a man attain to greater happiness on this earth than to stand at the end of life with Jesus in his arms and in his heart, set free from all earthly ties, and through with this world? When life's long, hard workday ends that way, when all puzzling questions get that kind of answer, then life's evening is bright indeed. Then autumn is more beautiful than spring, and age is happier than youth.

Not all old people are as happy as Simeon. Many suffer because children and other relatives have forgotten them, or treat them shabbily. But most of them are badly off because they have not found Jesus. So they try with all their might to cling to this life, and desire to forget the day that they must depart. But their vitality goes steadily downward, and then their cheerfulness dwindles, they complain and are dissatisfied. The world they do not wish to let go of, glides away from them, and they do not know the way to a better land. Then getting old is a dreary business. Then autumn is sour and cold and dark.

Happy is that person who sees the Savior and heaven more clearly as the years become many! Then all ties that bind us to earth are loosened more and more. Then that which is oppressive and makes one struggle in old age becomes as nothing compared to the glory that we shall receive. Then the evening of life is the gate to eternal day with God.

Let us, O Lord, be faithful
With Simeon to the end,
That so his dying song may
From all our hearts ascend:
"O Lord, let now Thy servant
Depart in peace for aye,
Since I have seen my Savior,
Have here beheld His day."

Anniversaries and Birthdays